# MODERN PRODUCTS LIABILITY LAW

*New Titles from*
*QUORUM BOOKS*

The Uses of Psychiatry in the Law: A Clinical View of Forensic Psychiatry
WALTER BROMBERG

Abuse on Wall Street: Conflicts of Interest in the Securities Markets
TWENTIETH CENTURY FUND

The Politics of Taxation
THOMAS J. REESE

# MODERN PRODUCTS LIABILITY LAW

RICHARD A. EPSTEIN

Quorum Books
Westport, Connecticut • London, England

**Library of Congress Cataloging in Publication Data**

Epstein, Richard Allen, 1943-
Modern products liability law.

Bibliography: p.
Includes index.
1. Products liability—United States. I. Title
KF1296.E67 376.7303'82 80-11486
ISBN 0-89930-002-2 (lib. bdg.)



Library of Congress Catalog Card Number: 80-11486
ISBN: 0-89930-002-2

First published in 1980 by Quorum Books

Greenwood Press
A division of Congressional Information Service, Inc.
88 Post Road West, Westport, Connecticut 06881

Printed in the United States of America

10 9 8 7 6 5 4 3 2 1

# CONTENTS

# FOREWORD

Richard Epstein's book should become a major source in the study of product liability law. It began as a more modest research endeavor undertaken in 1976 at the request of the American Insurance Association. The two previous years had produced unprecedented financial underwriting losses for the property/casualty insurance industry. Analysis of those losses showed that changes in legal doctrines were having a growing impact upon insurance companies, their policyholders, and those who based claims for injuries on defective products.

To develop an understanding of the causes and possible consequences of the changes in product liability law, the American Insurance Association commissioned a study scheduled for completion in 1977. After extensive search of the academic and legal communities, the association selected Professor Epstein because of his seasoned scholarship in tort law, his expertise in economics, and his independence from the insurance business.

Detours developed. We drafted Professor Epstein to help our committees prepare proposals for change in product liability statutes and moderate the extensive discussions of need and rationalization for each proposal. In the process of addressing what many regarded as an insurance crisis, we learned that the problems were more complex and subtle than we first suspected. What had begun as a limited inquiry by Professor Epstein blossomed into a major undertaking that has required constant revisions to match swiftly changing developments.

Although portions of the manuscript were read by association staff members and by experts in particular fields among our member companies, the choice of topics for study and the conclusions reached are those of Professor Epstein. Differences of opinion remain between the association and the author on some issues. Nevertheless, we are convinced that this work is a major contribution to the literature—and to the understanding—of product liability law, and we are proud to have had a role in its creation.

T. Lawrence Jones *President*
American Insurance Association

# ACKNOWLEDGMENTS

This book on products liability has been a long time in the writing. My serious thinking about the subject began in the fall of 1976 when I was asked by the American Insurance Association to assist its staff and member companies in preparation of a products liability package that was to contain statutes intended to remedy particular problems in the body of modern products liability law. After the statutory package was finally completed in the first half of 1977, I set about to write a book which was, and is, intended not so much as an exhaustive commentary on all the fine points of products liability law, but as a basic critique of its central assumptions and doctrines, including many issues not easily amenable to clear and proper resolution by legislative effort. The work on the book began while I was on leave from the University of Chicago as a fellow at the Center for Advanced Studies in Behavioral Sciences and has continued upon my return to the University of Chicago Law School. While the original work was commissioned by the American Insurance Association, the arguments advanced and the conclusions reached are solely my own.

During the preparation of earlier drafts of this manuscript I profited from the criticisms of many persons. In particular I should like to thank Walter Blum, William Landes, Robert McGuckin, and Paul Schupack for their helpful and insightful comments, Dennis Connolly of the American Insurance Association for his constant encouragement and support throughout the preparation of this manuscript, and Kathryn McCary and Judy Rose for their valuable research assistance. Lastly, I should like to give special thanks to Jeynean Porter, Christine Kondracik, and Susan Green for showing more patience than was due me during a long process of writing, revising, and updating.

Richard A. Epstein

# MODERN PRODUCTS LIABILITY LAW

CHAPTER

1

# RECURRENT THEMES

There is today an urgent need for a comprehensive reexamination of the law of products liability. It is important at the outset to state exactly why this is the case, for at one level the fresh inquiry seems to be clearly unwarranted. The law of products liability—although not always known by that name—has been with us in one form or another since the middle of the nineteenth century, if not before. From its inception, its central principles have been stated, examined, attacked, and defended many times. Repeated efforts have been made to show how these legal principles, once accepted, apply to those borderline cases that have proved troublesome either in theory or practice. The volume of work in the area has indeed been immense. Why, then, the need for yet another study?

The simplest answer is that the fundamental rules of the game have been radically altered in the past decade. No single opinion or statute has forever changed the face of products liability law. To the contrary, case law development reveals incremental changes, each of which, standing alone, is part of the gradual process of evolution and growth that long has been characteristic of the common law. Taken together, however, these small changes assume quite a different aspect. Although part of no grand, unified system, in combination they, almost without exception, have worked to expose manufacturers, distributors, and retailers to ever greater liability. The combined effect represents a legal revolution greater than the sum of the parts.

Evidence of the major shifts in products liability law is present everywhere. Ten or fifteen years ago products liability was but a tag end of the tort law curriculum, with teaching efforts largely devoted to the intricacies and confusions of the so-called privity limitation. Today products liability is a major topic in the first-year tort course, and in many law schools the subject of advanced treatment in upper-division courses and seminars. Ten or fifteen years ago there were few lawyers with a full-time practice in products liability litigation. Today individual lawyers, if not entire firms, specialize in products cases. Ten or fifteen years ago liability insurance for products of all kinds and descriptions was a casual extra, often offered to major customers free of charge as a special inducement for capturing other lines of business. Today products liability insurance is at least a three billion dollar business.[1] Ten or fifteen years ago a collision at an intersection generated suits between the drivers. Today that same collision will often inspire as well a suit against the manufacturer and retailer of either, or both, vehicles.

The remarkable expansion of products liability litigation has had profound social consequences. Whereas ten or fifteen years ago products liability was lawyer's law, today it is everyone's law and the subject of intense controversy and public debate. Hardly a week goes by without insistent demands for legislative reform that are in turn met with a spirited defense of the new legal order. The strong social interest in products liability law at this time of flux is what provides the motivation for a reexamination of the area. The real question today is not whether a reexamination is needed, but what it should cover and how it should proceed.

The structure of the reexamination takes us immediately to a fork in the road. One branch leads toward a detailed empirical examination of the "book" of products liability business.[2] Born of concern with the sharply higher cost and occasional unavailability of products liability insurance, this approach relies upon statistical and actuarial techniques to gather and interpret data about such matters as the number of products liability actions that have been brought; the time required to dispose of each; the number of cases in which the plaintiff goes home empty-handed and the number in which some payment is made; the number that are settled and the number that are tried; the distribution of claims with respect to type of products—drugs, machine tools, foods, and so on; the type of plaintiff—worker, consumer, bystander; the type of defendant—manufacturer, retailer, promoter, designer; and the like. A detailed profile of these aspects of products liability litigation can tell us much about what we do and where we have been. This information is indispensable for directing our attention to those areas of law (such as work-place injuries) in which the legal picture has greatly altered in recent years. Thus it might come as a surprise that food cases constitute

1. Note that there is no easy way to calculate the exact amount of premiums paid for past years because until very recently there has been no separate line for products liability premiums upon the insurance form. The three-billion-dollar figure seems, however, to be a good estimate of premiums paid, which are of course only a fraction of the total products liability bill. Still to be accounted for are amounts that must be paid by parties that are self-insured, in whole or in part, and the direct costs of defense that are not covered by insurance, the costs imposed by the law with respect to requirements of design, packaging, and marketing products, and the costs expended in efforts for general legislative changes.

2. *See, e.g.*, Insurance Services Office, *Product Liability Closed Claim Survey: A Technical Analysis of Survey Results* (1977) for an exhaustive analysis thereof. *See also* the Highlights thereof for a summary of the essential conclusions.

56 percent of the claims but only 2 percent of the claim dollars, while workplace accidents that give rise to claims against the product supplier constitute only 11 percent of the bodily injury claims but 42 percent of the bodily injury payments.[3] Figures like these give a firm background as to the dimensions and location of the problem, and when collected and refined, they may provide the data base upon which products liability insurance premiums should be determined and evaluated.

In spite of their evident usefulness, there are serious limitations as to what empirical studies of this nature, no matter how thoroughly conducted, can do. These studies cannot, in and of themselves, identify the doctrinal shifts that have taken place within the substantive law of products liability. They cannot provide any type of normative framework to evaluate the merits of the doctrinal developments so identified. To discharge these two tasks, the empirical research must be supplemented with a detailed analysis of the substantive law of products liability and its influence on product safety and development. The emphasis is not upon the delicate factual nuances that determine success or failure of individual cases at the legal margins; it is upon the legal rules that determine where these margins are to be found. The emphasis is not on inconsistent precedents regarding fine points of law, for these the common law has often faced and overcome; it is upon the central institutional choices which on a grand scale govern the operation of the legal system and shape its prospects for both success and survival.

To examine these structural themes, it is useful to trace products liability law through three main stages in its development. The first stage, from *Winterbottom v. Wright*[4] in 1842 until *MacPherson v. Buick Motor Co.*[5] in 1916, had as its major premise the belief that the grave administrative complications and adverse social consequences of products liability suits were so manifest that strenuous efforts were needed to fashion "fixed and definite" rules to prevent the economic ruin of product suppliers. In most cases, but not all, the result of this attitude was to place upon product users and consumers the burden of ferreting out and correcting all manner of product weaknesses and deficiencies. The privity rule—riddled with exceptions before it toppled—was a major tool, but by no means the only one, used to achieve that end. The need to prove the defendant's negligence helped insulate manufacturers from liability for defective products they placed upon the marketplace. The narrow conception of causal connection spared them liability whenever the negligence of other parties farther down the chain of distribution and use substantially contributed to the occurrence of injury. Strong affirmative defenses, whether of contributory negligence or assumption of risk, placed still further obstacles in the way of recovery, and rigorous requirements of proof everywhere blocked the plaintiff. The law

3. Insurance Services Office, Highlights, 5 (1977).
4. 10 M. &. W. 109, 152 Eng. Rep. 402 (Exch. 1842).
5. 217 N.Y. 382, 111 N.E. 1050 (1916).

was altogether too restrictive, as many of the barriers to recovery could not be justified either as a matter of substantive principle or administrative necessity.

The second stage of the development began with the epic decision in *MacPherson v. Buick* and continued until, roughly speaking, shortly after the publication in 1965 of the Restatement (Second) of Torts. In this period products liability law achieved what in retrospect appears to be the best balance between the dual constraints of substantive justice and administrative need. The manufacturer was required to supply the individual consumer with the product that had been promised or take the consequences if that product proved dangerous because it deviated from the manufacturer's own formula, design, or performance standards. The individual consumer or user was bound, as a condition of recovery, to treat that product with the respect that it deserved, to use it in the proper way and for its appropriate ends. The legal rules functioned like an elaborate set of implied contracts that carefully distributed losses from product-related accidents in accordance with the shared expectations of manufacturer and user. The privity limitation upon recovery was everywhere rejected; the negligence requirements were first eroded and then eliminated; the defect requirement in products liability actions was sensibly applied, if not always fully defined; and a workable set of affirmative defenses tied the fortunes of the injured party to his own conduct. While by no means perfect, the system evenly distributed the burdens of loss between manufacturers and consumers.

The third stage of development, which began sometime between 1968 and 1970, starts from totally different philosophical premises. Administrative necessities, which loomed all too large in the nineteenth century, are taken all too lightly by modern judges. In the surge toward ever greater public control, courts have radically redefined the relative obligations of manufacturers and consumers. The plaintiff must still show some defect in the defendant's product, but the defect concept has been expanded far beyond its traditional confines. No longer can a product escape legal scrutiny because it was supplied in the very condition in which the defendant represented it to be, for now in many jurisdictions a jury may treat that product as defective if it thinks that some alternative design or plan on balance is preferable. As a common law matter, the entire system cares much less for contractual models for setting liability and much more for public law models of regulation —judicial regulation to be sure, but regulation nonetheless.

The redefinition of the manufacturer's obligation has brought with it a correlative shift in the obligations of the product consumer. Whereas the consumer was once regarded as an essential and responsible link in the chain of product use, today he is often viewed more as an object of legal protection and less as a bearer of independent responsibilities. Instead of being held accountable for the consequences of his own misconduct, the consumer is all too often insulated from his own recklessness, foolishness, and neglect. In years past, a drunken driver could never dream of recovery against the manufacturer of his own automobile; today such recoveries can, and do, take place.

This history is painted with very broad strokes, and it needs some revision and qualification, and much elaboration and documentation. The more detailed account of that history is, moreover, rendered difficult if not treacherous by an elusive linguistic obstacle that is ever present in all common law subjects. At one level the basic legal doctrines never seem to change. Their familiar building blocks—negligence, strict liability, causation, assumption of risk, contributory negligence—were with us at the end of the nineteenth century. The same negligence tests used to justify restrictive nineteenth-century rules of privity are pressed into service to support the most exotic design defect case today. The leap from extreme to extreme shows just how difficult it is to break down the tyranny of legal concepts that can conceal the major substantive changes within the legal system. In order to penetrate verbal barriers, it is necessary to do legal history and legal analysis at the same time, maintaining our bearings throughout by constant reference to the detailed fact patterns of decided cases against which it is possible to identify and evaluate the changes in legal doctrine.

This, then, is an essay in interpretative legal theory. It combines a historical account of development of legal doctrine with an analytical account of its promise and shortcomings. The first half of the book traces the law of products liability through its first two periods, to the publication in 1965 of the Restatement (Second) of Torts. Chapter 2 begins with the account of the rise and fall of the privity limitation, which has had so much influence upon the growth and development of products liability law. Chapter 3 examines the development of the various common law theories of recovery-negligence, strict liability, express and implied warranty in the years between *MacPherson v. Buick* (1916) and *Escola v. Coca-Cola Bottling Co.* (1944)[6] Chapter 4 gives a detailed analysis of not only *Escola*, but of its companion case, *Greenman v. Yuba Power Products, Inc.*,[7] decided some eighteen years later. These two cases, both by what they decided and by how they decided it, ushered in the modern law of products liability. Chapter 5 is devoted to the question of the extent to which private parties may contract out of the products liability rules and examines in that connection the justifications for limiting contractual freedom advanced by the New Jersey Supreme Court in *Henningsen v. Bloomfield Motors, Inc.* (1960).[8] Chapter 6 completes the first part of the book and looks at the contribution of the Restatement (Second) of Torts, especially Section 402A, to the subsequent course of the tort law.

6. 24 Cal. 2d 453, 150 P.2d 436 (1944).
7. 59 Cal. 2d 57, 377 P.2d 897, 27 Cal. Rptr. 697 (1963).
8. 32 N.J. 358, 161 A.2d 69 (1960).

The second half of this book is devoted to an analysis of modern products liability actions. Chapter 7 addresses the complex issues associated with construction and design defect cases. Chapter 8 does the same for duty to warn actions. Chapter 9 examines the role of plaintiff's conduct which, under the guise of contributory negligence, product misuse, or assumption of risk, is so crucial to modern products liability litigation. Chapter 10 turns to some of the problems of procedure and proof associated with these modern products liability causes of action. Last, Chapter 11 looks at some issues of actual and punitive damages. These chapters are not meant as a substitute for a comprehensive treatise on the law of products liability. They are, however, designed to chronicle the major themes of the products liability law as it emerged from its nineteenth-century origins to the present day.

CHAPTER

# 2

# PRIVITY

This study of the law of products liability begins, then, not with a survey of the current rules, but with a historical account of its development from the middle of the nineteenth century until, to pick a convenient date, the publication of the Restatement (Second) of Torts in 1965. This historical study serves two distinct functions. First, it gives some sense of the traditional structure of products liability law before the recent expansion within the field. Second, it gives a representative sample of factual situations from which it is possible to deduce sensible propositions about how the law of products liability should be organized today.

It is best to organize this historical account around the three themes which dominated the pre-Restatement cases. The first is the birth, development, and ultimate death of the privity limitation, which for a long time was the distinctive feature in the nascent law of products liability. The second is the complicated relationship among theories of negligence, strict liability, and implied warranty. The last is the basic account of causation and the related concept of product defect. These issues cannot be placed in watertight compartments, even if analytically distinct, but they do provide a serviceable framework of analysis. This chapter is devoted to privity.[1]

## THE PRIVITY LIMITATION

### STATEMENT

The privity limitation is a technical doctrine of tort law that has no apparent analogue in ordinary discourse. In essence it provides that the purchaser of any product may maintain an action for personal injury or property damage only against his immediate seller. Whether the defendant was a

1. On the growth and development of the privity limitation, *see* W. Prosser, *Handbook of the Law of Torts* §96 (4th ed. 1971), and Bohlen, *Liability of Manufacturers to Persons Other than Their Immediate Vendees*, 45 Law Q. Rev. 343 (1929).

retailer, distributor, or manufacturer, the principle is the same. An injured plaintiff must have a direct contractual relationship with a defendant in order to have any possibility of legal recourse against him. Persons further down in the chain of distribution, or the innocent bystanders outside it, must seek their remedies against other parties—or do without relief altogether.

The bare statement of this rule gives only a small clue as to its immense effect on the basic patterns of tort litigation in the nineteenth century. Taken without its later case law qualifications, the privity rule insulated the typical manufacturer or supplier from virtually all actions for personal injury, death, or property damage caused by a defective product. There were two major exceptions to this blanket immunity. By the first the manufacturer or supplier could be held accountable for harms to intermediate distributors—a comparative rarity, since these parties did not use the product itself but only shipped it farther along the stream of commerce. By the second the manufacturers or suppliers could be reached through a web of indemnity actions brought against them by others who, directly or indirectly, were required to make good the hurt suffered by injured consumers and users. The scope and interpretation of the privity limitation were the central features of nineteenth-century products liability. Indeed it was privity that gave products liability its distinctive intellectual cast and its separate doctrinal niche. Plaintiffs who could surmount the privity limitation were, to be sure, faced with the sharp common law limitations upon recovery—rigorous causal restrictions and powerful defenses of contributory negligence and assumption of risk. But the vast majority of injured plaintiffs who could not surmount the privity limitation were out of court wholly without regard to these substantive hurdles. The privity rule was indeed simple to state and simple to apply. And for cases within its grip, it foreclosed all prospect for plaintiff's recovery simply by asking, "Who sold what to whom?"

## ORIGINS

The power and breadth of the privity limitation should not be allowed to conceal the notable confusion about its intellectual origins. The key case in its history is *Winterbottom v. Wright.*[2] The plaintiff was the driver of the mail coach in the employ of one Atkinson. Atkinson had received the coach under contract with the crown—as represented by the postmaster general. The postmaster general in turn had entered into an agreement with the defendant under which the defendant assumed the "sole and exclusive duty" to see that the coaches were "kept in a fit, proper, safe and secure condition." The defendant—or so the complaint alleged—did his work so negligently that the coach was left in such an unsafe condition that it broke down while in use, throwing the plaintiff to the ground and injuring him.

2. 10 M. & W. 109, 152 Eng. Rep. 402 (Ex. 1842)

The court held that the plaintiff's allegations disclosed no cause of action and accordingly dismissed the complaint. Crucial for understanding the decision are the two separate types of reasons—conceptual and administrative—that were offered to justify that result. The conceptual argument was an effort to show that the action was unsound as a matter of justice even if it created no unacceptable administrative burdens for the courts. The administrative argument was intended to show that, however sound the plaintiff's cause of action in theory, it had to be rejected because of the great uncertainty and massive litigation costs that would follow in its wake.

The justice argument was that recognition of the plaintiff's cause of action would do violence to whatever contract existed between the defendant and the postmaster general. Lord Abinger, the chief justice, noted:

> By permitting this action, we should be working this injustice, that after the defendant had done every thing to the satisfaction of his employer, and after all matters between them had been adjusted, and all accounts settled on the footing of their contract, we should subject them to be ripped open by this action of tort being brought against him.[3]

Likewise Baron Rolfe:

> The duty, therefore, is shewn to have arisen solely from the contract; and the fallacy consists in the use of that word "duty." If a duty to the Postmaster-General be meant, that is true; but if a duty to the plaintiff be intended (and in that sense the word is evidently used), there was none. This is one of those unfortunate cases in which there certainly has been damnum, but it is damnum absque iniuriâ. . . .[4]

Both these passages suffer from an important conceptual error. The contract between the defendant and the postmaster general was in no way essential for or relevant to the plaintiff's action against the defendant. The court was quite correct in noting that this contract does not (particularly in a jurisdiction like England which still does not generally recognize any actions by intended third-party beneficiaries)[5] cast upon the defendant any obligations toward the plaintiff. Yet, by the same token, the contract between

3. Id. at 115, 152 Eng. Rep. at 405.

4. Id. at 116, 152 Eng. Rep. at 405. The reference to damnum absque iniuriâ is the Latin tag for those harms that are not compensable even though they leave the plaintiff worse off than before. The concept is quite out of place here, given the obvious physical injuries to the plaintiff. Its chief relevance is to economic harms caused by competition.

5. *See, e.g.*, G. C. Chesire and C. H. S. Fifoot, *The Law of Contract* pt. 6, ch. 1, §1 (7th ed. 1969), for a statement of the rule that only parties to a contract can enforce an action for a breach of promise. Such third-party beneficiary contracts have been enforceable in American courts since the nineteenth century. *See Lawrence v. Fox*, 20 N.Y. 268 (1859). It is, of course, doubtful that the coachman was regarded, as the modern American contract law would require, as an "intended" beneficiary of the defendant's promise.

the crown and the defendant could not *limit* whatever actions were available to the plaintiff. He was a stranger to that contract, and so by traditional theory is not bound by its terms.

Suppose that the defendant had entered into a contract with the postmaster general whereby the former agreed to shoot game for the latter. If in the course of his duties the defendant shot the plaintiff, he could surely not plead his contractual obligation to the postmaster general (to shoot, say, in a lawful and careful manner) as a defense to the plaintiff's action, no matter whether the plaintiff's action is based upon strict liability or upon negligence. With the negligence theory the plaintiff must show that the defendant owed him a duty of care, but that duty is always imposed by operation of law and not by special agreement. The plaintiff must make out that duty in exactly the same way (whatever that might be) whether or not there had been any agreement between the defendant and the postmaster general. Alternatively, if strict liability controlled the shooting case, then the defendant owed the plaintiff an absolute duty not to invade his person; simply shooting the plaintiff violates that legal duty wholly without regard to the admitted contract between the defendant and the third party.

The difference between the defective coach and the shooting does not rest on the question of legal duty. It rests rather on the length of the causal chain. True, in the coach case there was no trespass, no direct application of force by the defendant to the plaintiff. Yet even in the nineteenth century, courts accepted the "action on the case" for consequential, or indirect, harms.[6] And if the plaintiff could recover because the defendant left a log in the road (to follow the famous example)[7] even if in breach of defendant's contract with some third party, then so too he should be able to recover in *Winterbottom* so long as his case is sufficient under the tort law. It is, therefore, wholly incorrect to argue that something inherent in the nature of the duty concept makes the plaintiff's cause of action not only unwise, but also legally unintelligible. To the extent that the judges in *Winterbottom v. Wright* rely on this argument, they bet their all on a loser. Let the debate about the privity limitation end here, and the entire concept should without question be consigned to the dustbin of historical curiosities.

The problem, however, is not so simple, because we must still consider the evident administrative fears of the judges, and these prove themselves to be more resistant to clear analysis. Lord Abinger said that judgment must be given for the defendant. "We ought not to permit a doubt to rest upon

6. *See*, for an account of the relationship between trespass and case, W. Prosser, *Handbook of the Law of Torts*, §7 (4th ed. 1971). For historical accounts of the subject, *see generally* C. H. S. Fifoot, *History and Sources of the Common Law* 66-73 (1949); Oliver Wendell Holmes, Jr., *The Common Law* 90-91 (1881).

7. *Reynolds v. Clarke*, 1 Str. 634, 92 Eng. Rep. 410 (K. B. 1726) (per Fortescue, J.).

this subject, for our doing so might be the means of letting in upon us an infinity of actions."[8] Again:

> If the plaintiff can sue, every passenger, or even any person passing along the road, who was injured by the upsetting of the coach, might bring a similar action. Unless we confine the operation of such contracts as this to the parties who entered into them, the most absurd and outrageous consequences, to which I can see no limit, would ensue.[9]

So, too, the fears of Baron Alderson:

> If we were to hold that the plaintiff could sue in such a case, there is no point at which such actions would stop. The only safe rule is to confine the right to recover to those who enter into the contract: if we go one step beyond that, there is no reason why we should not go fifty.[10]

The merits of the individual case were not uppermost in the minds of the judges. For them the crucial question was how they could limit the business of the courts without the faithful application of the privity doctrine. "Hard cases, it has been frequently observed, are apt to introduce bad law."[11]

Floodgate arguments have not been viewed with much sympathy by twentieth-century judges, who often regard them as flimsy excuses for not discharging the paramount judicial duty of deciding cases upon their in-

8. *Winterbottom v. Wright*, 10 M. & W. at 113, 152 Eng. Rep. at 404 (Ex. 1842). *Winterbottom v. Wright* should not be read in historical isolation on this point. Just five years earlier, Lord Abinger delivered the lead opinion in *Priestly v. Fowler*, 3 M. & W. 1, 150 Eng. Rep. 1030 (Ex. 1837), which adopted the so-called fellow servant or common employment doctrine. The gist of this doctrine was that an employer could not be sued by one of his employees for the injuries caused to him by another servant also within the employ of the master. In his opinion, Abinger noted that under such a proposed rule "[t]he master, for example, would be liable to the servant for the negligence of the chambermaid for putting him into a damp bed," and concluded with the familiar flourish: "The inconvenience, not to say the absurdity of these consequences, afford a sufficient argument against the application of this principle to the present case."

The common employment rule also had a firm hold on the American courts during the nineteenth century, with the key opinion being that of Chief Justice Shaw, one of the most respected judges of his time, in *Farwell v. The Boston & Worcester R.R. Corp.*, 45 Mass. (4 Metc.) 49 (1842). The rule was in the process of disintegration when its importance was removed by the passage of the workers' compensation laws in the first part of the twentieth century.

9. Id. at 114, 152 Eng. Rep. at 405.

10. Id. at 115, 152 Eng. Rep. at 405.

11. Id. at 116, 152 Eng. Rep. at 406.

dividual merits.[12] There is, however, for both the nineteenth and the twentieth centuries the terrible but inescapable trade-off presented every time administrative arguments of the *Winterbottom* stripe are advanced to cut back upon causes of action otherwise regarded as just. The sharp rule—here privity—helps eliminate the abuses and excesses of the system. Its price is always the simultaneous removal from the system of valid causes of action, even before the plaintiff is allowed his day in court. The plaintiff's plight looks all the more appealing because less drastic techniques are, in principle, available to weed out the frivolous from the respectable claims. Courts can allow the actions but raise the standard of proof, keep out certain types of evidence, or allocate certain costs to victorious defendants. Yet a note of caution must enter, for these less drastic devices themselves take time and money, and in some instances may not provide sufficient protection against pervasive abuses. Everything now depends upon the number and quality of the cases that are kept out by the rule. Where the adverse impact upon sound cases is commonplace, the "protective rule" becomes less attractive; where mainly frivolous cases are suppressed, that same rule has a far greater appeal.[13]

To elaborate: If it could be shown that 90 percent of the cases blocked by the privity rule should be decided for the defendant even in its absence, the rule would undoubtedly be a good one. It would clearly cut down on the costs of litigation without doing much, if any, violence to the results that justice requires. True, 10 percent of the cases are necessarily decided incorrectly; but what about the alternative? Let all the cases go to trial and the ideal result will be reached only if 10 percent of the cases are decided for plaintiff. Yet even the proper 90-10 split does not guarantee results that are superior to those generated by the automatic rule, for case-by-case adjudication is superior to the blanket rule only if the *right* 10 percent of the cases

12. *See, e.g.*, Tobriner, J. in *Dillon v. Legg*, 68 Cal. 2d 728, 441 P.2d 912, 69 Cal. Rptr. 72 (1968). "Courts not only compromise their basic responsibility to decide the merits of each case individually but destroy the public's confidence in them by using the broad broom of 'administrative convenience' to sweep away a class of claims a number of which are admittedly meritorious." 68 Cal. 2d at 737, 441 P.2d at 918, 69 Cal. Rptr. at 78 (1968). In *Dillon* the California Supreme Court allowed individuals who suffered from negligently inflicted nervous shock to recover even though they were not within the "zone of danger" of the person injured. The subsequent cases, largely for administrative reasons, have narrowly confined the scope of recovery to those who witnessed the harm to another person. *See, e.g.*, *Hair v. County of Monterey*, 45 Cal. App. 3d 538, 119 Cal. Rptr. 639 (1975).

13. The cases of nervous shock apart from physical injury again illustrate the point. A medical-legal study of 301 nervous shock cases indicated that recovery was appropriate only about 30 percent of the time, while defendants were in fact only able to prevail in about one-sixth of the suits. "Taking all cases decided between 1850 and 1944," the study concludes, "the net balance of justice would have been greater had all courts denied damages for injury imputed to psychic stimuli alone." Smith, *Relation of Emotions to Injury and Disease: Legal Liability for Psychic Stimuli*, 30 Va. L. Rev. 193, 285 (1944).

are in fact decided for the plaintiff. The blanket rule will in all likelihood combine the best of all worlds by yielding on balance the best attainable results at the lowest possible cost. Allowing all the actions to proceed to judgment would yield errors in 12 percent of the cases, if only four of the right ten plaintiffs recovered. In essence, the rejection of the blanket rule could well require increased expenditures to reach worse results. We must not, however, push this line of argument too far if the error costs of the overbroad privity rule were 50 or 60 percent; then its attraction fades. In this situation, the less drastic techniques of error control just mentioned could well represent more sensible ways to minimize the combination of decision error and administrative costs.

This administrative argument in favor of privity is, therefore, not subject to a clean conceptual refutation, because it is not a clean conceptual argument. The question to be investigated is whether the price that is paid for the privity rule is simply too high. The nineteenth-century judges' mistake was that they sought to answer this question without considering alternative substantive tort rules that might be brought to the nascent products liability area. These alternative approaches were but slowly understood and only after experience with the common forms of products actions. In order to get a better sense of what the judges in *Winterbottom v. Wright* missed, it is necessary to look at some of the cases whose factual patterns persuaded judges to create exceptions to the remorseless privity rule.

## EXCEPTIONS

The major exceptions to the privity rule developed one at a time in the last half of the nineteenth century. In their classical form they were summarized by Judge Sanborn in the important if somewhat neglected case of *Huset v. J. I. Case Threshing Machine Co.* as follows:

> The first is that an act of negligence of a manufacturer or vendor which is imminently dangerous to the life or health of mankind, and which is committed in the preparation or sale of an article intended to preserve, destroy, or affect human life, is actionable by third parties who suffer from the negligence.
>
> The second exception is that an owner's act of negligence which causes injury to one who is invited by him to use his defective appliance upon the owner's premises may form the basis of an action against the owner.
>
> The third exception to the rule is that one who sells or delivers an article which he knows to be imminently dangerous to life or limb to another without notice of its qualities is liable to any person who suffers an injury therefrom which might have been reasonably anticipated, whether there were any contractual relations between the parties or not.[14]

Let us consider these in order.

14. 120 F. 865, 870-71 (8th Cir. 1903).

INHERENTLY DANGEROUS PRODUCTS

The most important illustration of the first exception is *Thomas v. Winchester*,[15] an 1852 New York case. The plaintiff was seriously injured when she took a small quantity of belladonna that had been mislabeled by the defendant's employee as dandelion extract. Belladonna is a powerful poison, and dandelion extract is but "simple and harmless medicine." The difficulty with the plaintiff's cause of action was that her husband had purchased the belladonna for her from a local druggist who in turn had purchased it from the defendant. The defendant relied on *Winterbottom v. Wright*, which the court generally approved of in these words:

> If A. build a wagon and sell it to B., who sells it to C., and C. hires it to D., who in consequence of the gross negligence of A. in building the wagon is overturned and injured, D. cannot recover damages against A., the builder. A.'s obligation to build the wagon faithfully, arises solely out of his contract with B. The public have nothing to do with it.[16]

These words notwithstanding, the court then refused to apply *Winterbottom* to a mislabeled poisonous drug placed by the defendant in the stream of commerce. The method of escape is crucial. Originally, the privity doctrine was a "duty" limitation. No duty could run toward the plaintiff on the strength of a contractual undertaking to a third party, here the defendant's immediate vendee. *Thomas v. Winchester* transformed privity into a causation rule by treating it as a concrete illustration of the general common law principle that the defendant is accountable only for "the natural and necessary" consequences of his negligence. To show that the plaintiff's injury was the natural and necessary consequence of mislabeling the belladonna, the court had to find some way to overcome the fact that it passed through the hands of intermediate parties. It did so by noting that the sale of the substance in the original container created an "imminent danger" only to the ultimate user. In language that anticipates much of what Cardozo was to say in *MacPherson v. Buick*, it noted: "In the present case the sale of the poisonous article was made to a dealer in drugs, and not to a consumer. The injury therefore was not likely to fall on him, or on his vendee who was also a dealer; but much more likely to be visited on a remote purchaser, as actually happened."[17]

This argument is, in fact, *too* persuasive. It may explain why the privity limitation is inappropriate in cases of poisonous drugs, but it does not explain why it makes sense for a broken-down coach, which is likely to cause harm not to the retailer or distributor that first purchased it, but to its

15. 6 N.Y. 397 (1852).
16. Id. at 408.
17. Id. at 409.

ultimate user upon the highway. The two situations cannot, then, be distinguished upon conceptual grounds. Nonetheless, there are important differences in the types of proof needed in the two situations that do suggest a possible administrative distinction, with *Thomas v. Winchester* surely presenting the more attractive case for the plaintiff. The belladonna clearly remained in its original condition until its use caused the plaintiff's injury. Likewise there is no sign of culpable conduct by any of the intermediate parties in the chain of distribution, as all of them, including the plaintiff, were ignorant of the belladonna's true qualities and did nothing to make it more dangerous. On causal grounds, then, there is nothing to distinguish *Thomas* from a case in which the defendant first contracts for the sale of the belladonna directly with the plaintiff, only to ship it by messenger.

*Winterbottom* presents a more complicated causal picture. While the coach may well have remained in its original condition until the moment of injury, such is not necessarily the case. The coach may have been driven for months or years before the injury took place. The user of the coach might have modified it for his own purposes or allowed it to fall into a sad state of disrepair, and its driver might have neglected obvious and common safety precautions. What is to be made of these possible complications is of course unclear because the barrier created by the privity limitation prevents any of these issues from being raised at trial. For all we know, the proof of causal connection in *Winterbottom* could have been as simple as that in *Thomas*; the differences between the two cases go solely to questions of proof and thus raise issues not of kind but of degree. The sharp opposition between *Thomas* and *Winterbottom*, however, is not necessarily improper, because the cumulative differences between the cases may, for the administrative reasons noted above, warrant this treatment. Such indeed was the opinion of Judge Sanborn in *Huset v. Case*, who not only defended the privity rule on remoteness-of-damage grounds but offered this independent justification as well:

> [P]erhaps more than all this, [the action is never allowed] for the reason that a wise and conservative public policy has impressed the courts with the view that there must be a fixed and definite limitation to the liability of manufacturers and vendors for negligence in the construction and sale of complicated machines and structures which are to be operated or used by the intelligent and the ignorant, the skillful and the incompetent, the watchful and the careless, parties that cannot be known to the manufacturers or vendors, and who use the articles all over the country hundreds of miles distant from the place of their manufacture or original sale. . . .[18]

Today the privity limitation is long gone, but the problems raised by Sanborn's arguments are not.

18. 120 F. 865, 867 (1903).

## INVITATIONS TO USE DEFECTIVE PRODUCTS ON THE DEFENDANT'S PREMISES

The second exception in *Huset*, involving the owner's act of negligence that causes injury to one invited by him to use his defective appliance upon the owner's premises, also illustrates the halting way in which relaxation of the privity rule permitted recovery where the plaintiff's causal case was strong and its administrative complications but slight. In *Devlin v. Smith* the plaintiff workman was injured in a fall from a defective scaffold which was supplied to his employer by the defendant for use in painting the inside of the dome of the county courthouse.[19] The absence of any direct relationship between the injured employee and the supplier of the scaffold brought the case squarely within the privity limitation. Yet the New York court, cognizant of the fact that the scaffold in its original condition could not support the weight of a man working on it, allowed the plaintiff's action under what amounted to an implied contract created when the defendant supplied the scaffold for the benefit of the plaintiff. The case is, in causal terms, a close relative to *Thomas v. Winchester*. Indeed the only difference between them is that poison works its harm by initiating chemical changes upon ingestion, whereas the scaffold brings about damage because of its weak condition at great height and in ordinary use. At stake, then, is only the *mode* of causation, not the more fundamental question of remoteness of damages. Gravity and poisons work in different ways, but both cause damage.

> Stevenson [the defendant who made the scaffold] undertook to build a scaffold ninety feet in height for the express purpose of enabling the workmen of Smith [the plaintiff's employer] to stand upon it to paint the interior of the dome. Any defect or negligence in its construction, which should cause it to give way, would naturally result in these men being precipitated from that great height. A stronger case where misfortune to third persons not parties to the contract would be a natural and necessary consequence of the builder's negligence, can hardly be supposed, nor is it easy to imagine a more apt illustration of a case where such negligence would be an act imminently dangerous to human life. These circumstances seem to us to bring the case fairly within the principle of *Thomas v. Winchester*.[20]

However powerful this rationale, it must be noted that *Devlin v. Smith* does *not* fall within Sanborn's second exception because the accident did not take place upon the defendant's premises, as had been, for example, the situation in the key New York case of *Coughtry v. Globe Woolen Co.*,[21]

19. 89 N.Y. 470 (1872). There is also the English decision in *Heaven v. Pender*, 11 Q.B. 503 (1883), which, on similar facts, was decided the same way as *Devlin v. Smith*.

20. *Devlin v. Smith*, 89 N.Y. 470, 478 (1882).

21. 56 N.Y. 124 (1874). Judge Rapalio, who wrote the opinions in both cases, had no difficulty in extending the scope of this second exception. "It is true there was in [Coughtry] the additional fact that the scaffold was erected by the defendant upon its own premises, but the case did not depend wholly upon that point." 89 N.Y. at 478.

decided for the plaintiff some eight years before *Devlin v. Smith*. This rejection of *Devlin* was especially puzzling because Sanborn took such pains to rationalize the privity limitation as a specific application of the causal rules of remoteness of damage. Yet the location of the accident does not increase the probabilities of its occurrence. It is as though the plaintiff could recover in *Thomas* only if she consumed the belladonna on the defendant's premises. The second exception to the privity rule, then, illustrates the same unresolved tensions as the first. The conceptual arguments fail, and the administrative concerns of unending liability simply do not make any sense with cases in which the plaintiff's injuries result from a fall from a defective scaffold.

### THINGS KNOWN TO BE IMMINENTLY DANGEROUS

The gist of the last exception to the privity rule is that the injured plaintiff may recover from a remote defendant "who sells or delivers an article which he knows to be imminently dangerous to life or limb to another without notice of its qualities." The exception was first formulated in the 1837 English case *Langridge v. Levy*,[22] decided before *Winterbottom v. Wright*. The plaintiff was a young boy whose father had purchased a gun for his use from the defendant. The defendant represented that the gun was safe for use, and that it had been made by one Nock, a well-known gunmaker; in fact, the gun was made not by Nock but by an inferior gunmaker. Owing to a weakness in its barrel, the gun exploded while being fired, blowing off the plaintiff's hand. The plaintiff's cause of action rested on two alternative theories. The first, reminiscent of the arguments raised in *Winterbottom v. Wright*, was that the defendant's contractual warranty made him accountable to any person injured by his defective goods, a position that the court declined to adopt because of the enormous expansion of liability that it seemed to entail. The second and narrower position turned upon the express fraudulent representations about the gun's origin and condition made when delivering the gun to the father for the son's use. Of crucial importance for this exception is the question of whether liability should attach to representations that are implied on the one hand and innocent on the other.

With respect to the first of these questions, general legal theory always treats in identical fashion both express and implied-in-fact representations, and there is no reason to depart from this point of view with products liability actions. True, the danger always lurks that implied-in-fact representations will be converted by zealous judges into representations fictiously implied by operation of law. Yet even the possibility of that abuse cannot blunt the observation that in many cases—just think of foodstuffs sold in their original packages—the presentation of the product itself carries the implicit representation of its fitness for use *direct* from maker to user.

The social importance of these implicit representations cannot be under-

22. M. & W. 519, 150 Eng. Rep. 863 (Ex. 1837).

estimated. The plaintiff was successful in *Langridge v. Levy* only because the court found that the injured son was the "real party in interest," inasmuch as the father purchased the gun for his benefit and use. Yet if a family friend had used the gun in precisely the same way, under the same impressions about its fitness, the "real party" representation theory of *Langridge* fails, even though the switch in the plaintiff's identity creates no real causal complication. By 1900 any insistence upon the express nature of the representations had faded, and no specific mention of that requirement is made by Sanborn. A sale with knowledge suffices. The real task with each alleged implied representation is to determine its precise content and the conditions under which it is applicable, for far from guaranteeing safety, many products warn of danger. The medium is indeed the message.

The second implicit limitation upon this last exception, that only fraud (inferred from a sale with knowledge) would carry the day for the plaintiff, also raises important questions of both fact and theory. This limitation is consistent with the late nineteenth-century view which required proof of fraud to recover pecuniary losses incurred by acting on the faith of the defendant's false representation.[23] Yet the point is not decisive, as the physical injury cases provide the closer analogies. *Thomas v. Winchester*, the poison case, turned on misrepresentation by mislabeling, and yet recovery was allowed on proof of negligence alone. *Devlin v. Smith* rested upon the implied representation that the scaffold could carry the weight of a man; yet, here too recovery was allowed simply upon a showing that the scaffold was defectively or carelessly constructed. The cases in the third exception depend upon similar representations. In the California case of *Lewis v. Terry*,[24] the plaintiff suffered a broken arm and internal injuries when pinned inside a folding bed which closed upon her when she lay upon it, and the plaintiff in *Huset v. Case* sustained injuries when he fell through a metal cover of a threshing machine which was allegedly "insufficient to hold the weight of any man" even though standing on the cover was necessary for operation of the machine. The knowledge requirement of this last exception seems particularly hard and unprincipled in these two situations, which both have all the ingredients of a strong design defect case today. That neither the bed nor the thresher conformed to its own designated performance standards should suffice. Knowledge is quite immaterial.

It is now time to take stock of the privity rule and its nineteenth-century exceptions. The knowledge limitation in the third exception, and the premises limitation in the second, were all that was left of the privity rule. Without these two artificial barriers to recovery, the three exceptions together cover all possible cases, with *Winterbottom v. Wright* falling, for example, securely

23. *Derry v. Peek*, 14 App. Cas. 337 (H.L. 1889).
24. 111 Cal. 39, 43 P. 398 (1896).

into the expanded third exception. The older cases thus came within an ace of overcoming the privity limitation by expanding the exceptions to it. They did not, however, perceive and act upon the implicit causal unities in products cases. The stage was set for *MacPherson v. Buick.*[25]

## THE OVERTURNING OF PRIVITY

The facts of *MacPherson* are as follows. The defendant was the manufacturer of an automobile, which it sold to a dealer, who in turn sold it to the plaintiff. While the car was moving eight miles per hour on a good road, a wheel, manufactured by a reputable subcontractor, suddenly broke and collapsed. The plaintiff was thrown out of the car and injured. The question was whether the plaintiff had a good cause of action against the manufacturer of the finished product, even though there was no direct contract between them.

On these facts *Winterbottom v. Wright* controls, for none of the three basic exceptions announced in *Huset* applies. An automobile is not an inherently dangerous thing like poisons and explosives; the possession and control of the automobile, unlike the scaffold, far from remaining with the defendant, passed irrevocably to the plaintiff; and the defendant neither knew of the defect nor made any effort to conceal it. These arguments were, moreover, very forcefully presented in the now forgotten dissent of Chief Justice Bartlett:

> In the case at bar the defective wheel on an automobile moving only eight miles an hour was not any more dangerous to the occupants of the car than a similarly defective wheel would be to the occupants of a carriage drawn by a horse at the same speed; and yet unless the courts have been all wrong on this question up to the present time there would be no liability to strangers to the original sale. . . .[26]

The world, however, belongs to the future and not to the past. It is thus appropriate and necessary to examine the masterful technique adopted by Judge Cardozo to escape a large body of adverse precedent. Cardozo ignored the direct challenge of Bartlett. What controlled in the previous cases, he insisted, was not the mass of decisions applying the privity rule but two issues of immediate and paramount importance. The first was whether, in the circumstances of the case, the vendor had knowledge that the thing would be used by a person other than its immediate purchaser. Here the answer, reminiscent of *Thomas v. Winchester*, is clear:

> The maker of this car supplied it for the use of purchasers from the dealer just as plainly as the contractor in *Devlin v. Smith* supplied the scaffold for use by the

25. 217 N.Y. 382, 111 N.E. 1050 (1916).
26. Id. at 400, 111 N.E. at 1056-57.

servants of the owner. The dealer was indeed the one person of whom it might be said with some approach to certainty that by him the car would not be used. Yet the defendant would have us say that he was the one person whom it was under a legal duty to protect. The law does not lead us to so inconsequent a conclusion.[27]

The second issue is whether the product held out danger to life and limb. Here Cardozo refused to draw "subtle distinctions" between things "inherently dangerous and things imminently dangerous." He rightly insisted that the basic tort doctrines of foresight and remoteness of damage do not admit of a principled distinction between the two different kinds of dangerously defective conditions. The elaborate classification sanctioned by *Huset v. Case* was a thing of the past. Liability was properly denied in the earlier cases only where remoteness of damage tests, freed of any false associations with privity, mandated that result. The other decisions simply represented a misapplication of the general principles of causation and foresight. Cardozo observes:

Judge Sanborn says . . . that the contractor who builds a bridge, or the manufacturer who builds a car, cannot ordinarily foresee injury to other persons than the owner as the probable result. . . . [citation omitted] We take a different view. We think that injury to others is to be foreseen not merely as a possible, but as an almost inevitable result.[28]

The rejection of the privity limitation required Cardozo to address next the question of the defendant's negligence and its causal relationship to plaintiff's harm. His treatment of these issues is, unlike his masterful analysis of privity, both unsure and uneven. His views do, however, demand serious examination for the clues they provide about the future growth of the law.

The issue of defendant's negligence, for example, confronted Cardozo with no simple problem. The defective wheel was made by a reputable contractor, not by the defendant's own servants. Thus it is attractive, indeed correct, to argue that the defendant's selection of a competent contractor discharged its duty of care to the plaintiff, as reasonable care—not all possible care—is all that a negligence standard requires. If the defendant knows that a skilled specialist has both produced and inspected the wheels, it hardly seems sensible for the defendant to inspect them anew upon receipt, especially when, as Bartlett observed, the supplier "furnished the defendant with eighty thousand wheels, none of which had proved to be made of defective wood prior to the accident in the present case."[29]

Cardozo was quite conscious of this difficulty, and his response to it was

27. Id. at 391, 111 N.E. at 1053.
28. Id. at 392, 111 N.E. at 1054.
29. Id. at 395, 111 N.E. at 1055.

simply to assert that the general manufacturer "was not at liberty to put the finished product on the market without subjecting the component parts to ordinary and simple tests."[30] His result is correct, but is best supported by appeal to principles of vicarious liability, parallel to those applicable to independent contractors,[31] that hold the manufacturer of the finished product responsible for the defects of any of the components incorporated into the product, whether made by his employees or by independent contractors. As vicarious liability has always rested upon strict liability principles, a new and distinct duty of inspection need not be invented in order to "find" the negligence thought necessary for Buick's tortious liability. The simple solution is also the more elegant one because it allows the courts, at least in this corner of the law, to escape the question of *how much* inspection is necessary to discharge the duty of inspection imposed by operation of law.

A frank use of vicarious liability principles also could have spared Cardozo a further confusion on the remoteness of damages issue as it relates to the manufacturers of both the component part and the final product. Thus Cardozo is curiously uncertain about the wheelmaker's liability for the accident because he thought, under the narrow causal tests used at that time,[32] that Buick's failure to inspect might amount to intervening negligence defeating liability. The case for the opposite result is, however, clearly overwhelming. The wheelmaker made the bad wheel; Buick only incorporated it into its product. Likewise, the wheelmaker clearly had had better control over the quality of its product, which remained unchanged in all material respects until the time of injury. Buick has an action for indemnity against the wheel manufacturer for any tort judgment Buick pays to the injured party. The direct action for the injured party, therefore, is appropriate if only to avoid the multiplicity of suits. That conclusion is, moreover, made crystal clear once it is accepted that Buick's liability rests on vicarious liability and not causal principles; the nonexistent "duty" to inspect and its hypothetical breach could not possibly insulate the wheelmaker on remoteness of damages grounds. Indeed Cardozo's unjustified caution survived for but a very short time, for by 1932 the New York Court of Appeals, in *Smith v. Peerless Glass Co.*, speaking of the liability of component part manufacturers, held: "Whatever was shadowy then in respect to the principles both of negligence and of causation has vanished in the light of subsequent decisions."[33]

30. Id. at 394, 111 N.E. at 1055.

31. The parallel is that employers, while not normally held for the torts of their independent contractors, become responsible for them when, for example, they are engaged in work, such as excavation, upon the defendant's premises. *See generally* on the scope of this liability, W. Prosser, *Handbook of the Law of Torts* §71 (4th ed. 1971).

32. One such test was the so-called "last wrongdoer test," whereby the negligence of Buick would have insulated the wheelmaker from suit.

33. 259 N.Y. 292, 295, 181 N.E. 576, 577 (1932).

The second dimension to the causal question—one of considerably more importance and difficulty—concerns the responsibility of the manufacturer of the finished product for events that occur after the product leaves its possession and control. Here Cardozo dramatized his own concern about the potential reach of liability under a generalized and unqualified foresight test for remoteness of damage. Knowledge of the danger must be "not merely possible, but probable. It is possible to use almost anything in a way that will make it dangerous if defective. That is not enough to charge the manufacturer with a duty independent of his contract."[34] The key point was that shared expectations of intermediate inspection precluded the possibility of unlimited liability. "We are dealing," he says, "now [in *MacPherson*] with the liability of the manufacturer of the finished product who puts it on the market to be used without inspection by his customers."[35]

The abrogation of the privity doctrine did not, under Cardozo's careful formulation of the rule, open the floodgates to massive litigation. The caution over causation and especially the concern with "downstream" conduct both served to keep the law within manageable boundaries. Indeed it can be argued that even after *MacPherson* the rules of recovery were too restrictive. The history and justification for their relaxation in the next generation forms the proper subject of the next chapter.

34. 217 N.Y. 382, 389, 111 N.E. 1050, 1053 (1916).
35. Id. at 390, 111 N.E. at 1053.

CHAPTER

3

# FROM PRIVITY TO STRICT LIABILITY

## THE "STRONG" CAUSE OF ACTION

The progression from *Winterbottom v. Wright*[1] to *MacPherson v. Buick*[2] clearly shows how the administrative arguments for the privity doctrine crumbled under the onslaught directed against them. The factual patterns in those decided cases show, moreover, that it is possible to identify certain recurrent features of a basic cause of action that has the "fixed and definite limitations" upon liability rightly demanded in *Huset v. Case.*[3] The elements of that "strong" cause of action are as follows.

First, there must be a *defect*, whether of design or construction, in the product in its original condition. The wheel in *MacPherson* contained a construction defect, and the threshing machine in *Huset* allegedly a design defect, because neither could bear the weight that the manufacturer represented it could sustain.

Second, the defect must *persist* in its original form until the time of injury. There must be no question of modification or alteration of the product, and no question of whether it had reached or passed the limits of ordinary wear and tear. Both points are easily satisfied in both *MacPherson* and *Huset*.

Third, the defect in the product must be *latent* in that the plaintiff could not have discovered it by simple visual inspection. The point is true for both cases.

Fourth, the plaintiff's use of the product must be consistent with its normal and intended function and must place upon it no stresses and strains other than those which it had to bear in order to be used at all; again, the point is true for both cases.

There is one curious omission from this list—the defendant's *negligence*, the ostensible basis of plaintiff action in all the cases discussed. This omis-

1. 10 M. & W. 109, 152 Eng. Rep. 402 (Exch. 1842).
2. 217 N.Y. 382, 111 N.E. 1050 (1916).
3. 120 F. 865 (8th Cir. 1903).

sion, however surprising, is eminently defensible in principle, but only—and the point will become increasingly clear—if the defect and causation notions are properly defined and limited, if burdens of proof are properly assigned, and if affirmative defenses are properly recognized. The relative unimportance of the negligence requirement can be best understood by first setting out the relationships among the three dominant theories used in products liability actions: negligence, warranty (both express and implied), and strict liability. In historical terms this task can be most easily accomplished by tracing the development of the products liability law from *MacPherson v. Buick* to the two California opinions written by Justice Traynor: *Escola v. Coca-Cola Bottling Company*,[4] decided in 1944, and *Greenman v. Yuba Power Products, Inc.*,[5] decided in 1962.

## NEGLIGENCE AND STRICT LIABILITY

Establishing the correct relationship between negligence and strict liability is one of the dominant concerns, not only of the law of products liability, but of the entire law of tort.[6] Is it enough for the plaintiff to allege only that the conduct of the defendant caused harm to the plaintiff's person or property? Or is it necessary in addition to allege that the harm so caused could have been prevented by the defendant's exercise of reasonable care? Where the extent of defendant's care (including all possible care) is regarded as immaterial, the case proceeds on a theory of strict liability. Where the want of reasonable care must be shown, the case proceeds on a theory of negligence, which, because it demands everything required of a plaintiff under a strict liability theory and more, is—analytically at least—the more restrictive theory of recovery.

The striking feature of tort theory around the turn of the century is that most academic writers thought that a uniform theory of negligence should in principle govern all physical injury cases.[7] The argument made in favor of that position essentially proceeded on moral terms. The defendant it was said was entitled to be free from burdensome litigation unless it could be shown that he was at fault in the occurrence of harm. Simply showing that he caused the harm was not, the argument continued, sufficient to establish the element of "fault" or personal "wrong," even if it did establish the

4. 24 Cal. 2d 453, 150 P.2d 436 (1944).

5. 59 Cal. 2d 57, 377 P.2d 897, 27 Cal. Rptr. 697 (1963).

6. For more extended discussions of the same issue, *see* Epstein, *A Theory of Strict Liability*, 2 J. Legal Stud. 151 (1973); Epstein, *Medical Malpractice: The Case for Contract*, 1976 Am. Bar Foundation Research J. 87 (1976).

7. *See, e.g.*, Oliver Wendell Holmes, Jr., *The Common Law*, Lecture III (1881); J. Salmond, *Salmond on Torts* §118 (1st ed. 1907); Ames, *Law and Morals*, 22 Harv. L. Rev. 97 (1908).

element of causation. Ideally, proof of a conscious disregard of the interests of others was needed to establish this essential requisite of individual fault. But the difficulties of determining subjective states of mind, and the need to protect individuals from "the slips and falls" of their neighbors combined to move the law toward the "objective" reasonable man standard of conduct: the defendant could be held responsible for the harm caused even if he did not have the personal attributes necessary to prevent its occurrence, so long as that harm could have been prevented by the reasonable man in the defendant's shoes.

This synthesis of the negligence law looks more imposing upon first appearance than it really is. Thus, it was clear that even during the late nineteenth and early twentieth centuries, strict liability principles continued to play an important role in cases involving injuries to real estate, whether by trespass or nuisance,[8] and to dominate other related areas of law—defamation,[9] and conversion of personal property.[10]

This persistence of strict liability might be explained on many grounds, but one point of special importance is this: even if the law of torts is thought to respond primarily to moral concerns, a negligence system need not command universal and unquestioning assent. The point is particularly clear in cases involving persons who before the occurrence of the accident were strangers to each other, that is strangers on the highway or neighboring landowners, but not parties who have voluntarily come together—to physician and patient, or landowner and invited visitor. With situations involving strangers, the law of negligence in its mature formation provided, in effect, that the defendant's benefits from his own conduct formed a valid excuse for not paying the plaintiff for the harm that such conduct caused. A theory of strict liability, however, sharply disputes this central premise: if the gains derived from certain activities are indeed as great as the defendant contends, there is all the more reason why he should pay for the harm those activities caused to the person or property of another, for, as against an innocent plaintiff who has nothing to do with the creation of the harm in question, it is only too clear that the defendant who captures the entire benefit of his own activities should, to the extent that the law can make it so, also bear its entire costs.

Now the complete force behind this particular argument rests upon the assumption that the defendant alone benefits from the activities that cause the harm. Where there is, however, a consensual relationship between the parties, the assumption no longer holds: now the defendant acts for the

8. *See e.g.*, the discussion in *Fletcher v. Rylands*, L.R. 1 Ex. 265 (1866), aff'd in *Rylands v. Fletcher*, L. R. 3 E. & I. App. 330 (1868).

9. *E. Hulton & Co. v. Jones*, [1909] 2 K.B. 444; [1910] A.C. 20; *Peck v. Tribune Co.*, 214 U.S. 185 (1909).

10. *Hollins v. Fowler*, L.R. 7 Q.B. 616 (1872); *Poggi v. Scott*, 167 Cal. 372, 139 P. 815 (1914).

benefit of both parties to the relationship. Under these circumstances the goal of the tort law is not to devise legal sanctions that prevent the "externalization" of harm upon innocent parties, but rather to allocate risks ex ante so as best to improve the position of both parties. In this last connection, the answers are not always clear-cut. In some circumstances it may well be that the retention of a strict liability rule makes eminent sense. Yet in others—just think of medical practice—the sensible rule may well be that the plaintiff assumes by implication the risks of certain harms, at least those which were not negligently caused.[11]

The arguments just made on behalf of strict liability, even if conclusive in cases involving strangers, to which they apply, are therefore of but limited relevance in products liability situations. They say in effect that strict liability and not negligence should govern whenever an innocent bystander is injured by a defective product made and marketed by the defendant. These same arguments are, however, of no particular relevance to the vast bulk of products liability actions brought by purchasers, users, and consumers of particular products. Here the passing of the privity requirement necessarily implies that the injured party should be treated as if he were in *direct* consensual relationship with the remote defendant. Contract arguments, not tort arguments, should govern. The choice between negligence and strict liability is thus clouded by assumption of risk elements, and thereby becomes more problematic in principle. In many products liability cases, at least, that choice is largely determined by a fresh set of difficulties that has always frustrated the proper application of the negligence standard.

The basic negligence standard requires a determination of whether the defendant has acted with reasonable care, which in turn raises the question of how much care must a defendant use toward a given plaintiff before he is excused from liability? Where the standard of care is determined in whole or in part by statute and custom, some external standard gives partial guidance on the ultimate issue. Nonetheless, even these aids have not prevented negligence from being inescapably defined in terms of a deceptively simple "cost-benefit" relationship. Do the benefits from the defendant's actions outweigh their associated costs to the plaintiff?

The classical formulation of the negligence rule, articulated after some earlier halting efforts, is that of Learned Hand in *United States v. Carroll Towing Co.*[12] Hand claimed that conduct is negligent where the probability of an accident (P) multiplied by the expected loss (L) of the accident exceeds the burdens (B) of its prevention. There follows a nice inequality, $PL \lessgtr B$.

11. *See, e.g.*, Epstein, *Medical Malpractice: The Case for Contract*, 1976 Am. Bar Foundation Research J. 87 (1976); McCoid, *The Care Required of Medical Practitioners*, 12 Vand. L. Rev. 549 (1959).

12. 159 F.2d 169 (2d Cir. 1947). An earlier version of the test can be found in Terry, *Negligence*, 29 Harv. L. Rev. 40 (1915), and the most thoroughgoing economic analysis of the formula is Posner, *A Theory of Negligence*, 1 J. Legal Stud. 29 (1972).

The formula is, of couse, subject to a number of objections, not the least of which is the obvious point of how to determine the appropriate numbers in any given case. Even more to the point here is the obvious instability that the formula produces in marginal cases, even if we assume that the formula is endowed with a precision that it does not, in fact, possess. Suppose that there is a 1 percent probability of a $10,000 accident that therefore bears an expected cost of $100. Now assume that the costs of prevention are but $99. From this it follows that the defendant is negligent, and hence liable for $10,000 if the accident occurs. Now change the cost of prevention to $101 and the situation shifts totally: as the costs of prevention now exceed the expected costs of the accident, no negligence is involved. It takes no great instinct to sense that something is very wrong with a system in which tiny shifts in the estimates of prevention costs can produce massive shifts in legal results. The same uneasiness is reinforced by the parallel instability created by the measurement of damages. Thus it seems odd in the extreme for the plaintiff to recover in full if the damages are placed at $10,001 but to go home empty handed if they are $2 less. A system of strict liability avoids both these embarrassments. It ignores the issue of precautions. In the first example the liability is for $10,000 no matter whether the costs of prevention are $99, $101, or for that matter $1,000,000, so long as causal connection is established. And it treats the differences in damages as irrelevant to the question of liability, bearing only on the extent of recovery. The plaintiff with $10,001 in damages will recover in exactly the same situations as the plaintiff with $9,999. The two-dollar difference in damages means only a two-dollar difference in recovery.

This instability of the negligence system suggests that individualized determinations of negligence must place strong administrative strains upon the legal system. Cost-benefit analyses, even unreliable ones, are not cheap to do. When they are done, they must reduce the percentage of cases in which recovery is granted while increasing the costs of determining whether recovery is in fact appropriate. Even if compensation of all injured parties is *not* a goal of the tort system, there is still a strong private sentiment, not to mention an insistent social pressure, to see that those dollars committed to the tort system go to injured parties rather than to the lawyers and experts needed to keep the system in operation. A strict liability rule has both these desirable effects.

Looking, then, at both the theoretical and administrative difficulties of a rigorous negligence system, one would expect that the negligence element is not part of the strong products liability cause of action. For the same reasons, it is not surprising that nineteenth-century judges never really took the negligence issue all that seriously in the cases they decided. In *Thomas v. Winchester*[13] mislabeling the poisonous drug was negligent, and no one asked

13. 6 N.Y. 397 (1852).

whether reasonable care had been used to see if the proper labels had been affixed. In *Huset v. Case* building a machine that could not hold the weight of the man who stepped on it was negligent, and no one asked whether reasonable care was taken to build it strong enough. And in *MacPherson v. Buick*, Buick's not inspecting was deemed negligent, as was the contractor's building those wheels out of bad wood.

These, and other nineteenth-century cases, implicitly equated the defendant's negligence with the creation of dangerous and defective products. The abrogation of the privity limitation, however, moved the negligence issue to center stage. The central question was whether an explicit negligence standard could withstand over the years the ambiguity of its application and use. The short answer is that it did not. And while the method of legal changes was often stumbling and uncertain, the movement in the years before the Second Restatement was all in the direction of strict liability for defective products.[14]

Three themes need special attention. The first concerns the legal strategies adopted to bring about the desired changes in the law of negligence and warranty. The second concerns the consequences of the changes for the decided cases. And the third concerns the emergence of "product defect" as the central concept in products liability litigation.

## THE DECLINE OF NEGLIGENCE

Two separate means were used to move from negligence to strict liability standards. By the first the standard of care applicable in negligence cases was progressively redefined to raise the levels of performance demanded of product manufacturers and sellers. By the second, the skillful use of presumptions, mainly associated with the doctrine of res ipsa loquitur, was used to limit the ability of the defendant to rebut any allegation of negligence made against him. Let us examine them in order.

### STANDARD OF CARE

The first method used to attenuate the negligence requirement needs little comment or explanation. The courts simply held that manufacturers, particularly of foodstuffs, owed the ultimate consumer a very high standard of care. Such was reasonable under the circumstances, given "the imperative need of consumers of food stuffs to rely upon the care of manufacturers thereof, and the inability of consumers . . . to detect injurious impurities or poisonous substances therein, and the complex system of modern production and distribution. . . ."[15] The distinction between highest possible care and

14. *See*, on these developments, James, *Products Liability*, 34 Texas L. Rev. 44 (1966); Prosser, *The Assault Upon the Citadel (Strict Liability to the Consumer)*, 69 Yale L. J. 1099 (1960).

15. *Hertzler v. Manshum*, 228 Mich. 416, 422, 200 N.W. 155, 156 (1924).

strict liability was not formally abolished, as food may be poisonous even when highest care has been observed in its preparation. But now it became more attractive for firms to defend themselves—as surely they must be allowed to do—by showing that the food was safe and wholesome instead of by showing that, although it was poisoned or spoiled, they had taken all possible care to make it safe and wholesome. The ever more exacting negligence standard tended to push the defect requirement to the fore.

The negligence standard was undermined in yet another way as courts weakened the close tie between negligence and custom. Here, in developments that paralleled those in other areas of tort law, courts refused to regard the custom in the defendant's trade or business as necessarily setting the ultimate standard of care.[16] All firms within a given industry (whether or not acting in collusion), it was said, may have failed to adopt appropriate safety standards. This, moreover, the jury was allowed to find as a matter of fact, thereby reducing common industry practice to but one piece of evidence bearing on the ultimate standard of care.

Where the defect requirement is strongly maintained—as it is in cases of contaminated food—the major criticism of the judicial attack upon custom is that it does not go far enough. The rule that gives custom presumptive and not conclusive effect can only increase the costs of litigation. Yet that same rule still permits a jury to find that custom was indeed appropriate in a given case or that, if some higher standard was required, it was in fact met. Subordinating custom may have narrowed the gap between negligence and strict liability; what was needed was a rule that eliminated the gap altogether.

### RES IPSA LOQUITUR

The second method for undermining the negligence requirement, at least in foodstuff cases, involved the doctrine of res ipsa loquitur. Under this doctrine the burden was shifted to the defendant to show, with the defect established, that he was not negligent. The classical statement of the proposition, attributable originally to Wigmore but today followed everywhere, is as follows: (1) the event must be of a kind which ordinarily does not occur in the absence of someone's negligence; (2) it must be caused by an agency or instrumentality within the exclusive control of the defendant; (3) it must not have been due to any voluntary action or contribution on the part of the plaintiff.[17] The technique is well illustrated by a 1924 case, *Richenbacher v. California Packing Corporation*.[18] The plaintiff was injured when she cut her mouth on some heavy, gray glass found in a can of spinach packaged and marketed by the defendant under its Del Monte label. The plaintiff's

16. *The T. J. Hooper*, 60 F.2d 737 (2d Cir. 1932).

17. *See* Wigmore, vol. 4, *Evidence* §2509 (1st ed. 1905); W. Prosser, *Handbook of the Law of Torts* §39 (4th ed. 1971).

18. 250 Mass. 198, 145 N.E. 281 (1924).

evidence showed that she and her husband handled the can in such a manner that the glass could not have entered the spinach after it left the can. There was no specific evidence of the defendant's negligence in preparing the spinach; yet, the court found negligence because of the unexplained "fact that the glass was in the can when it was sealed at the defendant's factory."[19] The exhaustive evidence presented by the defendant "as to the manner the spinach is handled in the factory before it is placed in sealed cans for sale and distribution for human consumption did not establish that it was impossible that the glass was in the can when it was sealed, but only that it was not feasible if proper care were used. . . ."[20] The net effect of this decision was that the proof of defect and causation—the foreign substance in the food at the time of the packing—was decisive on the question of prima facie liability. The "explanation" in principle open to the defendant will never be established because it can never show that *all* of its employees *always* observed the required safety techniques. The only effective escape from liability is a demonstration that the glass came into the sealed container after it was opened, but this line of proof goes not to negligence, but to the more basic issues of defect and causation, which together remain a successful avenue of defense even under strict liability: Yet no manufacturer is liable because a customer mixes spinach with broken glass.

## IMPLIED WARRANTIES

The erosion of the negligence requirements in products cases was hastened by developments in yet another quarter of the law, that of the liability of sellers (whether or not manufacturers) under theories of implied warranty. The great advantage of all warranty theories for plantiffs is that they impose strict obligations upon the sellers of goods; performance, not effort, is the measure, and there is no excuse even if the seller took all possible care to see that the goods were as represented. Negligence, unless explicitly introduced by agreement, is not part of the plaintiff's prima facie case for recovery.

The major constraint upon the warranty action stemmed from its narrow reach, for here again we are confronted with the renewed influence of the privity doctrine. *Chysky v. Drake*,[21] decided by the New York Court of Appeals—Cardozo concurring—some four years after *MacPherson* is a clear indication of privity's grip. The plaintiff suffered injuries to her mouth after she bit into a cake containing a concealed nail; the cake had been manufactured by the defendants. She had received the cake for her lunch from her employer, who in turn had purchased it from the defendant. Had the plaintiff herself purchased the cake directly from the defendant, she could

19. Id. at 201, 145 N.E. at 282, *quoted* from Supreme Court opinion.
20. Id. at 202-03, 145 N.E. at 282.
21. *Chysky v. Drake Brothers Co.*, 235 N.Y. 468, 139 N.E. 576 (1923).

have recovered under the New York Sales Act on the strength of a breach of an implied warranty that the product was reasonably fit for its intended purpose. A unanimous court, however, held that it was fatal to her cause of action that her employer, and not she, had purchased the cake from the defendant. The matter was resolved with these conclusive words: "unless there be privity of contract, there can be no implied warranty."[22]

*Chysky v. Drake* instantly became the focus of critical attack. On its facts, the plaintiff's case satisfies all the essential requisites of the strong products liability action: the defect was created by the defendant when the nail was baked into the cake; that nail remained there until the time of injury; it was latent; and the plaintiff relied upon the benign appearance of the cake to her detriment. Chysky's case is at least as attractive as MacPherson's. Why, then, was her action denied? The most likely explanation for this apparent legal anomaly stems from the uneasiness of the judges about the boundaries that separate the different causes of action. The decision in *Chysky* does not hearken an incipient twentieth-century revival of special pleading. Rather, the case presented the judicial dilemma that allowing the plaintiff's warranty action against the remote vendor necessarily undermined the negligence requirement of *MacPherson v. Buick.* Stripping the privity limitation from implied warranty cases thus outflanks *MacPherson*; users and consumers could escape the obligation to prove negligence by using an implied—and strict—warranty theory.

The fragile accommodation reached in *Chysky v. Drake* did not endure, however, because it was nourished not by a sense of the justice of the case, but only by the demands of legal symmetry. In the years that followed the decision, courts commonly escaped its unfortunate implications by placing, if only by brute force or obvious fiction, the injured plaintiff in privity with the defendant.[23] Thus, let the mother buy the cake and the child bite the nail, and the courts, in a manner reminiscent of *Langridge v. Levy*, were prepared to insist that the child was "the real party" to the contract. If the technique of real purchaser did not work, others could be summoned. Warranties of implied fitness were made to run with the goods, on the analogy of covenants running with the land. The dealer was held to "assign" his cause of action to the injured consumer, although it was never explained why the consumer was not limited under the assignment to the dealer's damages. Third-party beneficiary contracts were solemnly found, even though the identity of the third-party beneficiary was discovered only after, not before, the injury took place. This is not the place to defend any of these clever artifices. It is sufficient to note that none of them would have been necessary if the thoroughgoing theory of strict liability had been recog-

22. Id. at 472, 139 N.E. at 578.

23. The tale is recounted in greater detail in Prosser, *The Assault Upon the Citadel (Strict Liability to the Consumer)*, 69 Yale L. J. 1099 (1960).

nized as the proper tort theory in *MacPherson v. Buick*. The cake does say "eat me," and the courts made sure that it said "eat me" to whoever happened to eat it.

In New York the end of an era came thirty-eight years later in 1961, when the Court of Appeals in *Greenberg v. Lorenz*[24] in effect overruled *Chysky*. An action was brought against a retailer when hidden slivers of metal cut the mouth of a woman whose father had purchased the offending tin of salmon. The court treated the injustice in the *Chysky* rule as a given, and reinterpreted its sales statute to allow any injured person to maintain the action for the implied warranty. By the time that *Greenberg* had come down, the principle of strict liability was very much in the air, and the decision in *Greenberg* well illustrates the proposition that regardless of labels, there is no substantive difference whatsoever between the "contractual" theories of implied warranty on the one hand and the "tort" theories of strict products liability on the other. Where the plaintiff's case is treated as sounding in warranty, the explicit emphasis is given to the implied-in-fact representation about the condition of the defendant's product that is the source of the implied-in-law warranty. Yet the theory has its distinctive bite only because it is understood, if not stated, that the most meticulous defendant will not be excused if his product does not match the warranty under which it was sold. The strict liability theory, however, reaches the same result from the opposite direction. The name of the theory stresses that the exercise of all possible care will not excuse the defendant whose defective product causes harm to the plaintiff's person or property. Yet, the cause of action requires as well proof of product defect, which in turn is implicitly established by comparing the product as sold with the product as represented. At the end, therefore, the choice between the two theories is, at best, a matter of verbal preference, and the matter can lead to no real harm so long as the way in which the case is described does not determine in whole or in part the substantive and procedural rules by which it is governed.

## EXPRESS WARRANTIES

The previous pages have been devoted to a discussion of implied warranties. While they are the most important for modern developments, some mention should also be made of the early treatment of express warranties, whose relationship to contractual principles is, of course, unquestioned. The key illustrative case is *Baxter v. Ford Motor Co.*, decided by the Washington court in 1932.[25] The plaintiff was allowed a cause of action on a theory of an express warranty or misrepresentation. Through its booklets

24. 9 N.Y. 2d 195, 173 N.E. 2d 773, 213 N.Y.S. 2d 39 (1961). The importance to be attached to bringing suit against the retailer instead of the manufacturer is discussed infra at ch. 6.

25. 168 Wash. 456, 12 P.2d 409 (1932).

and its dealers the defendant manufacturer had represented that the windshield of its Ford Model A contained shatterproof Triplex glass. The plaintiff, relying on these representations, purchased the car and was injured when the windshield shattered after being struck with a pebble that had been kicked up from the road. The opinion made continual reference to the direct marketing techniques that the defendant used to sell its products:

> Radio, billboards and the products of the printing press have become the means of creating a large part of the demand that causes goods to depart from factories to the ultimate consumer. It would be unjust to recognize a rule that would permit manufacturers of goods to create a demand for their products by representing that they possess qualities which they, in fact, do not possess; and then, because there is no privity of contract existing between the consumer and the manufacturer, deny the consumer the right to recover if damages result from the absence of those qualities, when such absence is not readily noticeable.[26]

The argument of the court makes unassailable good sense, in that it recognizes that representations do not lose their force when acted upon at a distance. Even if based upon strict liability principles, the express warranty action is, however, of limited usefulness. Most products, particularly foodstuffs and the like, are sold without any specific contractual provisions at all, and those cases that involve express representations are apt to be troublesome because of the need, stressed in *Baxter*, to show the plaintiff's reliance on the representation. Then, too, the cause of action contains its own implicit limitations. Since the warranty is express, it should be subject to express limitations and conditions under which the defendant will be bound. These conditions could, for example, state that only the immediate purchaser was entitled to the benefits of the express warranty or that the purchaser's recovery is conditioned upon his prudent and proper use of the automobile. Despite their practical limitations, express warranties again show the awkwardness of the privity limitation in cases of implied warranty: if a defendant is bound to all who rely upon an express warranty, then should he not be bound to those same parties where his warranty is implied, not in law, but in fact?

The doctrinal developments in the quarter century following *MacPherson v. Buick* illustrate the uneasy way in which the courts groped toward a general principle of strict liability in products liability cases. It fell, however, to Justice Traynor of the California Supreme Court, speaking first for himself in *Escola v. Coca-Cola Bottling Co.* and later for a unanimous court in *Greenman v. Yuba Power Products, Inc.*, to make explicit the emerging preference for strict liability. We turn now to an examination of those cases, as they mark the close of one era of judicial activity and the opening of another.

26. Id. at 462-63, 12 P. 2d at 412.

CHAPTER

# 4

# *ESCOLA* AND *GREENMAN*

## THE FIRST TRIUMPH OF STRICT LIABILITY

Although *Escola v. Coca-Cola Bottling Co.*,[1] and *Greenman v. Yuba Power Products, Inc.*[2] were decided some eighteen years apart, they represent the bridge between the old and the new law of products liability. Regarded in terms of their factual patterns, both easily satisfy the exacting conditions for the strong products liability suits set out at the beginning of the last chapter. Examined for their delineation of the elements of the plaintiff's cause of action, they are models of good sense and careful legal craftsmanship. Yet, understood as an expression of the larger principles of tort theory, they contain discordant and disturbing elements with the potential for great—and unwarranted—extensions of defendant's liability in products cases. It is important to consider in turn the facts, the legal theories, and the rationales of these two epic cases.

### *ESCOLA* AND *GREENMAN:* THE FACTS

In *Escola* the plaintiff was a waitress in a restaurant. Bottles of Coca-Cola, manufactured by the defendant, had been delivered to the restaurant some thirty-six hours previously. While the plaintiff was placing these bottles in the refrigerator one of them exploded, severely injuring her hand. After the explosion, the remains of the bottle were thrown away by a fellow employee. The plaintiff's complaint alleged that the defendant had been negligent in selling "bottles containing said beverage which on account of excessive pressure of gas or by reason of some defect in the bottle was dangerous . . . and likely to explode."[3] The plaintiff testified about the way in which the bottle had been handled from the moment that it was delivered to

1. 24 Cal. 2d 453, 150 P.2d 436 (1944).
2. 59 Cal. 2d 57, 377 P. 2d 897, 27 Cal. Rptr. 697 (1963).
3. 24 Cal. 2d at 456, 150 P.2d at 437 (1944).

the restaurant until it exploded, but she offered no direct evidence whatsoever about the defendant's negligence in the manufacture and preparation of the bottle. The defendant through expert witnesses offered detailed evidence about the procedures under which the bottles were made and marketed. The trial court allowed the case to go to the jury, which awarded damages to the plaintiff. On appeal, the California Supreme Court in an able, if somewhat heroic, opinion by Chief Justice Gibson affirmed the judgment for the plaintiff from the lower court, resting it squarely upon the doctrine of res ipsa loquitur. The case was rightly left to the jury, for the record contained "evidence permitting a reasonable inference that it [the bottle] was not accessible to extraneous harmful forces and that it was carefully handled by plaintiff or any third person who may have moved or touched it."[4] The extensive evidence introduced by the defendant on the issue of negligence did not control, for "it is ordinarily a question of fact for the jury to determine whether the inference [created by the presumption] has been dispelled."[5]

As was the earlier Massachusetts case of *Richenbacher v. California Packing Corp.*,[6] this case is the paradigmatic strong products liability action: a latent defect in the product's original condition; no third-party intervention; ordinary and proper use by the plaintiff. With these as givens, the movement toward strict liability scarcely places a ripple upon the placid waters of the law.

The facts in *Greenman*, though slightly more exotic than those in *Escola*, reveal the same essential truths. The plaintiff in *Greenman* was injured by a Shopsmith, a combination power tool manufactured and marketed by the defendant, and purchased for him by his wife. While he was using the tool as a lathe, a piece of wood "suddenly flew out of the machine and struck him on the forehead, inflicting serious injuries."[7] The defect alleged was that the Shopsmith had set screws of insufficient strength to hold the wood in place when the machine was in ordinary use. The plaintiff failed on his negligence count, and the defendant contended that the actions for express or implied warranty were barred as well because the plaintiff did not furnish to the seller notice of the accident within a "reasonable time," required under the Sales Act as a condition precedent to such action.[8] In order to escape the complications of the Sales Act, Judge Traynor characterized the plaintiff's action as one for strict liability in tort. That it could be couched as well in implied warranty seems clear enough, as Traynor himself noted that the plaintiff's action did not depend upon the fact that he happened to

4. Id. at 458, 150 P.2d at 439.
5. Id. at 461, 150 P.2d at 440.
6. 250 Mass. 198 145 N.E. 281 (1924), discussed supra at 31.
7. 59 Cal. 2d 57, 59, 377 P.2d 897, 898, 27 Cal. Rptr. 697, 698 (1963).
8. California Civil Code §1789. This section was repealed and superseded in 1963 when California adopted the Uniform Commercial Code.

read the manufacturer's brochure. "Implicit in the machine's presence on the market, however, was a *representation*"—upon which implied warranty could rest—"that it would safely do the jobs for which it was built."[9] The question of its precise characterization aside, *Greenman* in reality involves the same issues as *Huset v. Case.*[10] A powerful design defect theory governs both cases; in each the plaintiff's case is that the defendant's product did not live up to its own performance standards. The shift from negligence to strict liability may have eased the plaintiff's burden, but it posed no threat to the institutional integrity of the basic tort system. Approached, then, from their precise factual patterns, *Greenman* and *Escola* are anchored securely in the past.

### *ESCOLA* AND *GREENMAN*: THE RULE OF THE LAW

The conservatism of these two great cases is also mirrored in their controlling legal rules: The crucial passages from Traynor's concurrence in *Escola* read as follows:

> In my opinion it should now be recognized that a manufacturer incurs an absolute liability when an article that he has placed on the market, knowing that it is to be used without inspection, proves to have a defect that causes injury to human beings.[11]

This "absolute" liability is clarified at the end of the opinion:

> The manufacturer's liability snould, of course, be defined in terms of the safety of the product in normal and proper use, and should not extend to injuries that cannot be traced to the product as it reached the market.[12]

In *Greenman* the rule is cast in a somewhat different verbal form.

> A manufacturer is strictly liable in tort when an article he places on the market, knowing that it is to be used without inspection for defects, proves to have a defect that causes injury to a human being. Recognized first in the case of unwholesome food products, such liability has now been extended to a variety of other products that create as great or greater hazards if defective.[13]

And again there is this qualification:

9. 59 Cal. 2d 57, 64, 377 P. 2d 897, 901, 27 Cal. Rptr. 697, 701 (1963). (Italics added.)
10. 120 F.865 (8th Cir. 1903).
11. 24 Cal. 2d 453, 461, 150 P.2d 436, 440 (1944).
12. Id. at 468, 150 P. 2d at 444.
13. 59 Cal. 2d at 62, 377 P.2d at 900, 27 Cal. Rptr. at 700.

To establish the manufacturer's liability it was sufficient that plaintiff proved that he was injured while using the Shopsmith in a way it was intended to be used as a result of a defect in design and manufacture of which plaintiff was not aware that made the Shopsmith unsafe for its intended use.[14]

As written, both these opinions leave certain important questions unanswered. Neither, for example, contains a complete account of the critical term product defect, although it does seem clear that both tied it closely to the representations, both explicit and implicit, that the defendant made about his products. And both opinions can be criticized as well because they did not indicate whether the traditional negligence cause of action survived and, if so, under what circumstances. Yet, these points aside, it seems clear beyond a doubt that both these decisions represent extremely narrow theories of recovery, based upon the failure of a product to meet its own standard of design or performance while involved in ordinary use. The strict liability cause of action announced in these two opinions gives no hint as to the enormous explosion in products liability law—an explosion that has led to a repudiation of most of the limitations of recovery contained in the rules of decision in these two cases.[15] To understand the source of the doctrinal revolution, it is necessary to turn in detail to the social justifications offered for the strict liability rule in these two cases.

## *ESCOLA* AND *GREENMAN*: THEORETICAL IMPLICATIONS

Both *Escola* and *Greenman* present an abundance of justifications for the new strict liability doctrine. Thus, in *Escola*, Traynor writes:

Even if there is no negligence, however, public policy demands that responsibility be fixed wherever it will most effectively reduce the hazards to life and health inherent in defective products that reach the market. It is evident that the manufacturer can anticipate some hazards and guard against the recurrence of others, as the public cannot. Those who suffer injury from defective products are unprepared to meet its consequences. The cost of an injury and the loss of time or health may be an overwhelming misfortune to the person injured, and a needless one, for the risk of injury can be insured by the manufacturer and distributed among the public as a cost of doing business. It is to the public interest to prevent the marketing of products having defects that are a menace to the public. If such products nevertheless find their

14. Thus consider these changes. The requirement of intermediate inspection has passed from the law. *See Balido v. Improved Machinery, Inc.*, 29 Cal. App. 3d 633, 105 Cal. Rptr. 890 (1972).

15. *See, e.g., Barker v. Lull Engineering Co.*, 20 Cal. 3d 413, 573 P.2d 443, 143 Cal. Rptr. 225 (1978), which rejects both the *Greenman* account of product defect and the normal and proper limitation as being too restrictive upon recovery. Indeed the chapters on design defects, the duty to warn, and plaintiff's conduct are best regarded as commentaries upon the shape of the products liability law after the repudiation of the doctrinal rules in *Greenman* and *Escola*.

way into the market it is to the public interest to place the responsibility for whatever injury they may cause upon the manufacturer, who, even if he is not negligent in the manufacture of the product, is responsible for its reaching the market. However intermittently such injuries may occur and however haphazardly they may strike, the risk of their occurrence is a constant risk and a general one. Against such a risk there should be general and constant protection and the manufacturer is best situated to afford such protection.[16]

The single most important sentence in the *Greenman* opinion reads simply:

The purpose of [strict] liability is to insure that the costs of injuries resulting from defective products are borne by the manufacturers that put such products on the market rather than by the injured persons who are powerless to protect themselves.[17]

It is possible to isolate four separate arguments in the passages just quoted. The first goes to the desirable incentive effects of the strict liability doctrine; the second to the hardships that alternative legal theories impose upon accident victims; the third to the relevance of liability insurance, and the last to the administrative benefits of the strict liability theory. We take them up in order.

*Incentive Effects*

The first argument is that the adoption of strict liability is a good thing because it reduces both the number of dangerous products that reach the market and the damage that they cause. As an initial point it seems that the argument cannot carry this great weight for the simple reason that the specialized rules of negligence law such as high standards of care and res ipsa loquitur, coupled with theories of implied warranty, already have led the tort system to the verge of strict liability. If ninety-nine cases out of a hundred will be decided the same way no matter what liability rule is adopted, then the shift in rules simply cannot make that great a difference in the behavior of the parties whose conduct is governed by them. Therefore, in order even to explore the implications of the difference in liability rules, we shall have to assume that the outcomes of some substantial number of cases will be dependent upon the theory of liability used to decide them. Yet, even with this assumption the incentive implications are much less straightforward than Traynor's confident assertions might suggest.

First, there is good reason to assume that the only difference between negligence and strict liability will be not the number of accidents that occur but the number of accidents that receive compensation. Thus if the rule of negligence is defined in terms of a classical cost-benefit analysis, the

16. 24 Cal. 2d at 462, 150 P.2d at 440-41.
17. 59 Cal. 2d at 63, 377 P.2d at 901, 27 Cal. Rptr. at 701.

defendant will cease to take precautions when it becomes cheaper socially to permit accidents than it is to avoid them. Under a strict liability system the defendant will in theory opt for the same point of safety, ceasing to take precautions when they are no longer cost-effective, even if he will have to pay for the accidents that do occur. The only difference between the two rules therefore goes to the issue of compensation for victims, which, however important, only involves the wealth distribution between parties *after* accidents and not the conduct of parties *before* them.[18] With the negligence rule the defendant who takes cost-effective precautions need never pay damages. With strict liability, the defendant must pay damages no matter what precautions are taken. The differences between the two theories do raise serious ethical issues, but those are by definition immaterial in an inquiry that focuses solely upon incentive effects.

Second, the incentive effects of any rule of defendant's liability are greatly muddied when placed in their proper institutional context. One obvious point is that most of the products commonly involved in tort actions—food, drugs, machine tools, airplanes, and automobiles—have long been subject to many forms of direct federal, state, and local regulation. The avowed aim of such regulation is often public safety, and in many cases the regulators can and do impose direct administrative sanctions or money fines upon noncomplying parties, without proof of damage in individual cases. The presence of such regulatory schemes—some effective, others unused, some well-planned, others positively dangerous—makes it very difficult for courts (or even legislators) to determine the safety incentives for *all* products attributable to an uncertain shift in liability rules. Courts have from time to time talked about the integration of private products liability actions with direct public regulation,[19] but they have been unable to do anything with the idea, in large measure because of the host of intractable empirical questions raised by any systematic inquiry into the issue.

Third, there is the problem of complementary incentives. To establish Traynor's position that strict liability improves safety incentives, it is not sufficient to show that strict liability will encourage manufacturers to take greater safety precautions. It is also necessary to show that the strict liability rule will not *remove* or *undermine* incentives toward safety which otherwise would fall upon other parties in the chain of distribution and use. The question of interlocking incentives is one that can only be adequately explored

18. *See, e.g.*, Demsetz, *When Does the Rule of Liability Matter?*, 1. J. Legal Stud. 13 (1972).

19. *Goldberg v. Kollsman Instrument Corp.*, 12 N.Y. 2d 432, 191 N.E. 2d 81, 240 N.Y.S. 2d 592 (1963) (Burke, J. dissenting), where the question is asked of strict liability in the context of airlines subject to the direct regulation of the Federal Aviation Administration (F.A.A.). *See, also*, for a discussion of the same issue in connection with F.A.A. and modern design defect litigation, *Wilson v. Piper Aircraft Corp.*, 282 Or.61, 577 P.2d 1322 (1978). (Linde, J. concurring).

(if at all) with sophisticated knowledge of mathematical game theory; but even without such esoteric aids it is possible to point out the difficulties of Traynor's incentive argument. If, for example, strict liability is imposed upon a manufacturer, the proprietor of a commercial establishment that uses the manufacturer's products can be expected to exercise somewhat less care in the maintenance and repair of his equipment, precisely because he knows that his exposure to tortious liability will be reduced by the presence of another defendant. Likewise consumers who know that the use of any product carries with it substantial insurance against major injury may also be either less careful in the selection of goods or less careful in their manner in the maintenance and use of the goods that are selected. The benefits of strict liability may thus be offset by the reduction in the market importance of manufacturer's reputation in the choice of goods or by a relaxation of consumer vigilance.[20]

Those who believe that the prospect of injury is sufficient deterrence against carelessness *by users*, an obvious and common sense position, may doubt this last point. On reflection, however, the argument seems flawed because it assumes that shifts in liability rules that have no effect upon the *average* consumer also will exert no influence upon the *marginal* consumer. Yet, here we need only note that *some* consumers at *some* times will be influenced by the changes in relative costs and benefits associated with legal change to undertake riskier courses of action. Thus, the strong enforcement of the speeding laws, sanctioned by only fairly small fines (or remote chances of license suspension) can have a major effect upon driving habits and accident rates. Why, then, will the prospect of a large damage award have no influence on behavior? Traynor may be right, but thus far the evidence suggests at the very most that the Scottish verdict of "not proven" is in order.

We must, however, be careful to recognize the limitations of this "not proven" verdict for strict liability, for it is clear that other strong implications *do* follow from Traynor's concern with safety incentives. Thus, these incentive arguments do account for the "normal and proper" limitation that he engrafted without explanation onto his formulation of the rule. Recall that Judge Sanborn in *Huset v. Case*,[21] thought that the decisive argument against any relaxation of the privity requirement was that it would expose the manufacturer to the follies and foibles of all persons—the skillful and the untrained, the wise and the simple—who happened to use his machinery. The point is, of course, a powerful one no matter whether the original defendant's liability is based upon negligence or strict liability.

20. *See*, Oi, *The Economics of Product Safety*, 4 Bell Journal of Economics 3 (1973).

21. 120 F. 865 (8th Cir. 1903).

Yet, it can be met (at the cost of some increased litigation complexity) by keeping out of the system all those cases in which the plaintiff has not made normal and proper use of the product. In effect, this "normal and proper use" limitation thus furthers Traynor's incentive justifications because it identifies one large class of injuries that at least by rough approximation can be better avoided by precautions at the user level. That Traynor saw this point in *Escola* seems tolerably clear by his recognition that the manufacturer could foresee and guard against *some* hazards, as the public cannot.

Fourth, incentive arguments bring to the front the issue of *retrospective* application of the legal rule, an issue not addressed by Traynor in these two cases and one much ignored in the subsequent literature. Discussions of torts law yield to a strong but unwise temptation to assume that liability rules announced by any court will only influence the future conduct of private parties. In those common instances of "snapshot" torts—the typical road accident or slip-and-fall case comes to mind—the general assertion represents, with trivial exceptions, the whole truth. Indeed even in the products liability area the point is essentially true with respect to the Coke bottle involved in *Escola*, but *not* the power tool in *Greenman*. The very expansion of products liability beyond food and drink to heavy machinery and other capital goods brings the question of retrospective effects to the fore. Even if the rules announced have prospective application with respect to the *plaintiff's injuries*, they nonetheless have retrospective application with respect to the *defendant's product and conduct*: a machine tool may have a useful life of thirty or forty years or more, depending of course on the level of maintenance accorded the machinery and other factors. With old, long-lived products new stringent liability rules can have little or no incentive effect upon the manufacturer's behavior, as he does not control, does not have access to, in fact, does not even know the fate of equipment sent into the marketplace years before. The injured party and those who remain in possession and control of the goods are far more responsive to incentives than the defendant.

Where the shift is simply from negligence to strict liability, the magnitude of the retrospective change is apt to be de minimis, because so little is at stake in the choice of the liability rules. But any alteration as to the definition of what counts as a defect (as with duty to warn and design defect cases) or in the appropriate standards of plaintiff or third-party conduct cannot be taken into account by the defendant, except at prohibitive cost. Traynor's concern with incentive arguments points therefore to a distinction between prospective and retrospective effects of legal change, one that is much more easily achieved by legislation than by judicial decision. The "backlog" problem—of old products now judged by new rules—will not, however, go away simply because we ignore it. Some special legislation is needed to limit the severe dislocations created by major substantive expansions of liability that are given, as to defendants, retrospective effect.[22]

The incentive rationales, therefore, have borne mixed fruit. They do not account in any clear way for the preference for strict liability over negligence, but they do account for the "normal and proper" use limitation, and they do suggest that some special treatment should be given to cases involving older products in the marketplace before the advent of the new rules.

### *Hardship Effects*

The second rationale that Traynor offered for the strict liability rule may be described as the hardship rationale. Its implications are much more troublesome for the structure of the tort law than the incentive arguments. Thus, when Traynor argues that individual parties may be "ill-prepared" to meet the "overwhelming consequences" of injury, he justifies not only strict liability in defective products cases but also the broader, and indefensible, proposition that manufacturers and others should always be liable simply by virtue of a product-associated injury. The fatal weakness with

22. The problem of retrospective application is, moreover, confronted in very explicit form in connection with the "outside" statutes of limitations (sometimes called "statutes of repose") that have been both proposed and passed in recent years. In essence these statutes provide that in most instances a product seller cannot be held liable in a products liability case for harms that are caused, roughly speaking, ten years after the product was first placed into the stream of commerce. As drafted, the statutes usually provide exceptions where the product was sold with an express warranty or where the seller engaged in some deliberate effort to conceal a defect in his product or otherwise misrepresent its condition. And it would be advisable to include in these statutes some provision that insures that the statutes do not insulate a product seller from duties that arise *after* the product has been sold, as where some new warning must be issued about a dangerous side effect of a drug, unknown when the product was first marketed.

In order to be effective, such outside statutes of limitations should provide an absolute defense in the cases to which they apply, even if they will in some cases work to deny a plaintiff a meritorious claim against a given seller (but not, it must be noted, against other parties in possession of the product). In essence the justification for this statute is that time is such a good proxy for nonliability in most cases that the passage of the statute will both reduce the errors in decision and the costs of administering the system. The privity limitation, discussed in ch. 2, was of course a very bad proxy with which this statute should be usefully contrasted.

Outside statutes of limitations have been passed in many states. *See, e.g.*, Fla. Stat. Ann. §95.031(2) (Supp. 1979); Ind. Code Ann. §34-4-20A-5 (Burns) (Supp. 1979). In some instances these statutes are confined to strict liability claims only, Ariz. Rev. Stat. Ann. §12-551 (Supp. 1978), a limitation of considerable dimensions given that most strict liability claims can, with the aid of res ipsa loquitur, be brought as negligence suits. In other instances the impact of the outside statute of limitations is softened to a presumption, Colo. Rev. Stat. §13-21-403(3) (Supp. 1978), and Model Uniform Product Liability Act, §110(B). While this approach might prevent the occasional injustice tolerated by the absolute bar, it will create many others by undermining the administrative and error reduction rationales behind the statute.

For a criticism of the absolute bar, *see* Phillips, *An Analysis of Proposed Reform of Products Liability Statutes of Limitations*, 56 N. Car. L. Rev. 663 (1978).

this line of argument is that it offers no principled ground to limit liability to the narrow type of circumstances that were involved in the *Escola* case. Remove the defect in the bottle, and the misfortune remains. Remove the "normal and proper use" requirement, and the need for compensation continues unabated. Therefore, the injection of the hardship element works this profound revolution in tort theory: all "no liability" defenses become suspect as the seriousness of the injury now helps to establish liability, even though traditionally, the seriousness of the plaintiff's need went to the question of damages only after liability had been established on independent grounds. The hardship arguments have within them the capacity for untold mischief because they facilitate the implicit conversion of a tort system of corrective justice for wrongs committed by the defendant against the plaintiff into a system of universal entitlement for the needy plaintiff.

The weakness of this hardship rationale is, moreover, clearly revealed from another vantage point when we evaluate the empirical foundations for Traynor's claim that individuals are ill-prepared to meet the consequences of misfortune. In some cases the proposition is true. But other truths dominate. The very large portion of serious illnesses and accidents arise in contexts in which today there is still no trace of tortious liability. In these situations major social institutions—health insurance and workers' compensation to name but two—have been designed to insure that injured parties receive limited benefits to cushion them against the financial misfortune, but not to make them whole. *Escola* itself was a classic worker's compensation case. Thus, if the hardship rationale governs products liability, we should expect to find two major modifications in the law of damages that will convert this branch of the law from a tort to a compensation system. First, there should be a systematic denial of recovery for pain and suffering and perhaps a flat ceiling on the level of recoverable damages. Second, there should be a systematic reckoning of the impact of collateral benefits upon the financial condition of the injured party. Recovery should be reduced by the level of such benefits and at some point perhaps even eliminated.

The products liability cases that have confronted these two issues have, of course, gone in precisely the opposite direction: the traditional tort arguments on damages hold sway. The plaintiff's measure of damages, liability established, is the amount needed to make him whole, to the extent that money can do so. Ceilings are regarded with hostility,[23] and the jury is always instructed to award damages for pain and suffering; the usual common law rule is followed on collateral benefits, so that the defendant wrongdoer is not allowed to convert his victim's thrift to his own financial advantage. However influential the hardship rationale, its negative implications

23. Indeed when they have been enacted for medical malpractice cases, they have been held unconstitutional. *See, e.g., Wright v. Central Du Page Hospital Ass'n*, 63 Ill. 2d 313, 347 N.E. 2d 736 (1976).

are always ignored on damages, even though there is no more expensive, clumsy, and erratic method of comprehensive social insurance than tort litigation, where the preoccupation with defect, causation, and plaintiff's conduct directs massive inquiries toward issues manifestly irrelevant to the hardship question. Justice Traynor notes in his opinion that as the risk of injury is "general and constant," so too should be the protection against it. No sensible set of tort liability rules can provide that general and constant coverage; if desired, first-party compensation systems, and to a lesser extent workers' compensation, can. The hardship arguments rob tort law of its form and structure. They should receive no weight in the formation of tort doctrine.

*Ease of Insurance*

A third strand of the argument in *Escola*—one made more explicit in later cases—closely dovetails with the hardship issue. It is that strict liability is justified because the manufacturer or other defendant can better procure insurance against the risk, passing on its premiums to purchasers as part of its general cost of doing business. In an explicitly instrumental manner, the manufacturer is pressed into service as a convenient insurance vehicle, to whom individual purchasers make small contributions in order to receive protection against the prospect of large losses. There is at first blush an undeniable appeal to the insurance rationale, but, as with the rationales already examined, it is subject to manifold complications that, in the end, render it problematic, if not wrong.

The first point is that this insurance argument reverses the traditional relationship between liability insurance and the tort law. In the usual common law context, the court first determines what the liabilities of a given enterprise ought to be (usually upon fairness or efficiency grounds) after which the defendant goes into the marketplace to purchase, if desired, liability insurance to cover the identified risk. Risk pooling, risk management, and loss prevention are the sensible private responses to tort obligations. The reversal of that relationship between tort and insurance creates problems in identifying the firm to transmit the losses, particularly when no firm is ideally suited to spread losses in an orderly fashion. Two points are of particular importance.

First, it is by no means clear that *any* firm stands in the best position to distribute losses through the insurance mechanism. It may well be that the individual harmed, not any of the many firms that might harm him, forms the best unit around which to organize the insurance function. The transactions costs are clearly lower, for there is no tort suit, and the individual affected has (because of an intimate awareness of his personal and financial situation) a far better sense of the level of coverage that he wants against certain specific contingencies, such as death or disability.

Second, even if some enterprise is the better unit through which to organize insurance protection, the question is which of the many firms should assume that risk. Here the choices are by no means easy. It is possible to demand, as is in fact done today, that each firm carry liability insurance for risks associated with its products. Yet, this rule gives rise to very complicated situations in which many different parties are sued with respect to any given accident, creating huge administrative costs that can match in magnitude the amount of damage awards paid to injured parties. An alternative to this possibility is to select one firm among many to bear the special entrepreneurial risks, but here there are simply no satisfactory criteria of selection. The point was discussed at length in 1963 in *Goldberg v. Kollsman Instrument Corp.* where the court had to decide in a typical modern situation how to divide up liability among an airplane manufacturer, its altimeter submanufacturer, and an airline carrier.[24] All can insure, and all have knowledge of some risks but not of others. We are no nearer a definitive solution to this question today than we were then, and it is idle to think that sophisticated economic analysis (which is far better at posing problems than at solving them) will materially aid in the solution of this essential task. Insurance functions well as the response to tortious liability, but not as the reason for its creation.

There is a second problem of perhaps greater importance. The ability of any particular firm to shoulder the risks of liability insurance depends in very large measure upon the substantive content of the products liability law for which the insurance is written. Where, as in cases like *Escola* and *Greenman*, the manufacturer is in essence held liable for products which fail to live up to his own standards of construction or performance, it should not be too difficult to calculate the risk associated with marketing a defective product and to test or inspect the product in advance of sale in order to reduce the likelihood of the occurrence of the insurable event. The substantive tort liability rule applied in *Escola* therefore lends itself to a manageable calculation of premiums because there is a high proportion of known as against unknown and unknowable elements.

The recent extensions of products liability law have, however, vastly complicated the task of underwriting. Where, for example, a manufacturer can be held responsible because a jury in its unfettered wisdom decides that its product—say a machine tool—could have been designed better than it was,[25] or sold with warnings more comprehensive than those provided,[26] it becomes difficult if not impossible for the usual techniques of inspection and underwriting to yield any adequate assessment of the additional risks to be insured. When product modifications do not insulate the manufacturer

24. 12 N.Y. 2d 432, 191 N.E. 2d 81, 240 N.Y.S. 2d 592 (1963).

25. *See* ch. 7 for a discussion of the modern design defect cases that adopt this view.

26. *See* ch. 8 for a discussion of the modern duty to warn cases.

from responsibility for subsequent injuries, the underwriting judgment must not only take into account the dangers in the product as it is, but also the dangers of the product as it might be transformed.[27] And when all forms of "foreseeable" misuse no longer constitute a defense against liability, the risk involved—and the premium to be charged—depends as much on the skill and training of the user as it does on the intrinsic merit of the product.

These and other substantive difficulties are further compounded because the product liability rules apply not only to new products but also to those long in the stream of commerce. If it is a nightmare to estimate the contingent liability costs for ancient machines in unknown condition and in unknown hands, those difficulties are *not* solved by the institution of insurance. Insurance only transfers and pools the risks. It cannot reduce the costs associated with those risks or the uncertainties involved in their measurement.

The imposition of modern liability rules on products already in the marketplace also calls into question the ability of the manufacturer or retailer to recover the additional cost of insurance by increasing the price of its new products. In economic terms, "sunk costs" are not recoverable. The purchasers of current products simply will not assume any portion of the manufacturer's exposure for old products which they would not be required to bear in the absence of a purchase. The problem of old products remains, therefore, with the parties subject to liability and with their shareholders. A purchaser of equipment will not pay more because he learns that the seller is charged with heavy back taxes on an unrelated transaction. So, too, a purchaser will not assume a firm's prior debts, no matter what the structure (competitive or monopolistic or anywhere in between) of the manufacturer's product market. The losses remain on the manufacturer, whether or not he obtains liability insurance, which simply cannot do all the things demanded of it. The loss-spreading rationale cannot support the edifice that has been constructed upon it.

### *Administrative Arguments*

The last consideration that Traynor raised in support of the strict liability rule breaks no new ground. The elimination of negligence reduces the complexity of individual suits and eliminates the need for strained interpretations of res ipsa loquitur. The direct action against the manufacturer tends to bypass complicated indemnity actions with retailers and distributors. These administrative gains seem to be both real and substantial, and no offsetting considerations becloud the issue. The problem has been discussed already and need not be recanvassed. Where Traynor is least innovative, he is also soundest. Simple is best.

27. *See, e.g., Price v. Niagara Machine & Tool Works*, 136 Cal. Rptr. 535 (1977), *deleted from official reporter*.

CHAPTER

5

# FREEDOM OF CONTRACT AND THE GROWTH OF PRODUCTS LIABILITY LAW

To complete this historical examination of products liability law, it is necessary to consider one last question which thus far has been given scant attention: To what extent may private parties *contract out* of products liability rules that are otherwise imposed by judicial command? In principle, this very question could have been raised at any point in the history of the products liability law, but as a practical matter it was of little importance throughout the nineteenth century. During that era the judicial rules themselves so limited the scope of recovery that there was little if any reason for private parties to incur the additional expenses of consensually limiting the available causes of action. The expansion of products liability actions in the twentieth century, however, has added urgency to the matter of contracting out of tort law. Indeed, it is an issue on which it is possible to detect a revolution in judicial thought which perhaps shares pride of place with the parallel changes in the substantive rules of products liability.[1]

The fundamental nature of the shift can be summarized in a few sentences. The earlier position accepted the dominance of consensual arrangements in two ways: first, on the tort side, in its unqualified recognition of assumption of risk, particularly in its express form, as a valid defense; second, in a general unwillingness on the contract side to allow anything but fraud, duress, or incompetence as reasons to set aside contracts between two parties.[2] Today the language of inequality of bargaining power, contracts of adhesion, standard form contracts, public policy, and unconscionability, all rarely

1. The analogous set of issues arises in connection with medical malpractice law, where again the importance of private contract has been declining. For a criticism of the modern developments, *see* Epstein, *Medical Malpractice: The Case for Contract*, 1976 Am. Bar Foundation Research J. 87 (1976).

2. For a defense of the older position on its merits, *see* Epstein, *Unconscionability: A Critical Reappraisal*, 18 J. L. & Econ. 293 (1975).

invoked in the nineteenth century, dominate judicial decisions.[3] The shift in attitude is revealed by a discussion of two cases, *Baxter v. Ford Motor Company*[4] and *Henningsen v. Bloomfield Motors, Inc.*,[5] perhaps the one case that more than others inaugurated the modern age of products liability.

In *Baxter* the plaintiff brought (in addition to his suit against Ford) a second cause of action against St. John Motors, the dealer who sold him the car. That action failed because the court held as controlling the following provision in the Baxter-St. John contract: "It is further agreed that no warranty either express or implied is made by the dealer under this order or otherwise covering said car."[6] The plaintiff's effort to escape the effect of this clause was succinctly met by the court: "To have permitted the introduction of the testimony in question [about St. John's representations] as against St. John Motors, would have been to have countenanced an attempt to vary the terms of the written instrument by parol testimony."[7] The clear implication is that Ford Motor Company could have claimed the benefit of this clause if it had been party to the agreement. There is no trace in the opinion of any dissatisfaction with the current law: fraud and duress were clearly no part of this routine transaction, and the court showed no willingness to import doctrines of unconscionability, economic duress, or unequal bargaining power into the case. Mass advertising was discussed, but only in order to establish the actionability of Ford's representations, and not to exclude the possibility of limiting the effect of those representations by express language at the time of purchase. We have the lull before the storm.

By 1960, when *Henningsen* was decided, the world was, according to the New Jersey Supreme Court, a very different place. In *Henningsen* the plaintiff's husband purchased for her a new Plymouth automobile from Bloomfield Motors. Within ten days of the original purchase, when the car had

3. Perhaps the most influential article written in support of the modern tradition is, Kessler, *Contracts of Adhesion—Some Thoughts About Freedom of Contract*, 43 Colum. L. Rev. 629 (1943).

4. 168 Wash. 456, 12 P.2d 409 (1932).

5. 32 N.J. 358, 161 A.2d 69 (1960). The importance of Henningsen at the time it was handed down was immense. Of that decision Prosser wrote, "In the field of products liability, the date of the fall of the citadel of privity [i.e., the onset of the modern era] can be fixed with some certainty. It was May 9, 1960, when the Supreme Court of New Jersey announced the decision in *Henningsen v. Bloomfield Motors, Inc.*" Prosser, *The Fall of the Citadel (Strict Liability to the Consumer)*, 50 Minn. L. Rev. 791 (1966).

Today the popularity of the implied warranty theory is much reduced. Thus in *Austin v. Ford Motor Co.*, 86 Wis. 2d 628, 644, 273 N.W. 2d 233, 240 (1978), the implied warranty theory was described as a "transitional rationale" that is no longer required after section 402A of the Restatement (Second) of Torts. And the Model Uniform Product Liability Act, 44 Federal Register, A212, 62714-15, section 104, organizes the basic products liability actions without reference to the concept.

6. 168 Wash. 456, 459, 12 P.2d 409, 411 (1932).

7. Id. at 459, 12 P.2d at 411.

been driven less than five hundred miles, the plaintiff was injured when the car went out of control and into a tree when its steering mechanism failed. Treated simply as a products liability action, this case satisfies all basic criteria for the strong plaintiff's case. The defect was latent, the use was normal, and the short period that the car had been in service made it unlikely that the defect was attributable to events that took place after the time of sale.

It was, however, the treatment of the contract issue that gave *Henningsen* its explosive quality. The separate contracts between the plaintiff's husband and both Chrysler and Bloomfield Motors each contained clauses that excluded all liability for personal injuries. Both contracts further provided that the original purchaser's sole remedy in the event of difficulty was the replacement of those parts found defective within the first four thousand miles of driving upon delivery at customer's expense to the factory. The limits of the clause are obvious. The purchaser cannot recover either for personal injuries or for consequential damages; he cannot recover in the event that good parts are assembled in a defective manner; and subsequent owners can recover nothing. "The terms of the warranty are," the court concluded, "a sad commentary upon the automobile manufacturers' marketing practices."[8]

The court was equally troubled by the manner in which the limitations upon liability were set out in the various printed forms signed by the purchaser. Both in the size of type and in the location of crucial terms, these forms worked to keep their terms secret from all but the most observing and inquiring buyer; in fact Mr. Henningsen testified that he had not read any of the printed agreements.

The court also took offense at the common practice whereby automobile manufacturers "undertook to withdraw from actual and direct contractual contact with the buyer" by selling cars through independent dealers.[9] Finally, the court was much concerned with the impact of modern advertising, which in its view persuaded individual consumers to buy certain products, such as automobiles, without first acquiring the independent knowledge necessary to make an informed decision.

These circumstances in combination were sufficient to persuade the New Jersey court to take drastic measures to counteract the marketing practices in the automobile industry. Holding that the benefits of the limitations upon liability were "not fairly obtained," the court struck them down. It then endorsed the theory that an implied warranty of fitness, actionable without proof of negligence, ran toward the original purchaser regardless of the expressed intentions of the parties. This solution still left the plaintiff short of recovery because she was the wife of the original purchaser. There-

8. 32 N.J. 358, 375, 161 A.2d 69, 78 (1960).
9. Id. at 372-73; 161 A.2d at 77.

fore the court, noting the realities of modern marketing, insisted further that sound social policy required an extension of its implied warranties to her as well. The fusion of warranty and strict liability implicit in the earlier decisions had explicitly taken place.

To evaluate the soundness of the *Henningsen* opinion, we must distinguish carefully between the two separate lines of argument it contains. Looking first at the basic question of disclosure (that is, small type and such factors), something can be said for the court's position that the limitations upon liability were not brought home to the purchaser (provided we do not dwell on the common-sense point that no one ever reads the small print because everyone knows in advance exactly what it says). Yet even with this defect in contract formation, the appropriate remedy is *not* to strike down the exemption clause. Instead, the preferred approach—one well tailored to the perceived wrong—requires the manufacturer to print the offending clauses in bold type, such that, with the restrictions brought home, the consumer can decide for himself whether they are too onerous.[10] Under this approach, the net effect of *Henningsen* upon the law of products liability would have been minor. In the short run, firms would have been spurred to hire communications experts to make sure that all essential terms were so clearly and forcefully stated that most future misunderstandings would be avoided. And if, as the self-interest of consumers might well dictate, the restrictive terms were accepted by those with knowledge of their content, very little else would be changed. At best, some increase in transaction costs, trivial in comparison with the total cost of selling automobiles, would result in some greater, if undemanded, clarity in the original agreement.[11]

Perhaps sensing the weakness of its disclosure rationales, the court went on to hold that in all events the contractual releases could not be honored at all because they were unfairly obtained. Asserting an inequality of bargaining power between the parties, the court insisted that it was not a fair bargain for the manufacturer to substitute a limited warranty for the comprehensive general warranty the law would otherwise imply. Taking this view, mere disclosure will not do: judicial revision of warranty terms is imperative.

10. Such was the intention in the drafting of the original unconscionability provisions of the Uniform Commercial Code. *See* U.C.C., §2-302 (1978 version), and the comments thereto.

11. Here it is also necessary to take issue with one of the most common rules of interpretation in modern contract law, that the terms of a standard form agreement should be construed against the firm that drafted them and in favor of the individual consumer. *See, e.g., Gray v. Zurich Insurance Co.*, 65 Cal. 2d 263, 419 P.2d 168, 54 Cal. Rptr. 104 (1966), where the principle was applied to an insurance contract. While the principle in question might aid consumers in individual cases, its long-run effects are to complicate the drafting of contractual documents, as firms are required to introduce an ever-increasing number of qualifications in order to shape the contract as they (and their consumers) ex ante would have it.

However popular the *Henningsen* approach might be today,[12] it remains clearly flawed in all its essentials. First, the court offered no reasons as to why it thought the contract had been unfairly obtained, apart from those which go to the original disclosure issue. Fraud and duress were absent, and inequality of bargaining power is but an unsupported conclusion that does not explain why some individuals buy elsewhere or buy only if they can obtain satisfactory price concessions from the dealer. Automobile manufacturers are not the government; no matter what their net assets, they do not enjoy the power to conscript unwilling persons as their customers.

Second, the argument of the court has unacceptable implications. If sale agreements are indeed "unfairly obtained," then *none* of their terms should escape judicial nullification. In the standard case of duress or fraud the aggrieved party, whether buyer or seller, is permitted to set aside the *entire* arrangement without making any showing that all or any of its terms are unfair in some objective sense. If the economic pressures upon the buyer are tantamount either to fraud or duress, the court, far from limiting its intervention to liability terms, should be free, if not compelled, to rip open the entire agreement. Terms relating to price, delivery, service, color, and so on should all be subject to review and revision.

Third, the court improperly identifies the elements that constitute the quid pro quo when it looks to warranty terms of the agreement in isolation. It is, of course, improper to say that the limited warranty is an even swap for the comprehensive warranty. Yet it is too clear for argument that the complete transaction involved the sale of a car with its limited warranty in exchange for the price. The quid pro quo for the limited warranty is not confined therefore to the rejected comprehensive warranty but includes as well the reduction in purchase price for the automobile: a price that will be greater with the full warranty than with the limited one. Warranties are but one form of benefit which may be separately priced. A car with a radio costs more than the same car without the radio, and so too with warranties.

The court in *Henningsen* compounded this last error by making yet another methodological mistake. The court looked at the transaction only as one in which the seller of the car got in essence something for nothing. The court never asked itself whether the limited warranty might benefit *both* parties, even though that is the only explanation that can account for the market durability of such arrangements. The manufacturer limits his exposure; the

12. A recitation of the countless ways in which *Henningsen* has influenced the growth of other areas of the law is quite beyond the scope of this essay. For but one example of its versatility, *see Javins v. First National Realty Corp.*, 428 F.2d 1071 (D.C. Cir. 1970), where *Henningsen* was used to support the judicial determination that an implied warranty of habitability is to be read into the terms of the standard apartment lease, even where such warranty is expressly negatived by the terms of the lease itself. The arguments of general consumer incompetence and the inability of private markets to function for the provision of necessities were both stressed in the opinion.

buyer saves that portion of the purchase price that otherwise must be set aside to fund the warranty obligation; both parties benefit from the administrative savings that follow from the elimination of expensive and time-consuming lawsuits. This strict allocation of risk will, in all likelihood, cut out some cases in which, ex ante, both parties might desire to allow recovery, inasmuch as administrative savings always substitute broad, if rough, approximations for detailed inquiries into the facts of each case. Yet, by the same token, these broad rules do eliminate a second form of error—expensive and possibly frivolous lawsuits—that will emerge if the full warranties are required by law. If bodily protection to the purchaser is desired, it is better secured in a separate transaction, perhaps through private health or disability insurance, on either an individual or a group basis, so that each person can choose the level of benefits that best fits his needs. The limited warranty is a sensible expression of the joint willingness *not* to treat health and accident insurance as tied to the purchase of an automobile.

The radical case for contract abrogation advanced in *Henningsen* thus fails for a number of sufficient reasons. It does not follow, however, that any comprehensive common law theory of products liability can place exclusive or even dominant reliance upon private agreements. Still another objection to this contractual approach, not discussed in *Henningsen*, highlights its troubled application to products liability cases. The basic problem is that many, perhaps most, product injuries occur to persons not in privity with the products defendant. *Henningsen* itself is such a situation, inasmuch as the injured party was the wife, who was not under orthodox contract theory bound by the terms of an agreement between her husband and Chrysler. Of even greater institutional importance, virtually all work-place accidents involve injured employees who are not in the chain of purchase with the original seller.[13] And the same point applies to cars, machinery, and like products that are resold years after their original purchase. The chain of contracts cannot keep up with the rapid motion of products between persons and over time.

The hard question is what to make of these impediments to voluntary contracts. One possible approach is to allow contractual limitations upon liability to prevail whenever they are found but to permit ordinary products liability actions when these limitations are absent. That solution, however, creates the unstable anomaly that Mr. Henningsen is barred from suit even though his wife, or an injured occupant, remains free to press a claim for full damages. The objection may not be decisive, for it may well be better that contracts be allowed to govern in the areas to which they apply, leaving the courts to fashion implied contracts only where they do not.

What is more, the differences between purchasers and users can be re-

13. For the complications that follow *see* Epstein, *Coordination of Workers' Compensation Benefits with Tort Damage Awards*, 13 The Forum 464 (1978).

solved in yet another manner that would mark the end of much of products liability law. Since it is probable that most purchasers would in fact accept limitations upon liability as being in their own self-interest, it could be presumed that other parties similarly situated would have agreed to the same limitations if direct negotiations had not been blocked by high transaction costs. The necessary implication is that Mrs. Henningsen should be barred by the limited warranty to which her husband agreed. This radical position, however, is by no means beyond challenge even on contractual grounds. While an immediate purchaser will receive a reduction in price for the release of all, or most, tort liability, a stranger to the agreement will not. The possibility exists that this market imperfection would induce manufacturers to take unwarranted risks with the safety of consumers generally, although it is not altogether clear how it could be effectively exploited.

The problems with both these restrictive solutions suggest a third solution, one that disregards the contract between manufacturer and ultimate buyer so that a uniform tort solution exists in all cases. That solution itself has very substantial costs in the necessary disruption of private expectations and in the huge administrative costs it imposes upon all participants to the tort system. Yet when all this has been said, today it is tilting at windmills to fight the anticontractual bias found not only in *Henningsen* but in the legion of cases that have followed it.

The practical implications of *Henningsen* are yet another matter. Here it is necessary to distinguish between its long- and short-term effects. For the short term, the decision may have produced no net social benefits, but by the same token it provoked no great social dislocations. The underlying fact pattern in *Henningsen* was essentially that of the strong products liability case, so that the judicial cause of action created no undue strains upon the administration of the torts system. The judicial rules of the 1960s may not have matched the contractual ideal, but chances are that they were very close to it. If the adverse effects of judicial regulation are measured by the spread between the imposed result and the contractual one, then *Henningsen* had little immediate effect. Products liability insurance rates remained a small matter in the decade after *Henningsen*.[14] The underlying products liability law had not moved much in an institutional sense, even with the

14. *See, e.g.*, Note, *Product Liability and the Choice of Law*, 78 Harv. L. Rev. 1452, 1456 (1965), where it was reported as follows:

> Indeed, current insurance practices permit a manufacturer to insure his products at roughly the same cost whether he makes them in a negligence state or a strict [liability] state. [Strict liability] has not yet forced [insurance companies] to readjust their system of imposing a single insurance rate for a single sort of product throughout the country.

Jeffrey O'Connell has observed that the total products liability premiums in 1970 were estimated to be $125 million dollars, a fivefold increase from 1950, but a small sum none the less. *See* O'Connell, *Expanding No-Fault Beyond Auto Insurance: Some Proposals*, 59 Va. L. Rev. 749,755 (1973).

newly created limitations upon freedom of contract and the early adoption of strict liability principles.

The long-term implications of the decision are another matter entirely. *Henningsen* rests upon the implicit premise that the standard American practices of manufacturing and marketing were not only suspect but perhaps corrupt. From that premise it was easy to move into an aggressive posture on substantive products liability doctrines, which after *Henningsen* became matters of proper judicial intervention. Two consequences followed. First, *Henningsen* neutralized the possibility that private contracts could check judicial excesses. Second, *Henningsen* undermined the traditionally cautious judicial attitudes on doctrinal issues in products liability cases. As late as 1965 the original rules in the Restatement (Second) of Torts were sensible enough, even with their rejection of privity and their acceptance of strict liability principles. The enormous transformation of the law since 1965 has created substantive doctrines that are far less desirable, and the consequent dislocations have been more severe. We must look, therefore, first to the Restatement and then to the subsequent case law development of the next generation.

CHAPTER

# 6

# THE RESTATEMENT (SECOND)OF TORTS: 402A

The publication of the Restatement (Second) of Torts in 1965 marks a major turning point in the history of products liability. The applicable provisions, grouped together in a chapter quaintly entitled "Liability of Persons Supplying Chattels for the Use of Others,"[1] represent a peculiar amalgam of the old and the new. One full topic, "Persons Supplying Chattels to be Used for their Business Purposes,"[2] deals with a very improbable situation of virtually no importance in practice today. Other sections and their comments are directed toward the obligations of suppliers who are neither manufacturers nor retailers;[3] and these too are historical curiosities of recent vintage. Closer to the modern law, the Restatement gives detailed treatments of various issues of liability under the negligence rules, many of which remain important to this very day.[4] And in one exceptionally important provision, Section 402A, the Restatement accepts the arguments of Justice Traynor in *Escola* and candidly imposes a "special" strict liability upon the sellers of defective products which cause physical harm to users and consumers. It is not possible in this book to go into all the remote corners and dead ends explored with such loving care in the Restatement, but it is vital to analyze in detail both the text of Section 402A and the exhaustive comments on it. Such an analysis shows what departures from traditional negligence principles were wrought by the Restatement rule of strict liability; and it provides a benchmark against which to measure the changes, sometimes bold, sometimes timid, that are the Restatement's contribution to today's law. The complete text of Section 402A (and its three caveats) is as follows:

1. Restatement (Second) of Torts, ch. 14 (heading).
2. Id., ch. 14, topic 2. §§391-93.
3. Id. §§388-90. (ch. 14, topic 1. "Rules Applicable to All Suppliers").
4. Id. §395 (ch. 14, topic 3. "Manufacturers of Chattels").

**402A Special Liability of Seller of Product for Physical Harm to User or Consumer**

(1) One who sells any product in a defective condition unreasonably dangerous to the user or consumer or to his property is subject to liability for physical harm thereby caused to the ultimate user or consumer, or to his property, if
   (a) the seller is engaged in the business of selling such a product, and
   (b) it is expected to and does reach the user or consumer without substantial change in the condition in which it is sold.

(2) The rule stated in Subsection (1) applies although
   (a) the seller has exercised all possible care in the preparation and sale of his product, and
   (b) the user or consumer has not bought the product from or entered into any contractual relation with the seller.

Caveat:

The Institute expresses no opinion as to whether the rules stated in this Section may not apply

(1) to harm to persons other than users or consumers;
(2) to the seller of a product expected to be processed or otherwise substantially changed before it reaches the user or consumer; or
(3) to the seller of a component part of a product to be assembled.

## TWO CLEAR POINTS

There are several important points to make about the general structure of the section. In the first place the rule makes two things explicit: that negligence is irrelevant to liability under this section and that the privity limitation can never bar recovery. The first of these tasks is accomplished neatly by the language of subsection (2) (a), which asserts that the basic rule applies even though "the seller has exercised all possible care in the preparation and sale of his product." The second is accomplished in the next clause which treats the absence of a direct contractual relationship between the seller and the injured party as immaterial to the basic cause of action. The first point confirmed the growing trend; the second ratified past law. No further comment need be made about them, as their implications have already been discussed in the historical sections of this book.

## THREE CAVEATS

Several other features of the text of Section 402A do, however, require further comment. In particular, it is instructive to note the cautious tone of the three caveats to the basic section. The first caveat raises a doubt as to whether the rule of strict liability extends to actions brought by injured bystanders. Comment *o* gives the unsatisfactory explanation that, however much the basic rule is warranted for users and consumers, consumer pressures for strict liability do not create "the same demand for the protection of casual strangers." The hesitation on this point is puzzling, and the comment's guess about some unidentified public demand is speculative and unsupported. We have already commented upon the rationales that might be used for strict liability. No matter which of them is accepted, strict liability should apply to actions brought by bystanders just as it applies to those brought by users or consumers. Administrative savings still can be realized by elimination of the negligence issue; the proper incentives still can be placed upon the defendant; and loss-spreading objectives (however dubious) still can be achieved. Indeed the strict liability principle works even where the account of product defect rests upon a theory of express or implied representations about product fitness. The defendant represented to a third party that he, the third party, could use the defendant's product with safety when he could not so use it. The false representation made to the third party is sufficient to impute his actions to the original product supplier. The plaintiff's causal case need not depend upon the supplier's representation to the injured plaintiff. Indeed, there is one additional reason why the bystander is, of all possible plaintiffs, the one most entitled to protection. Actions brought by users or consumers may well be barred by assumption of risk arguments, given the opportunity to inspect the product. This issue is quite remote in bystander suits, as the plaintiff never takes the product into his own possession. He is a stranger to the chain of distribution, entitled prima facie to protection from miscarriages within it. The argument for bystander recovery, subject only to the defenses generally appropriate in stranger cases, is indeed overwhelming. While no reasoned decisions applied strict products liability doctrines in favor of bystanders before the publication of the Second Restatement, from 1969 or so a uniform line of cases has properly allowed the bystander cause of action under Section 402A.[5]

Similar observations apply to the second caveat, as the prospect of product processing or modification only raises the question of whether the defect originally in the product persisted until it helped cause plaintiff's physical injury. That question is, of course, interesting and important, but it arises whether or not strict liability principles supplant the older rules of negligence. For the purposes of the Restatement it should have been sufficient to carry over the traditional causal limitations based on third-party intervention, developed in the negligence context, to the new strict liability action. As with the bystander issue, the initial doubts expressed in this caveat have given way to a proper acceptance of strict liability.

5. *See, e.g.*, the strong opinion of Peters, J. in *Elmore v. American Motors Corp.*, 70 Cal. 2d 578, 451 P.2d 84, 75 Cal. Rptr. 652 (1969); *Codling v. Paglia*, 32 N.Y. 2d 330, 298 N.E. 2d 622, 345 N.Y.S. 2d 461 (1973), where the ordinary defense of contributory negligence was preserved. For law review comment, *see* Noel, *Defective Products: Extension of Strict Liability to Bystanders*, 38 Tenn. L. Rev. 1 (1970); Comment, *Strict Products Liability to the Bystander: A Study in Common Law Determinism*, 38 U. Chi. L. Rev. 625 (1971).

The last caveat, concerning the liability of component part manufacturers, also represents an unaccountable bit of caution. The analogous liability under negligence principles was well established in the pre-Restatement cases.[6] The Restatement's treatment of products liability under negligence expressly held the manufacturer of the finished product responsible for the negligence of the component part manufacturers.[7] All basic justifications for strict liability apply to component part manufacturers, who are analogous in all respects to manufacturers of completed products. As with the two previous caveats, time has rightly passed by the Restatement on this question.[8]

## THE LIABILITY OF "SELLERS"

One of the most important innovations of Section 402A concerns the class of defendants to which its "special" liability rules apply. The text of the section, heavily influenced by the history of warranty law, limits liability to the "seller" of a product. Comment *f* of the Restatement indicates the broad construction attached to the term by noting that it applies to any "wholesaler or retail dealer or distributor." This extension of strict liability principles to these intermediate parties works a startling, unheralded change of legal principle. The analogous Restatement provisions on negligence liability and the vast bulk of the pre-Restatement cases all recognized the limited liability of distributors and retailers of defective products which had been manufactured and packaged by others.

The exact nature of the obligations of the intermediates varied somewhat from jurisdiction to jurisdiction, but through all these local variations emerged the clear sense that the intermediate parties should not be responsible for product defects which they did not create and which they could not discover through the ordinary methods by which they prepared their products for customer sale.[9] In some cases the intermediate parties were treated like the shippers who moved the goods from one place to another. In other cases, where they assumed a more active role, they were treated in the same manner as manufacturers. One consequence of this position was that the intermediate parties could not, for example, be held responsible for the occasional impurities that found their way into packaged goods, at least if

6. *See* ch. 2 above at note 33.

7. *See* Restatement (Second) of Torts, §395, comment *m*. It remains of course true that the action against the manufacturer of the component part will require the plaintiff to overcome one more link in the causal chain, a point that is normally of no difficulty where the component is not modified or altered upon its incorporation into the completed product.

8. *Noel v. United Aircraft Corp.* 342 F.2d 232 (3d Cir. 1964).

9. *See, e.g., Hertzler v. Manshum.* "If defendant Manshum [the retailer] satisfies a jury that the flour was delivered by him to plaintiff's decedent in the same container, and exactly as furnished him by the manufacturer—in other words that the poison did not get into the flour while in his possession—then he is not liable, . . ." 228 Mich. 416, 423, 200 N.W. 155, 157 (1924).

these goods had been acquired from a reputable manufacturer or middleman. Another was that these parties could not be held accountable for any defect in design which could be identified and corrected only by parties possessing the technical skills of the original manufacturer. In light of these principles, the intermediate parties ran the risk of exposure when they did something that helped bring about the harm—leaving milk off ice, failing to conduct some safety inspection normally required of persons in their position, or representing that a particular product was appropriate for a task for which it was in fact ill suited. At no point, however, were these intermediate parties subject to vicarious liability for the wrongs of the manufacturer.

Without much discussion of this body of case law, the Restatement jettisoned all these restrictions in strict liability actions, even though it continued to respect them in the negligence context.[10] From a position of little or no exposure, the retailer came to be treated as the alter ego of the manufacturer. From the vantage point of this book, that shift requires major justification. The theory of express or implied representations, sufficient to attach strict liability to the manufacturer, does not work well with intermediate parties because, except in the situations just identified, there is no consumer expectation that they will do more than pass their products down the chain of distribution. Likewise, the administrative case for strict liability has no application to intermediaries that act purely as conduits. Strict liability of the manufacturer is useful as a means of eliminating complicated issues of negligence: it is hardly needed when there is no exposure in negligence to begin with. The reorientation of the Restatement's basic principle calls for a reasoned justification. The classic effort in that direction is that of Justice Traynor in *Vandermark v. Ford Motor Company*, where he states his arguments as follows:

> Retailers like manufacturers are engaged in the business of distributing goods to the public. They are an integral part of the overall producing and marketing enterprise that should bear the cost of injuries resulting from defective products. [Citations omitted.] In some cases the retailer may be the only member of that enterprise reasonably available to the injured plaintiff. In other cases the retailer himself may play a substantial part in insuring that the product is safe or may be in a position to exert pressure on the manufacturer to that end; the retailer's strict liability thus serves as an added incentive to safety. Strict liability on the manufacturer and retailer alike affords maximum protection to the injured plaintiff and works no injustice to the defendants, for they can adjust the costs of such protection between them in the course of their continuing business relationship. Accordingly, as a retailer engaged in the business of distributing goods to the public, Maywood Bell [the dealer] is strictly liable in tort for personal injuries caused by defects in cars sold by it. . . .[11]

10. Restatement §402A. comments *a* & *m*; §§388, 399, 402.
11. 61 Cal. 2d. 256, 262-63, 391 P.2d 168, 171-72, 37 Cal. Rptr., 896, 899-900 (1964).

Traynor's opinion insists that all intermediate parties should be charged with liability because they are part of the chain of producing and marketing goods, but often these parties have everything to do with marketing and nothing to do with other production or safety. It is, therefore, far from obvious that intermediate parties should be saddled with costs that are in no sense of their own making. But it is said that this new liability will create additional pressures for manufacturers to make safe products. The point may be true, but there are good reasons to think that it is not. Where the manufacturer alone is accountable for manufacturing defects, the injured party will have every incentive to pursue him. Where a retailer or wholesaler is jointly accountable, the force of the direct action against the manufacturer must, of necessity, be diluted by the opportunity of injured parties to press their claims against others in the chain of distribution. The reduction of direct pressure against the manufacturer may be offset by the actions for indemnity and contribution that these intermediate parties will in turn bring against the manufacturer, but it is far from obvious that the complicated incentives created by this divided system of responsibility are superior to those of a simple rule that directs the full brunt of the injured party's efforts against the manufacturer. Indeed in some of the hard cases that test the *Vandermark* rule—suits against retailers of products marketed in sealed containers or against distributors of completed machine tool presses—there is little, if anything, that distributors or retailers can do to influence the conduct of the manufacturer who has, after all, full control over the production process. In such cases we should expect, therefore, that the retailer's primary efforts will be directed *not* toward influencing the design and quality of the product, but toward obtaining "hold harmless" clauses from the manufacturer to reimburse him in the event that the original product is adjudged defective and harmful. These clauses are not costless to negotiate or to litigate, and *Vandermark* ironically fosters the multiplicity of actions which was one of the evils the original principle of strict liability sought to avoid. Finally, with respect to durable goods long in the marketplace, the rule works the great *retrospective* injustice of subjecting distributors and retailers to liabilities (for which there may be no action over against an insolvent or liquidated manufacturer) that were wholly uncontemplated at the time of the original sales transaction.

In the end, therefore, the only argument in favor of the generalized retailer's liability is that it affords the plaintiff an alternative remedy when the manufacturer is insulated, say by jurisdictional requirements, from direct action by injured parties. There is always something very uneasy about an argument which says that *A* should be held liable for certain harms simply because *B* cannot be. If this argument is, however, regarded as decisive under the doubtful loss distribution rationales of products liability, it should be subject to at least two limitations. First, it should not apply to durable products sent into the marketplace before the announcement of the new rules; and second, it should not apply whenever the manufacturer is amenable to suit in the jurisdiction in which the plaintiff is injured.[12] Where, of course, the suit against the retailer is for his own wrongs in connection with the preparation, storage, or distribution of the product, liability should proceed under ordinary tort principles.

The theoretical weaknesses in the *Vandermark* decision, moreover, are well exposed by the problems raised in the recent Oregon case of *Tillman v. Vance Equipment Co.*[13] There the plaintiff was injured when trying to grease the gears of a twenty-four-year-old crane. The crane in question had just been purchased by the plaintiff's employer on an "as is" basis from the defendant, who had acquired it on special order for resale to the employer, subject to his inspection and final approval. The defendant thus functioned more like a broker than the typical "seller" to whom Section 402A is directed. In light of the defendant's role, the Oregon court quite properly refused to subject him to the strict liability rules of that section, noting that its application would upset the delicate market arrangements that have developed over the years for the distribution of used products.

The court then sought to distinguish the defendant here from the ordinary retailer in *Vandermark*, arguing that the used products dealer is "entirely outside the ordinary chain of distribution," thereby making it difficult, if not impossible, to organize any systematic exchange of information between him and the original manufacturer. But of what value is the exchange of information between a manufacturer and a retailer in a design defect case? Or when a rusty nail is lodged inside a cake? What is it we expect the retailer to do? The sensible rule seems to be to hold both the retailer and the used-product seller responsible only when knowledge of and control over danger makes their conduct essential to the loss control process—a rule that will exonerate retailers and distributors almost, but not quite, as often as used-product sellers.

12. *See*, for a recent legislative attempt to enact these requirements, Ariz. Rev. Stat. Ann. §12-551.

The same attitude is also displayed in the Model Uniform Product Liability Act, prepared by the Department of Commerce, which deals with the question in section 105, which addresses the "Basic Standards of Responsibility for Product Sellers Other Than Manufacturers" and concludes that strict liability principles ought to govern only where the manufacturer proper is not able to respond in damages to claims brought against him.

13. 286 Or. 747, 596 P.2d 1299 (1979). Indeed a similar problem arises where specific products are made to the special order of the user. *See, e.g., Hunt v. Blasius*, 55 Ill. App. 3d 14, 370 N.E. 2d 617 (1977), where it was held that "bidders who comply strictly with governmental specifications should be shielded from liability in any respect in which the product complies [with such standards)." Id. at 20, 370 N.E. 2d at 621-22. The unresolved question is why suppliers to private users should not be entitled to the same protection when they make goods to special order.

The same point can be put in a somewhat different manner. The court in *Tillman* looked to the "implied representational" aspect of the defendant's used-products business, and concluded that no one—be he immediate purchaser or ultimate user—could ever regard this defendant as warranting the fitness of the product under Section 402A. That same representational theory works for the benefit of the retailer and distributor as well, even if they are in the ordinary chain of distribution: no one expects them to redesign products or open sealed containers. The unwillingness of the court in *Tillman* to extend Section 402A to this special class of sellers shows a solid appreciation of the basic concerns of products liability law that is not fully reflected in the text of the Restatement (Second) of Torts. The radical revision introduced by *Vandermark* and the Restatement (Second) in the treatment of intermediate parties should not be confused with the traditional form of strict liability. It is a dubious form of *vicarious* liability for the wrongs of others that serves none of the proper purposes of the products liability law.

## WHAT IS A "DEFECT"?

As already noted, one of the major consequences of the explicit abandonment of negligence in Section 402A was that it brought the defect concept to the fore. The question—strict liability for what?—demands identification of some product defect as a necessary component of the basic cause of action. Baseball bats can strike innocent people; guns can shoot them; hot coffee can burn them; aspirin can poison them; milk can drown them. Without the defect requirement, the manufacturer of any of these ordinary products could be held accountable for any harm associated in any way with any product. Clearly, the notion of product defect is the fundamental barrier to such grotesque results.

Section 402A accepts the defect requirement by limiting its strict liability action to "any product in a defective condition unreasonably dangerous to the user or consumer or to his property."[14] Its comments, however, indicate the narrow scope of the traditional defect concept. Thus, comment *h* begins:

> A product is not in a defective condition when it is safe for normal handling and consumption. If the injury results from abnormal handling, as where a bottled

14. *See* Restatement (Second) of Torts, §402A, comment *i*. These examples are suggestive of the narrow scope of the earlier drafts of §402A which limited its strict liability rule first to cases of food and drink and later to cases of products intended for intimate body use. By 1965 the case law had moved so rapidly that the section was changed to embrace all products, but no effort was made to see how the language of "defect" and "unreasonably dangerous" was influenced by the expansion of the basic provision. On this history, *see* Wade, *On the Nature of Strict Tort Liability for Products*, 44 Miss. L. J. 825, 830-31 (1973). On the complications that arise in connection with the integration of the defect definition and the assumption of risk defense, *see* ch. 9.

beverage is knocked against a radiator to remove the cap, or from abnormal preparation for use, as where too much salt is added to food, or from abnormal consumption, as where a child eats too much candy and is made ill, the seller is not liable.

Further examples illustrate the same theory. Comment *i* says that "whiskey containing a dangerous amount of fusel oil," or "tobacco containing something like marijuana" or "bad butter contaminated with poisonous fish oil," all qualify as dangerously defective products. Modest innovations extend the defect concept to "decay or deterioration of a product before sale," and to products marketed in a defective container. "Thus a carbonated beverage in a bottle which is so weak, or cracked, or jagged at the edges, or bottled under such excessive pressure that it may explode or otherwise cause harm to the person who handles it, is in a defective and dangerous condition."[15]

Section 402A appears to narrow the concept of defect further by the use of the words "unreasonably dangerous." On first reading, these words seem somewhat out of place. Reasonableness is the distinctive feature of the negligence concept; yet the major aim of Section 402A is to remove the negligence issue from products liability cases.[16] The section's comments indicate that one purpose of the "unreasonably dangerous" limitation was to protect the manufacturer from possible insurer's liability in the event of the misuse or overconsumption of the product. Since, however, the term "defective" already had been defined by a product's tendency to cause harm only in normal use, these words are at best unnecessary, and at worst mischievous. Their use was, however, thought appropriate for the large class of products that are highly beneficial even though not fully safe for ordinary consumption and use.[17] Thus, rabies vaccine should certainly be administered to persons bitten by rabid animal; even though it creates a distinct probability of an early death, it also represents the only hope for life. Less dramatically, blood transfusions may well be required in spite of the (at one time) irreducible possibility of hepatitis. Yet even here the words "unreasonably dangerous" do not ideally fit their chosen purpose.[18] The Restatement could have made the matter much clearer if it had explicitly recognized that the concept of product defect is intimately bound up with the deviation between the product as it is represented by the seller and the product as it exists when it is in fact sold. In essence, the selling of both blood and vaccine is without adverse legal consequences because all interested

15. Restatement (Second) of Torts, §402A, comment *h*.

16. Id., comment *i*.

17. Id., comment *h*.

18. A point made much of by the California Supreme Court in *Cronin v. J.B.E. Olson Corp.*, 8 Cal. 3d 121, 501 P.2d 1153, 104 Cal. Rptr. 433 (1972), where the point was used to read the words "unreasonably dangerous" out of the California law without taking into account all the consequences of the shift. *See also Azzarello v. Black Bros. Co., Inc.*, 480 Pa. 547, 391 A.2d 1020 (1978).

parties know of certain inherent risks that are assumed by the user on his own best judgment. Typically, no misrepresentation is involved. The question, therefore, of the "unreasonable danger" drops out of the legal calculation. Once the seller has delivered the product that was promised, the legal risk is with the user who is, in the typical situation, willing to take it in order to forestall the prospect of some greater harm.

The defect concept receives little analysis or elaboration in Section 402A, which gives no hint whatsoever of the expansive interpretation impressed upon it after 1970. Thus it is striking that Section 402A contains little discussion of the two other types of defect that today dominate products liability litigation. Design defect cases are not even mentioned, probably because the draftsmen thought that Section 398, dealing with liability for negligent design, covered the entire area. Duty to warn cases received a little attention, which suggested the apparent narrowness of their reach.[19] One example notes that a drug could be considered defective if marketed without information about its appropriate dosage levels, and another indicates that warnings might be appropriate where a small class of users might develop an allergic reaction to the product. Yet even in these circumstances, it is doubtful that strict liability principles governed duty to warn cases because there is both a cross-reference to the negligence rules of Section 398[20] and an explicit observation that the warnings are only demanded where the seller "has knowledge, or by the application of reasonable, developed human skill and foresight should have knowledge, of the presence of the ingredient and the danger."[21]

## PLAINTIFF'S CONDUCT

Curiously enough, one issue never confronted in the text of Section 402A involves the proper treatment of plaintiff's conduct in products liability actions. The issue is obliquely faced in the "normal use" element of the defect definition and specifically mentioned in comment *n* to the text. Ordinary contributory negligence was said to be no defense, and assumption of risk was said to apply only in cases in which there was a voluntary and unreasonable encounter of a known product defect. Comment *n*, to which we shall return, offers no justification for these restrictive rules, and the

19. Restatement (Second) of Torts, §402A, comment *j*.

20. Id., §388, especially in comments *i*, *j*, and *n*. Comments *i* & *j* deal with simple cases in which the seller does not disclose obvious defects (e.g., baking soda tins that explode) that infect some but not all members of a large lot. Comment *n* deals with the difficult question of what duties are imposed upon the seller where the product is not sold to the person who in fact makes immediate and direct use of it, as with the scaffold sold to the contractor for the benefit of his workmen. The entire discussion is predicated upon the application of negligence principles.

21. Restatement (Second) of Torts, §402A, comment *j*.

best explanation for this lapse is that the limited state of the law at the time of the Second Restatement gave no hint as to the future importance of the issue.

## THE AGENDA

This analysis of the Restatement both shows the substantive limitations of Section 402A and places on the agenda two major themes. The first theme involves the interpretation and application of the defect principle in the wide range of cases decided after publication of the Restatement. The second concerns the proper treatment of plaintiff's conduct in this new era of products liability actions. Chapters 7 and 8 are devoted to the first of these questions. Chapter 9 is devoted to the second of them. In both areas the true revolution was wrought, not by the Restatement, but after it.

CHAPTER

7

# CONSTRUCTION AND DESIGN DEFECTS

## CONSTRUCTION DEFECTS

There is little need at this juncture to dwell upon the law of construction defects. The essence of the plaintiff's case is always that the defendant's product deviated in some material way from the plans and specifications of its own original design. In the food cases, a construction defect is made out by showing contamination, adulteration, or spoilage. In the machine tool cases it is made out by showing that the product in question was not equipped, for example, with the seals or valves called for by its basic design. In a chemical or drug case, the case is made out by showing that the product was not prepared in accordance with its own formula. In all these cases the plaintiff holds the defendant only to the standards that he has chosen to impose upon himself.[1] That this standard may be higher than that set by industry practice or by statute is of no concern. The defendant has sold the product on the faith of his higher representation; presumably he has commanded a higher price for his superior product. The representation that serves him well when the product meets its standard should bind him when the product falls below that same standard. There can be no quarrel with a legal rule that binds any manufacturer or supplier to a self-imposed standard. The real problems in this area come in the design defect cases to which we now turn.

1. *See, e.g.*, for this suggestion of unfair penalty on a product seller, Twerski & Weinstein, "*A Critique of the Uniform Product Liability Law—A Rush to Judgment*," 28 Drake L. Rev. 221, 225 (1979). Note too the response of the Model Act that the high construction standards might benefit the manufacturers by insulating them from charges of design defect, a sensible observation given the very broad standards for design defect that are articulated in Section 104 of the Act. Federal Register, vol. 44, no. 212, pp. 62722-23 (October 31, 1979) and for the account of the product defect generally, Section 104, pp. 62721 ff.

## DESIGN DEFECTS

Design defect cases stand in sharp contrast to the construction defect cases just considered.[2] Construction defect cases presuppose that the design is safe but insist that the product is dangerous because it does not conform to the design. Design defect cases presuppose that the product conforms to design but insist that the design itself is unsafe. Construction defects arise because of occasional miscarriages in the manufacturing process; design defects necessarily pervade an entire line of products whose production was exactly as intended. Design defect cases thus create a potential for liability that is normally unmatched in the production defect area. The size of the stakes is no reason to shrink from imposing such liability whenever it is warranted in principle, but it is a reason to reexamine closely the basis upon which liability supposedly rests.

Discussions of design defect cases often have been marred by the implicit assumption that all such cases fall under a common rubric, and are thus subject to essentially the same considerations. In fact, it is possible to identify three major classes of design defect cases that call for different types of response, both at the judicial and at the legislative level. Cases in the first class, which we shall call "strong" design defect cases, rest upon the defendant's express or implicit representations about his product's design and performance. Cases in the second class rest upon the defendant's breach of the external standards, whether imposed by statute or by common practice. The last class, consisting of the "modern" design defect cases, identifies the product defect through extended use of cost-benefit formulas, generally by jury determination. For each class of cases it is necessary to speak of three separate issues. First, what counts as a product defect; second, whether the basis for design defect liability rests upon negligence or strict liability principles; and third, what causal determinations must be made to complete the prima facie case. Affirmative defenses are necessarily raised in this analysis, but their systematic examination will be postponed until this discussion of both design defect and duty to warn cases is completed.

### STRONG DESIGN DEFECT CASES

#### *Product Defect*

The strength of the strong design defect cases is best understood after first restating the two major reasons why construction defect cases are so

2. The literature on design defects is voluminous. For a critical account of the modern developments (to which this chapter owes much), *see* Henderson, *Judicial Review of Manufacturers' Conscious Design Choices: The Limits of Adjudication*, 73 Colum. L. Rev. 1531 (1973). For a strong statement of the opposite position, *see* Twerski, Weinstein, Donaher, & Piehler, *The Use and Abuse of Warnings in Products Liability—Design Defect Litigation Comes of Age*, 61 Cornell L. Rev. 495 (1976).

easily incorporated within the liability system. First, the very definition of a construction defect allows the plaintiff's case to rest upon the assertion that the manufacturer should be held responsible for the consequences of any misrepresentation about his product. Glass slivers in ice cream are not dangerous per se; they are dangerous only to persons misled by appearances. The point is underscored by the assumption of risk defense that, even today, bars recovery when the product defect is known to the plaintiff, who can then avoid the peril, for example, by not eating the ice cream. Second, construction defect cases do not require the judicial promulgation of independent standards for what constitutes defectiveness. Instead, the defendant is bound by his own express or implied specifications under which the product was marketed. Such standards are expressed in the detailed design specifications for a machine tool, and they are surely implicit with ice cream and other foodstuffs, even if the defendant never uttered a word about impurities.

Virtually all pre-Restatement design defect cases and many more recent ones possess these two desirable features of the construction defect case, as the previous accounts of both *Huset v. Case*[3] and *Greenman v. Yuba Power,*[4] both design defect cases, show. The close kinship between the design and the construction cases lies in the fact that in design defect cases the defendant expressly or impliedly represented that the product reached *performance* (as opposed to *design*) standards which made it safe for the uses for which it was constructed. The major difference between these two types of cases, design and construction, lies in the precision with which the appropriate standards of judgment can be identified and applied. It is usually a simple task in construction defect cases to determine product specifications, whether express or implied. With design defect cases the point is somewhat more problematic, because the applicable performance standards do not leap out to present themselves to the court or the jury. True, the task was easy enough in *Huset* and *Greenman*, given that the machines failed when used exactly as intended. Yet, some irreducible uncertainty remains whenever efforts are made in the heat of litigation to determine the expectations shared by manufacturers and users about both product uses and product limitations. Can the plaintiff recover if he injures himself by using a screwdriver to open a can of paint? It depends in part upon the size of the screwdriver and the force to which it is subjected. Can the plaintiff recover if he stands on a chair to change a lightbulb? Again, it depends on the size and shape of the chair, the person who stood on it, and the type of surface on which it rested. General rules will not solve all strong design defect cases, given the need for determining the "sense" of representations that a given product makes, as it were, about itself. The task is

3. 120 F. 865 (8th Cir. 1903), discussed in ch. 2.
4. 59 Cal. 2d 57, 377 P.2d 897, 27 Cal. Rptr. 697 (1963), discussed in ch. 4.

necessarily contextual, and the outcomes at the margin remain necessarily imprecise, providing the stuff of which jury trials are made. Justice Traynor caught one-half of the inquiry when he said in *Greenman v. Yuba Power* that "[i]mplicit in the machine's presence on the market, however, was a representation it would safely do the jobs for which it was built."[5] But a balanced view looks as well to the language of Judge Askren thirty-five years earlier in *Foster v. Ford Motor Company.* "The very appearance of a complicated piece of machinery, such as this [tractor], is in itself a sufficient warning to one who desires to use it, that he should acquaint himself with its power and possibilities."[6] Where both implied warnings and warranties are taken into account, there will be some doubtful ground and some wrong decisions, but there will be no threat to the institutional integrity of the system.

*Negligence or Strict Liability*

Turning to the next issue, we should not shrink in the classical design defect context from holding a defendant strictly liable for products that do not meet the performance standards under which they were expressly or impliedly marketed. Here, as elsewhere, negligence issues raise intractable questions of *how much* care the defendant must exercise in order to escape liability. There is no reason to allow this expensive and difficult inquiry for the benefit of a defendant who can protect himself by making clear the limits and capacities of the product that he produces. The issue of negligence—*why* was this product defective?—can only deflect the inquiry from its central issue—*was* this product defective? The clear and limited account of defect provides ample protection against the unlimited and unprincipled extensions of liability so feared by the nineteenth-century judges.

The strict liability standard works well even with some more complicated cases decided after the *Greenman* decision. Thus in *Dudley Sports Co. v. Schmitt,*[7] the defendant manufactured a baseball-pitching machine that

5. Id. at 64, 377 P.2d at 901, 27 Cal. Rptr. at 701.

6. 139 Wash. 341, 347-48, 246 P. 945, 947 (1926). One instance in which the limitations derived from appearance were not taken into account by the court is *DeSantis v. Parker Feeders, Inc.*, 547 F.2d 357 (7th Cir. 1976). There the plaintiff's father purchased the components for a cattle feeder from the defendant, which he then assembled for use on the family farm. The plaintiff, aged six, lost all of one leg and part of another when he and his brother had a water-gun fight around the machine while in operation. The court noted that the machine was always depicted in its promotional literature without a safety guard over the auger, and that it was stated, "Even a child can do your feeding." It is impossible to glean from these facts any assertion that the machine was safe for children's horseplay. With respect to the judicial efforts in that regard, the only answer is, "no, they did not mean that at all." The case is another illustration of the general soundness of the "open and obvious" rule, which, of course, it rejects. See, ch. 8 at 145.

7. 151 Ind. App. 217, 279 N.E.2d 266 (1972).

operated by both electrical and mechanical means. The cycle began when the machine's throwing arm was propelled forward at great speed by a mechanical spring. After the baseball was so released, the cycle was completed when the arm was returned to its original position by an electric motor. The salient characteristic of this machine was that when it was "at rest," the mechanical spring was in its *coiled* position. The plaintiff accidentally brushed against the machine, released its safety catch, and was severely injured when struck by the rapidly moving arm.

Strict liability principles should govern.[8] The machine as designed by the defendant contains a trap, a hidden danger that is in no way apparent from its benign outward appearance. The fact that the manufacturer took certain precautions may well have reduced the probability of accident, but it should not shift back to the innocent plaintiff the cost of those accidents that, in fact, happen. The court case is not the place to judge whether one sort of locking device was better than another. Once the court is satisfied that the machine was indeed a trap in such casual encounters, liability should be imposed even if the product was designed in conformity to the state of the art and in compliance with all statutes. Exacting standards of judgment are appropriate because the message carried by the appearance of the machine—that it would not spring into action when touched—takes precedence over any standard for defectiveness that might have been mandated in its absence.[9]

### *Causation*

There is, lastly, the causation issue, which also presents no problems that call into question the basic soundness of the strong design defect case.

8. The emphasis on strict liability for products that fail in ordinary use thus makes it possible to ignore the question of whether the precautions previously taken were adequate in light of the product modifications subsequently made by the defendant. *See, e.g., doCanto v. Ametek, Inc.*, 367 Mass. 776, 328 N.E. 2d 873 (1975), where the plaintiff's hand was caught between rollers of the iron manufactured by the defendant. The defendant showed that the plaintiff's hand was unusually tiny, and the plaintiff was allowed to introduce evidence of the way in which the defendant had redesigned the guard. This last bit of evidence might have been relevant under a negligence theory on the question of proper precautions (where its admissibility is subject to doubt, *see* ch. 10) but it should be quite irrelevant to the plaintiff's case given that the product failed in its ordinary use.

9. Note that the approach taken here differs from that of the Model Uniform Product Liability Act, § 104 (B) and the analysis thereof, where it is argued that a negligence standard might help to reduce the otherwise unbounded exposure created by the design defect standards. Yet that exposure comes only with the modern defect cases discussed in this chapter and not with those products that fail in ordinary use, as ordainarily understood. *See* infra at 76.

Yet the position of the model act seems both too broad and too narrow. In the traditional design defect cases the strict liability standard creates little peril because the actions are limited to products with latent defects that manifest themselves in ordinary use, as that term is ordinarily understood. And in the modern design defect cases, discussed below, the negligence standard does not do enough (unless it is very broadly applied) to counteract the enormous increase in exposure brought about by the unprecedented expansion of the defect concept.

There may be some question as to how much stress and strain a power tool should be able to withstand, but the plaintiff in *Greenman* did not exceed those limits; so too the plaintiff in *Huset* exerted only normal pressure on the engine covering where he was supposed to stand. The causal arguments are, finally, even easier in *Schmitt*, where the plaintiff only brushed against the machine and "triggered" a release of forces improperly designed into it. In all these strong design defect cases, the defendant, by representing how his product should be used or treated, should be viewed as if he struck the very blow that was the immediate cause of the plaintiff's injury. The subsequent actions of the intermediate parties were not only foreseeable but also intended and invited. The cases raise, therefore, no difficult problems for the plaintiff on the thorny remoteness-of-damage issue.

## STATUTES AND COMMON PRACTICE

Causes of action based on failure to comply with statutes or with common practice differ from the cases discussed so far in that the standard of judgment is externally imposed upon the defendant and not assumed voluntarily in the course of his business. In spite of their great importance today, the Restatement (Second) of Torts, Section 402A, does not address how either statutes or common practice are to be taken into account in determining product defect, although both issues have long been important in the general law of negligence. As the two types of standards differ both in their nature and their source, it is best to treat them separately. We turn first to statutes and then to common practice.

### *Statutory Violations*

Design defect cases predicated on noncompliance with statute present no special difficulties in the modern context. The applicable statutory or administrative standard is known to the defendant at the time the product is manufactured, thus precluding any claim of unfairness based upon its retrospective application. That standard can be ascertained by the jury in the ordinary course of trial, so that deciding what counts as a product defect is no more difficult than in a routine construction defect case, and probably somewhat simpler than in a strong design defect case. The statute or regulation may be wise or it may be foolish, but those are not judicial concerns. Bad statutes may have bad economic consequences, but they do not undermine the integrity of the tort system.

With the product defect simply and directly established, the other elements of the basic cause of action fall quickly into place. One question is whether the basic statute confers a private cause of action on an injured party. The point may well be settled by the statute itself; and where it is not the same, principles of construction applicable in other tort contexts should govern. There is next the issue of whether liability should rest upon negligence or strict liability principles. As the decisive advantage of strict liability—its elimination of "how much" questions from litigation—applies to statutory violations, there is no reason to return here to a negligence standard. The causation issue is more troublesome, particularly if the legislation requires the defendant to guard the plaintiff, wholly or in part, against certain stated contingencies, such as head-on automobile collisions. Here it will be necessary to know with great precision the nature of the forces that harmed the plaintiff (whether generated by the plaintiff himself or by third parties) and that portion of damages which would have occurred even if the defendant's product met all applicable statutory standards. But, given the relative ease with which defendant could have avoided all these legal complications, he can properly be made to litigate the causal questions, once the initial breach of statutory duty is established.

*Common Practice*

Products liability cases based upon the failure to design a product that conforms to common practice within the defendant's trade or business raise more complex issues. Again the initial question is how to determine the appropriate standard against which the defectiveness of the defendant's product should be measured. The determination is doubtless more uncertain than in statutory cases. Common practice shifts from place to place and from time to time, so that the evidence on its precise contours will often be uncertain and contradictory. Yet these difficulties can be overrated. The test of common practice should not be confused with a test which asks whether the defendant's product was designed in accordance with the then applicable "state of the art" within the industry, where that phrase is construed to allow the trier of fact to assess the multitude of technical and economic issues which bear on the relative merits of alternative designs. Instead, common practice looks not to what might or should have been done by firms within any given industry, but rather to what *was in fact done* by all, or some substantial fraction, of those firms. Observation, not calculation, is the basis of the test. While some litigation over what constitutes a common industrial practice must be expected, the long historical experience with both these rules—and the analogous rules on custom as a standard of medical malpractice[10]—suggests that they do not impose intolerable burdens upon the legal system. The standard of common practice, though uncertain at the edges, contains a core of good sense.

The more difficult point about common practice concerns its relationship to the express or implied representations that the defendant makes about his products. Where those representations are *higher* than common practice demands, then on contractual principles they govern in the particular case.

10. *See, e.g.*, McCoid, *The Care Required of Medical Practitioners*, 12 Vand. L. Rev. 549, 605-14 (1959).

The higher standard of excellence does not penalize the especially prudent manufacturer, who is able to command a higher price to compensate for the increased liability exposure. As with construction defect cases,[11] there is nothing to fear from demanding conformity with self-imposed standards. The alternative case, in which the defendant's standards are below those of the industry, is more difficult to evaluate. Thus it is quite possible to treat common practice, like all other forms of custom, as dispositive only in the absence of evidence of the contrary intention of the parties. Under this contractual approach it follows that, where the defective condition of which the plaintiff complains is open and obvious or otherwise known to the plaintiff, the common custom no longer controls on the question of design safety. This position was indeed dominant in the American case law until very recently,[12] and, when accepted, it limited the role of common practice to situations involving latent defects. Thus, in *Wells v. Web Machinery*,[13] for example, the defendant designed his punch press with only a single limit switch. The function of the switch was to prevent the press from closing on the operator's hands. When the original switch failed, it was replaced with another switch that was also defective. Thereafter, the plaintiff's hands were badly injured when the press unexpectedly came down on them. An alternative design that incorporated dual limit switches could have stopped the operation of the press when either limit switch failed and could have prevented the accident. Such dual switches were in fact standard in the defendant's industry, in order to guard against precisely this contingency. The defect was surely latent, and the machine's appearance gave no clue about its fail-safe capabilities. The manufacturer of the original machine was properly held liable for the loss, notwithstanding the intervention of the defective replacement switch. The common practice of the industry in effect served as the contractual standard that bound both parties.

Common practice may be used, however, not only as a tool of contractual interpretation but also, like statutes, as an instrument of direct public regulation. Assume that it is obvious to all concerned that a product possesses certain inherent dangers. Under the previous view of common practice, the obviousness of the condition, especially if communicated to the user, establishes either that the product is not defective or that, if it is, the user assumes the risk of any injury associated with that defect. Yet in its regulatory interpretation, common practice—not the implicit communication between manufacturer and product user—determines whether a product is defective and necessarily removes with it any contractual defense of assumption of risk.

This regulatory interpretation of common practice raises the question of

11. *See* note 1 above.

12. *See, e.g., Campo v. Scofield*, 301 N.Y. 468, 95 N.E. 2d 802 (1950), overruled in *Micallef v. Miehle Co.*, 39 N.Y. 2d 376, 348 N.E.2d 571, 384 N.Y.S.2d 115 (1976).

13. 20 Ill. App. 3d 545, 315 N.E.2d 301 (1974).

whether we can identify any market imperfections that justify preferring the judgment of the industry to the judgment of the parties in question. The point can be debated on both sides; yet what is important in this context is *not* how the problem is resolved, but what is at stake. The interplay between contractual freedom and regulatory control is a recurrent theme of the tort law. Limitations upon freedom of contract were part of the tort law long before the advent of the current products liability crisis, and the system could well survive and even flourish with these limitations. The standards of common practice are drawn from the industries which are to be regulated. Thus, there is the strong likelihood that over time such standards will achieve widespread acceptance and be both workable and efficient. The contractual view may be, as I believe, preferable, but the common practice standard is surely acceptable.

Once common practice has set the standard of product defect, it still remains necessary to complete the other elements in the plaintiff's cause of action. Here the discussion follows the treatment of the statutory cause of action on all relevant points. On the issue of negligence or strict liability, the latter seems clearly preferable. On the issue of causation, the same recurrent issues appear, as it is still necessary to ask, given the other circumstances of the case, whether and to what extent the plaintiff would have been protected from injury if the product had been made in accordance with common practice. All in all, the cause of action predicated upon common practice is perhaps more difficult than those we have previously considered, but it would still be a mistake to say that it unduly strains the institutional capabilities of the tort system.

### MODERN DESIGN DEFECT CASES

The types of design defect cases just discussed doubtless constitute a significant portion of the total volume of products liability actions. Yet it seems clear—although precise documentation is hard to find—that these cases constitute a small portion of the design defect cases that are today brought to trial and an insignificant fraction of appellate litigation. The major institutional controversies all arise when the courts attempt to go beyond defendant's representations, statutes, and common practice to fashion bolder and more aggressive rules for design defect cases.

The crux of the problem lies in the account of product defect used in these modern products liability actions. Whereas the older cases relied upon some standard established prior to the trial in order to measure the fitness of the defendant's product, the modern cases allow the jury a broad discretion at trial to determine the standard of fitness for all products. The newer versions of design defect liability rest on an extended concept of "foresight." The defendant's product may be found defective if it does not contain features to protect the plaintiff against misfortunes involving that product, so long as these are, to echo the language of classical negligence law, "reasonably foreseeable" and, we may add, preventable by the use of reasonable design techniques. The particular contingencies against which the defendant is under a "duty" to protect the plaintiff, of course, include those injuries that are associated with normal product use; more importantly they embrace those caused by product misuse, other neglect of the plaintiff, and all forms of third-party conduct. Whereas the traditional products liability rules restricted liability to cases where the steering wheel collapsed in ordinary driving, the more recent cases, beginning in 1968,[14] allow the jury to impose liability upon a defendant who has complied with all statutes and common practice, if further "reasonable" precautions could have protected the plaintiff against the injuries sustained in a head-on collision or brought on by his own drunken driving.[15]

The viability of this foresight formula is, of course, utterly dependent upon its reasonableness qualification. It is foreseeable that knives will cut, but they are not therefore defective. It is foreseeable that automobiles will be struck by heavy trucks; yet they need not be armor-plated. The extreme cases, of course, only illustrate the principle; they do not define its limits. Even if the product need not be absolutely safe, it must be reasonably safe. Note the ironic twist. The previous accounts of defect required us only to compare the product with an established design standard. Reasonableness language, long the bane of negligence law, played no role in the inquiry. Now, despite the explicit adoption of strict liability, reasonableness concepts are thrust back into the center of the stage, to define not the level of the defendant's care, but the safety of the defendant's product. There is thus a return to the unworkable, open-ended, cost-benefit analysis so characteristic of the traditional law of negligence. Thus in perhaps the most influential account of product defect in design cases, that of Professor Wade, we are told to take into account all of the following factors:

(1) The usefulness and desirability of the product—its utility to the user and to the public as a whole.

(2) The safety aspects of the product—the likelihood that it will cause injury, and the probable seriousness of the injury.

(3) The availability of a substitute product which would meet the same need and not be as unsafe.

(4) The manufacturer's ability to eliminate the unsafe character of the product without impairing its usefulness or making it too expensive to maintain its utility.

(5) The user's ability to avoid danger by the exercise of care in the use of the product.

(6) The user's anticipated awareness of the dangers inherent in the product and

14. *See, e.g., Larsen v. General Motors Corp.*, 391 F.2d 495 (8th Cir. 1968).

15. *See, e.g., Fields v. Volkswagen of America, Inc.*, 555 P.2d 48 (Okla. 1976).

their avoidability, because of general public knowledge of the obvious condition of the product, or of the existence of suitable warnings or instructions.

(7) The feasibility, on the part of the manufacturer, of spreading the loss by setting the price of the product or carrying liability insurance.[16]

Several points should immediately be obvious about the type of inquiry contemplated by Wade's account of a defect. First, it demands that we ask the very type of "how much" questions whose answers proved so elusive under the analogous tests of the traditional negligence law. Second, it demands that safety be viewed as a question of kind, even though it is in most contexts surely a matter of degree. Third, and in consequence of the first two, small differences in opinion about the value of any given variable are apt to "tip" the inquiry about product defect sharply to one side or the other.[17] Lastly, the standard itself is so open-ended that it must be very costly to administer and uncertain to apply in the course of any common law trial.

The formula then may foster a vast and unprincipled extension of products liability law. Yet of itself it need not plunge the entire system into chaos and confusion. So much depends upon the mode of its application. One simple comparison is with professional basketball. If the referee calls a "tight" game, all the players will foul out by the end of the first quarter. If he calls a somewhat looser one, order can be maintained on the court while the game progresses. Nothing in the formal rules indicates which type of game will be called. The basic rules of basketball, like the basic rules of products liability, do not eliminate all degrees of freedom for the actors within the system. In the same way, the formula Wade proposes may be consistently applied without any threat to institutional stability. A judge can remind the jury that reasonable safety, not absolute safety, is all that is required; that the manufacturer is not the insurer of product safety; that the trade-offs involved require the jury to take into account the full costs of product improvements and loss of productivity; that the untested suggestion of an improved design does not brand as defective the design in fact chosen; and that the plaintiff bears a heavy burden of proof in these extended design defect cases. These matters of degree can be strengthened in one way that no one can fail to understand. An appellate court can overturn jury verdicts in favor of the plaintiff on the grounds that they are not supported by the substantial evidence.

A good object lesson is found in the Arizona case of *Rogers v. Unimac*

16. Wade, *On the Nature of Strict Tort Liability for Products*, 44 Miss. L. J. 825, 837-38 (1973). A position similar to that proposed by Wade has recently been made in the Model Uniform Product Liability Act §104 (1979).

17. *See* the discussion of negligence tests in ch. 3, at 28-29.

*Co., Inc.*[18] The defendant had manufactured a washer-extractor unit that was used by plaintiff's employer to dry towels for the employer's car-wash business. The basic unit was originally equipped with a set of mechanical brake shoes capable of stopping the unit within ten seconds and activated by an electric micro-switch whenever the top of the basket (in which the drying towels were placed) was opened. An additional preset timing device turned the unit off at a specified moment, and allowed the basket to coast to a halt over a five-minute interval. The unit had been first installed some five and one-half years before the plaintiff's injuries. During the time of its operation it was allowed to fall into a state of complete and obvious disrepair, as the plaintiff's employer had refused to authorize any expenditures whatsoever for factory maintenance or repair. On the day of the plaintiff's injury, the mechanical brake shoes had repeatedly fallen off. The plaintiff's arm, wrist and hand were fractured when, following his employer's instructions, the plaintiff tried to stop the moving basket by pressing a towel down against the hub of the unit.

The plaintiff argued that the original unit was defective in design, in that it was not outfitted with an automatic lid-lock that would have kept the top fastened whenever the basket was still in motion. His expert witness noted that such lid-locks were called for by the guidelines for the laundry industry prepared by the American National Standards Institute but conceded on cross-examination that he had not compared the design of defendant's washer-extractor with those of its competitors, and that he had not assessed the impact of the proposed lid-lock standard upon the industry since it was first published in 1961. The defendant's assistant vice-president testified that his company had considered but rejected the institute's proposed standards because its own braking unit was "superior to anything we could find" with respect to safety, reliability, and braking capacity.

After taking all this evidence, the trial court entered a directed verdict for the defendant, which was sustained by the Arizona Supreme Court. In an earlier decision, *Byrns v. Riddell, Inc.*[19] that court had adopted in essence Wade's proposed tests of "unreasonably dangerous" design. Aggressively applied, those tests should have allowed the plaintiff to reach the jury on the question of whether a second safety device was cost-justified, as the

18. 115 Ariz. 304, 565 P.2d 181 (1977). This case also illustrates the application of the common-practice standard, as the defendant's safety devices were different from but superior to those standardly employed. In this case the "compensating" safety device surely makes up for the want of the traditional precaution. Indeed were this not the case, there would be no way in which customary standards could advance without innovators being taxed for the very benefits that they introduce.

19. 113 Ariz. 264, 550 P.2d 1065 (1976), where the court reversed a directed verdict for the defendant and allowed the plaintiff, who was injured in a football pileup, to pursue his design defect theory against the manufacturer of his football helmet. On remand the jury verdict was for the defendant.

neglect of repairs and circumvention of the built-in safety devices were, of course, foreseeable. The court, in a commendable display of good sense, abandoned its own abstract formula in favor of more specific tests. "That the Unimac Company could have adopted a different type of safety device, i.e., a lid lock, is not in itself sufficient evidence to establish defective design."[20] "The most the evidence presented by the plaintiff showed was improper maintenance and repair of the machine and not defective design. The safety features of the Unimac 202 were a reasonable preventative of injury so long as the machine was properly maintained. The manufacturer is not liable for lack of normal maintenance."[21] The first quotation shows that a court need not treat the possibility of alternative design as raising a triable issue on the defect question. The second, with its insistence upon normal and proper maintenance, shows that the suitability of a design cannot be measured by the foreseeable abuses to which it may be subjected. The importance of the "downstream" control (whether by the employer or the plaintiff) is fully recognized, under a set of facts which show that it is but a facile generalization to insist that the best place to control accidents is always in the original product design. The open-ended design defect test is thus hemmed in by a narrow set of supplementary rules that closes off in a clear and unambiguous way one possible avenue to unlimited design defect liability.

There is, of course, no guarantee that the design defect formula will always be applied in such a circumspect manner. The California Supreme Court in its decision in *Barker v. Lull Engineering Co.*[22] has shown how easy it is to move precipitously to the other extreme. The plaintiff was injured when struck by a falling piece of lumber as he attempted to jump from a High Lift Loader manufactured by the defendant Lull. The loader was a piece of heavy construction equipment that weighed about ten thousand pounds; it was designed to lift loads of up to five thousand pounds up to a height of thirty-two feet. The loader was equipped with levelers that allowed it to work on sloping terrain and a manual lock designed to prevent load slippage during the operation. The plaintiff, a substitute driver, had received only limited instruction in the operation of the loader and was at the time of injury using the lift on rugged terrain for which it was not designed. The regular operator of the loader had not reported for work on the day of the accident because he believed that a full-sized crane was necessary for the planned work. The evidence left it unclear whether the load fell because it exceeded the capacity of the equipment or because the plaintiff, having been panicked by a sudden shift in the load, let go the controls.

The plaintiff argued that, among other things, the loader was flawed by

20. 115 Ariz. 304, 307, 565 P.2d 181, 184 (1977).
21. Id. at 307, 565 P.2d at 184.
22. 20 Cal. 3d 413, 573 P.2d 443, 143 Cal. Rptr. 225 (1978).

four separate design defects. First, it was not equipped with a seatbelt. Second, it was not equipped with roll bars. Third, it was not equipped with "outriggers" to stabilize the basic unit under heavy loads. Fourth, it did not have a "park" position on its transmission. The defendant responded that the seatbelts could be a positive danger because they could chain the driver to the vehicle in the event of danger; that the roll bars were not necessary because the machine, owing to its broad base, could not tip over; that the outriggers were not necessary because the machine was stable when used on the proper terrain; and that no rival machine had the proposed outriggers or the "park" position.

The trial judge instructed the jury that the product could be found defective only if "unreasonably dangerous for its intended use," and that "in turn the unreasonableness of the danger must necessarily be derived from the state of the art at the time of the design."[23] The jury returned a verdict ten to two for the defendant. The California Supreme Court remanded for a new trial on two separate grounds. The "unreasonably dangerous" condition language introduced a false element of negligence into an area dominated by strict liability principles. And the "consumer expectations" test of *Greenman* properly functioned in its view as a floor but not a ceiling upon liability.[24] Under the proper rule of law, therefore, the court held that the jury was free to find a product defective whenever it decided the dangers of the challenged design exceeded its expected benefits. In the light of "hindsight," "a jury may consider," among other relevant factors, "the gravity of the danger posed by the challenged design, the likelihood that such a danger would occur, the mechanical feasibility of a safer alternative design, the financial cost of an improved design, and the adverse consequences to the product and to the consumer that would result from an alternative design."[25] As an added fillip, the court shifted to the defendant the burden of showing a cost justification for any challenged design *feature.*

The decision in *Barker v. Lull*, like the Wade formula on which it relies, may be criticized on several grounds. For one, the formula takes too lightly the consumer expectations test articulated in *Greenman v. Yuba Power*, dismissing it with the observation that "the expectations of the ordinary consumer cannot be viewed as the exclusive yardstick for evaluating design defectiveness because '[i]n many situations . . . the consumer would not know what to expect, because he would have no idea how safe the product

23. Id. at 422, n. 4, 573 P.2d at 449, n. 4, 143 Cal. Rptr. at 231, n.4.

24. The "consumer expectations" label for the *Greenman* position is, in fact, somewhat misleading, because it suggests that the test of the defect is solely what the user or consumer perceives and not what the manufacturer represents. The point of the difference could be material where the consumer is misled by his own misinformation or by the bad advice of some third party. In any event *Barker* is most instructive, as the California Supreme Court has in fact repudiated *Greenman*, by going beyond it.

25. 20 Cal. 3d 413, 430-31, 573 P.2d 443, 454-55, 143 Cal. Rptr. 225, 236-37.

could be made.' "[26] But the criticism does not explain why any given manufacturer should be expected to explain how safe the product *could* have been made. Instead, the real question seems to be, did the product conform to the performance standards under which it was sold, such that the comparison of the alternatives can be made by the consumer in the marketplace instead of by the jury in the courtroom? The expectations formula, sensibly understood, worked well in the traditional negligence cases that preceded *Greenman* and in the strict liability cases decided after it. It allows, indeed mandates, recovery in many cases, even if it absolutely bars the plaintiff in *Barker v. Lull.* While the formula has a certain indefiniteness at the margin, and is always subject to abuse by courts hostile to its negative implications,[27] it can, if fairly applied, yield an acceptable degree of predictability over the broad range of cases to which it must necessarily be applied. There seems no reason to reject it in favor of a formula which places no effective limits upon the power of courts or juries to second guess at their leisure the decisions of those who have made, marketed, purchased, and used the very products that are now subject to legal scrutiny.

What makes *Barker v. Lull* even more troublesome is that it goes beyond the Wade formula in two particular respects. First, the repeated emphasis upon "hindsight" instead of "foresight" further turns the screw against product manufacturers.[28] Second, the rejection of the "unreasonably dangerous" language provides in emphasis and tone a litigating edge for the plaintiff. The unprecedented (not to mention unjustified) shift of burden of proof from plaintiff to defendant complicates matters still further, because it may—though only time will tell—make it quite impossible for the defendant ever to obtain a directed verdict in a design defect case. A simple kitchen knife is presumptively defective, once the plaintiff can suggest that it be equipped with some untried safety guard, while complicated machinery of the sort involved in *Barker* can be subjected to endless hypothetical improvements. The *Barker* decision makes virtually any product-related injury the proper subject for a lawsuit, in a stunning reversal of the historical presumption that tort recovery is the exception rather than the rule.

26. Id. at 430, 573 P. 2d at 454, 143 Cal. Rptr. at 236.

27. *See, e.g., Turner v. General Motors Corp.*, 584 S.W. 2d 844 (Tex. 1979) where it was held that the plaintiff, whose car had rolled over after a major collision, could recover under a crashworthiness theory where the design defect was defined in terms of the "reasonable expectations" test. In such cases as this the test itself is no doubt best understood as requiring conformity to the rules of statute or common practice. It should not be construed to allow the court or jury to impose after the fact a set of expectations that is high enough to allow the plaintiff recovery no matter what the facts of any particular case. Note, too, that the possibility of such an extensive definition of product defect is much reduced if the "reasonable expectations" test is explicitly tied to expectations induced by the express or implied representations of performance standards. *See*, note 24 above.

28. 20 Cal. 3d 413, 430, 573 P.2d 443, 454, 143 Cal. Rptr. 225, 236, *quoting* Wade, *On the Nature of Strict Tort Liability for Products*, 44 Miss. L. J. 825, 829.

The chief objection to *Barker* lies, however, in its uncritical use of cost-benefit formulas for determining product defect. The problems with these formulas have already been illustrated in connection with the Hand formula so frequently used in negligence cases. The relevant difficulties do not change one whit simply because the cost-benefit inquiry is now directed toward the product defect question. All "tipping point" problems of the negligence law infect the broader definition of product defect. Yet far from being discussed, they are buried in a laundry list of assertedly relevant factors that are difficult to measure even under the best of circumstances. Nowhere does the *Barker* court recognize that rigorous application of its rule requires precise quantification of all relevant variables. The value, for example, associated with personal injury or loss of human life is subject to enormous dispute. Let the juries use previous torts awards (inflated perhaps for contingent fees and the hazards of litigation) to estimate the value of a life, and an endless set of precautions may seem cost-effective. But lower values for life or limb may be accepted by the worker himself or by various governmental agencies.[29] If so, products with fewer safety features are safe enough. Yet *Barker* gives no guidance on the proper choice of value for human life. Can a matter of recurrent importance in all personal injury cases be left to a jury which may not even be aware of its existence?

The potential scope of the *Barker* decision can well be seen in a case that rejects its extreme implications. In *Wilson v. Piper Aircraft Corporation*,[30] the plaintiff claimed that the light aircraft flown by the decedent was defective because it was equipped with an ordinary carburetion system instead of a more expensive fuel injection system. The defendant introduced undisputed evidence to show that between 80 and 90 percent of comparable aircraft were equipped with ordinary carburetion; yet the plaintiff contended that the crash might not have occurred because the fuel injection system would not have "iced" over. Given the conflicting evidence, the trial court entered a judgment for the plaintiff upon the jury verdict. The Supreme Court reversed and remanded for a new trial, making it clear that even though Federal Aviation Administration (F.A.A.) certification was not an absolute defense against allegations of defective design, it counted heavily in the case because the F.A.A. had addressed the icing problem and had decided that the use of such carburetion was not unduly dangerous. In the court's opinion the plaintiff's expert testimony was incomplete because it did not indicate the "effect the substitution of a fuel injection engine in this airplaine design would have had upon the airplane's cost, economy of operation, maintenance requirements, over-all performance, or safety in respects other than susceptibility to icing."[31]

29. The National Traffic and Highway Safety Commission uses a value of about $300,000 in determining its view of safety precautions.

30. 282 Or. 61, 577 P.2d 1322 (1978), *rehearing* 282 Or. 411, 579 P.2d 1287 (1978).

31. Id. at 70, 577 P.2d 1322 at 1327.

The plaintiff's request for rehearing was granted in light of *Barker v. Lull*, but the court, in a short opinion that stressed the differences between California and Oregon law, announced that it did not find *Barker* "persuasive."[32] The decision in *Wilson* represents a welcome and conscious departure from the extremes to which the California Supreme Court has taken the law. One can only speculate how *Wilson* would have been decided with the burden of proof squarely on the defendant. Nonetheless, *Wilson* is troublesome in at least these respects: it gives no principled reason why the F.A.A. standards should not be treated as conclusive; it sets no standards to indicate the way in which the *Wilson* case should be decided upon remand if the plaintiff presents a more comprehensive case; and it gives no guarantee of uniform results when the same fact question is raised in a similar case. *Wilson* is correct insofar as it says that cases like *Barker* take the design defect liability too far, but it gives us no proper guidance on the question, "How far is too far?"

The central problem in this area, whether it be with the unrestrained approach of *Barker* or the more guarded approach of *Wilson*, is that there is simply no sensible way to make the necessary judicial calculations of cost and benefit (not to mention the other factors that Wade mentions) that are thought determinative of the design defect question.

As James Henderson has forcefully and correctly argued,[33] the aggressive application of modern design defect standards places upon the trier of fact the impossible burden of making a whole set of complex *trade-offs*, because it is constantly asked, when all is said and done, whether some additional benefit is worth the additional cost it entails. The question can take many forms. In some instances, it is "simply" a matter of price; in others, it is a question of convenience; in still others, it is a question of trading one safety device for another. Yet no matter what form these trade-offs take, it seems fair to say that no judge or jury can make the multiple, delicate, *marginal* determinations appropriate to each and every product in each and every circumstance. The plaintiff in *Barker* proposed that roll bars be added to the equipment; must the jury make a detailed analysis of the structural changes in the basic unit that are required to support the additional weight of each of the possible roll-bar assemblies that might be added? Should it examine what changes must be made in the power plant in order to handle the increased weight of the vehicles? And should it inquire whether the gas tank must be relocated or redesigned because of the proposed changes? The plaintiff suggested that outriggers be added; do these influence the desirability of the roll bars? Do they create alternative hazards by increasing the size of the basic unit? Do they limit its usefulness on some

32. 282 Or. 411, 579 P.2d 1287 (1978).

33. Henderson, *Judicial Review of Manufacturers' Conscious Design Choices: The Limits of Adjudication*, 73 Colum. L. Rev. 1531 (1973).

work sites, if not upon all? To redesign the part, we must redesign the whole.[34]

The problems presented in *Barker* reappear everywhere. We can demand that automobiles be made strong and sturdy to protect their occupants in the event of crash; yet we thereby increase their cost, reduce their fuel efficiency, and increase the likelihood of serious injury to pedestrians or other motorists in the event of a collision. How much of each hazard is desirable? We can movc the gasoline tank farther from the exterior of the car to reduce the probability that it will explode in a collision, but we thereby increase the probability that any fire that does occur will invade the passenger compartment. Which is riskier? We can demand that football players wear heavy helmets to protect themselves in a pileup, but we thereby aggravate the damage to others butted by the heavier helmets. Which hazard is more ominous? If these questions go to the jury, a thousand necessary design choices can be the seeds of a thousand design defects.

We have mentioned, thus far, some obvious features of trade-offs. To understand better the full dimensions of the problem, consider in detail one "simple" product, the ladder. The ladder is chosen not only because it is the subject of innumerable products liability actions but because its design features have been intensely studied by the Federal Consumer Product Safety Commission, charged under federal law with developing standards for "safe" consumer products.[35] What is interesting is that the work of the Commission gives a good idea of the range of considerations that must be taken into account by all those including judges and juries, who conscientiously wish to set public standards of safe design.

There are first the unavoidable trade-offs of design features. How far apart should the rungs of the ladder be situated? One distance may be ideal for short people, another for tall ones. Is it possible to make a ladder that is equally suitable for all persons, under all the possible circumstances under which it will be used? Then, too, there are the common hazards associated with ladder use. One danger is that a ladder will collapse. Yet if it is made sturdy and rigid, the collapse may be avoided, but only at the cost of a treacherous slide.

The problem of trade-off, difficult enough where these design choices are involved, becomes far more complex after the relationship between price and consumer safety is explored. It is a truism that additional safety features often cost additional money; the question is which of these possible expenditures will be worthwhile. Safety features that are voluntarily incorporated are likely to be cost justified: most consumers pay for these precautions because they, with commendable fondness for their own skins,

34. For a judicial recognition of the basic problem, *see Garst v. General Motors Corp.*, 207 Kan. 2, 484 P.2d 47 (1971).

35. *See* the report on these deliberations in the Wall Street Journal, August 11, 1977, at 1, in an article entitled, "Setting Safety Rules For Products Proves Costly and Complicated."

want the safer product. The impact of safety standards imposed by direct regulation or by judicial fiat is much more problematic. Consumers have evidenced no willingness to pay for the additional safety features. For them the additional costs are for a product that is no better (and may be worse) than the product available in the unregulated market. This increase in product safety beyond what market preferences dictate may have the paradoxical effect of *reducing* overall consumer safety levels, even if it does insulate manufacturers from design defect suits. With ladders—and all other products—the dilemma is always this: if the regulation increases the cost of the ladder by mandating changes in design (or, we may add, warnings), it will thereby increase the ladder's price. With price increases come some decreases in sales, as some consumers will forego the superior ladder because they do not want to pay for its additional safety features. What, then, will happen with those people who decide not to purchase the safer ladders? They might avoid altogether those tasks for which ladders are used, thus increasing safety but at the cost of some consumer satisfaction. More disturbingly, they may choose more hazardous courses of conduct. Some consumers might use rickety old ladders; still others might decide to climb on hastily assembled piles of tables and chairs, a notorious source of danger.

The common assumption on safety is that the relevant choice is between the relatively unsafe products that are put out today and the safe products that can be "feasibly" manufactured under the new regulatory standards. In many cases, the choice will be much harder: it will be between the "risky" product that is now manufactured, and the *riskier*, if unidentified, substitute to which the potential user will turn when public regulation increases the price of a desired product. There are always knotty empirical questions about what types of substitution are induced by any given restriction upon consumer choice. Yet it may well be, with ladders and with other products, that many restrictions will increase the number of accidents. Fewer of the relatively safe products will reach the marketplace; the injuries caused by misused products still hurt even if no manufacturer can be held accountable for them.

The paradoxical effects of safety regulation also involve the safer products that have reached the ultimate consumer. The question then arises, what will be the influence, if any, that the safer ladder will have on consumer conduct? It is unlikely that the patterns of product use will remain unchanged; given the changes in relevant costs and benefits, the uses made of the ladders should vary until each consumer properly balances his own taste for utility and risk. If, for instance, the safer ladder is heavier than the traditional one, it may be used less often; some consumers will find it more difficult to move a ladder from place to place or to set it up in its proper position. Again the user may, at his own expense, alter or modify the design of the safe product in order to make it better suit his own purposes, thereby creating a product more dangerous than any that the manufacturer could have devised. It may well be (although the point is not as clear as could be hoped, given the reach of the "foreseeable misuse" doctrine) that the defendant will escape liability because the product was not defective in its original condition.[36] Yet if the goal is, as Justice Traynor reminds us, to minimize accidents and not to minimize manufacturer's liability for accidents, then the aggressive design standards have performed a great disservice.

The complications that stand in the way of adequate public standards of product safety are formidable indeed, and it is tempting to argue that the entire administrative apparatus should be discarded in favor of market solutions. The point may well be too extreme; and for these purposes it does not matter. The institutional integrity of the products liability law does not require repeal of all public safety regulation. If the government imposes unwise safety rules, whether by statute or regulation, their "only" adverse consequences will be on matters of resource allocation in general and accident levels in particular. Products liability exposure will still be kept within manageable levels, as manufacturers will be able to design products that conform to the regulatory standards whose adoption they may have opposed, perhaps with arguments of the sort made here. For liability issues, the crucial point, therefore, is one of institutional competence. Making the appropriate design choices is difficult enough in the administrative context; the task surely exceeds the capabilities of any judicial forum that must develop these standards in an uncertain and ad hoc matter. What chance is there of success when the task is undertaken in a bitter trial dominated by a host of other issues—such as causation, damages, and plaintiff's conduct—crucial to the outcome of the case but extraneous to the matter of safe design? It might be possible to identify the factors that are relevant to design choices, but it is impossible to combine them in any orderly fashion into a single formula that yields a simple conclusion of "safe" or "defective." The Model Uniform Product Liability Act, responsive to the current vogue, insists that the consumer is in all events entitled to a "reasonably safe" product, but its benign recommendation cannot be made operational.[37] The feature-

36. *But see Capasso v. Minster Machine Co.*, 532 F.2d 952 (3rd Cir. 1976), where a directed verdict for the defendant was reversed and the case remanded for new trial, when the plaintiff's employer had disconnected the hand presses originally provided by the defendant and connected the alternative foot treadle. The argument was that the machine was arguably defective because no suitable guard had been designed for the foot treadle (although a makeshift guard had been provided by the plaintiff's employer). Yet if no opportunity for the conversion of the machine had been provided, it may still have been converted, at even greater risk to its operator. *Capasso* is another instance where a combination of the product alteration and assumption of risk doctrines should mandate the directed verdict for the defendant.

37. *See* the introduction to the Model Act, 44 Federal Register p. 212, 62714-15. The reference to "reasonably safe products" also appears in the body of the statute, Section 103, where the importance of the goal is treated as an aid for the interpretation of doubtful cases that come under the statute.

less generality of those words does not have any bite in concrete situations, and they are rendered trivial by the vast discretion typically given to juries in design cases. Wade's broad-gauged formula and those of *Barker v. Lull* are incapable of rigorous and accurate application, while always holding out the prospect of much abuse.

But, it might be objected, it is a mistake to home in on the issue of judicial competence, for the very calculations demanded in design defect cases have been made for generations in ordinary negligence actions. In one sense there is truth in the criticism (and weakness in the negligence standard); but in practice there is a vital difference between the two situations. In the older negligence cases the plaintiff had to cross a clear, separate *causal* threshold before the alluring calculus of costs and benefits could be raised in a given case. The cost-benefit tests thus *limited* the scope of causal principles and thus of liability. The modern defect cases have, almost by inadvertence, removed that causal threshold. Now the controlling question is not what the defendant *did* to invade the person or property of the plaintiff but instead what the defendant *might have done* to protect the plaintiff against his own misdeeds or the misconduct of third parties.

The significance of this distinction runs through the length and breadth of the tort law. In highway cases there is no need even to consider the question of negligence until it is shown that the defendant struck the plaintiff, cut him off in traffic, or forced him off the road. In the stock cases of ice cream, the defendant can avoid the question of costs and benefits simply by keeping the glass out of the ice cream. In these contexts, it is quite proper to fictionalize the cost-benefit issue by the use of res ipsa loquitur. The safe harbor created by the older causal tests and the narrow definition of defect provided the defendant with all the protection needed. Yet today, if the defendant in a case like *Barker* wants to comply with the law, he has no possible way of knowing in advance whether he has properly weighed the imponderables of a cost-benefit analysis. What is needed today is some standard, be it wise or foolish, so that firms can know the rules of the game at the time of manufacture, and juries can know them at the time of trial.

The real question is why so many courts have in the last ten years rushed to embrace a form of liability that raises these manifold difficulties.[38] The problem is even more puzzling because most courts have some sense of the nature, if not the magnitude, of the problems that lurk beneath the polished exterior of the basic design defect formula: more than one court has noted that a "lawsuit is a poor way to design"[39] a complicated product. In the

38. *See, e.g., Huff v. White Motor Corp.* 565 F.2d 104 (7th Cir. 1977), where the Seventh Circuit repudiated its earlier decision in *Evans v. General Motors Corp.*, 359 F.2d 822 (7th Cir. 1966) which had once expressed the dominant view on the crashworthiness doctrine. A full compilation of the recent cases is found in the appendix to *Huff*, 565 F.2d at 110.

39. *See, e.g., Self v. General Motors Corp.*, 42 Cal. App. 3d 1, 7, 116 Cal. Rptr. 575, 579 (1974).

end, however, there are two clues that help to account for the adoption of the modern course. First, courts influenced by the false analogies between design defect and ordinary negligence cases have assumed that they were doing nothing novel when they applied "general tort principles" to design defect cases. Second, courts seem to sense that without judicial regulation of some sort, manufacturers will "not keep on their toes" and will "sit back" when it comes to matters of product safety. The point is not always made so colloquially, and its antecedents run back to the forceful language in *The T. J. Hooper*, recited with telling effect in many liability decisions:

> [I]n most cases reasonable prudence is in fact common prudence; but strictly it is never its measure; a whole calling may have unduly lagged in the adoption of new and available devices. It never may set its own tests, however persuasive be its usages. Courts must in the end say what is required; there are precautions so imperative that even their universal disregard will not excuse their omission.[40]

The central assumption of Hand's position, as applied to design defect cases, is that in the absence of judicial intervention firms will have incentives not to do their best on matters of safety. It is a truism, however, that much had been done to improve safety levels even before the recent expansion in products liability and before the onset of massive administrative safety regulation. The "lags" in safety can be shown only if, holding technology constant, there is some residual improvement in safety levels during the last decade or so attributable to judicial innovation. The position has by no means been established, and it is in large measure doubtful, given the counter-productive effects of direct regulation.

The modern faith in regulation should not, moreover, be allowed to obscure the strong impact of market incentives. Each firm when acting in its own self-interest will improve safety levels even in the absence of exposure to products liability suits. Machines that break down in ordinary use are responsible for losses in production, and they require expensive repairs. They reflect ill on the reputation of the parties that make and service them. The injuries attributable to these machines will hurt just as much, if not more, when no compensation is available from the manufacturer. Employers who face increases in workers' compensation insurance can be expected to shift to safer machines to the extent the additional costs of better equipment will reduce their insurance premiums; employees who suffer uncompensated or undercompensated injuries from these machines can be expected to shift employment if not given wage increases to offset the additional risks to which they are subject. Complacent firms run the risk of displacement and bankruptcy at the hands of competitors who provide better and safer products to their customers. The marketplace may not provide perfect information,

40. 60 F.2d 737, 740 (2d Cir. 1932).

and it may not have the capacity for instantaneous and perfect adjustment on safety matters. Yet, it would be a grave mistake to assume that individual parties whose profits and well-being are on the line will routinely allow manufacturers to "dictate" or "compel" the purchase of inferior equipment. Indeed, it is the commonest of occurrences for industrial equipment to be manufactured in accordance with purchaser specifications; and it is equally common for consumer goods to be sold with a full complement of optional safety features, such that the purchaser, with full knowledge of his own situation, can obtain for himself the best mix of safety, price, and convenience. Individual parties, firms, and unions all have sufficient competence that it is unlikely that they will patiently tolerate institutional arrangements that do not minimize the various costs associated with product-related accidents. And when legislative controls have—possibly—filled whatever gap is left by market institutions, it becomes doubtful in the extreme that any judicial process at reasonable cost can both identify and correct the *residual* imperfections in the substantive liability rules. Safety is indeed important, but there is little that aggressive judicial design standards can add to it.

*Strict Liability or Negligence*

The next order of business, after the design defect issue has been confronted, is to determine whether the basic cause of action is governed by negligence or strict liability principles. One argument in favor of the negligence standard is that it acts as a partial curb against the potential excesses of the modern design defect cases. Yet this prudential approach is subject to several objections. First, it again introduces the unprincipled "how much" questions into design defect cases. Second, it divides design defect cases into two classes, unless of course the strict liability principles of the case *Greenman* are repudiated as well, even with respect to products that fail in ordinary use. Third, it is doubtful that the negligence limitation is an effective limitation in these design defect cases. The earliest crashworthiness case, *Larsen v. General Motors Corp.*,[41] was decided explictly on negligence principles, as the court was unwilling in a diversity case to impose strict liability under Section 402A of the Restatement. And the first of the aggressive design defect cases in California, *Pike v. Frank G. Hough Co.*[42] (where the plaintiff insisted that the defendant's paydozer designed for heavy construction should have been outfitted with ringing bells and oversized mirrors), was also decided explicitly on negligence principles. Both these negligence cases do far more to expand liability than does Section 402A

41. 391 F.2d 495 (8th Cir. 1968).

42. 2 Cal. 3d 465, 467 P.2d 229, 85 Cal. Rptr. 629 (1970). For a more detailed criticism of this case, *see* Epstein, *Products Liability: The Search for the Middle Ground*, 56 N. Car. L. Rev. 643, 649-50 (1978).

of the Restatement. The protections afforded by the negligence rule, then, seem to be of little importance or consequence. The strict liability rule should, therefore, be adopted in these design defect cases, while the problem of judicial excesses should be directly confronted in setting and enforcing the appropriate standards for product defect.

*Causation*

The last set of issues in these design defect cases concerns the problem of causation. Here the most troublesome questions arise only because the defendant, in consequence of the broad defect definition, has a duty to protect the plaintiff against some external force generated by the plaintiff or by the third party. The immediate consequence of this broad duty is to deny the defendant all defenses based upon causal intervention. Since the defendant's product may be treated as defective because it does not protect the plaintiff against his own misconduct or the misconduct of a third party, both types of action complete, rather than break, the causal chain. The need to work these events back into the causal equation in turn makes it necessary to state very complex causal arguments, which at a minimum contain three separate elements. It is necessary to determine, first, the magnitude of the external force against which the defendant must protect the plaintiff; second, whether the force that was in fact applied exceeded the limits within which protection was necessary; and third, the extent to which the plaintiff would have suffered damages even if the defendant's product had in all relevant particulars reached or exceeded the standards of the "reasonably safe product."

The close interconnection of these three issues makes it important to specify with great particularity the performance standards for the defendant's product, however difficult that task may be, given the utter want of meaningful guidance as to what constitutes a product defect. In instructing the jury on the defect question alone, it may be sufficient to ask it to decide whether or not the product was unreasonably dangerous. But in evaluating the plaintiff's damages attributable to the defendant's conduct, it is absolutely necessary, to revert to *Barker v. Lull*, to know *just* how wide and heavy an outrigger is required, *just* how heavy a load was lifted by the plaintiff, and *just* what grade the defendant's lift should be able to negotiate.

The same degree of causal precision is required as well in the crashworthiness cases, where an accurate sense of the true state of affairs is found in *Self v. General Motors Corp.*[43] There the plaintiff sustained severe burn injuries when the Chevrolet station wagon in which she rode was struck in the left rear by another vehicle going somewhere between sixty-five and eighty-five miles per hour. In her action against General

43. 42 Cal. App. 3d 1, 116 Cal. Rptr. 575 (1974).

Motors she alleged that a safe positioning of the gas tank would have made it possible for her to escape her burn injuries, and she introduced expert testimony to the effect that if the tank had been located in the floor beneath the seats, "it would have been well protected by the structure of the automobile."[44] The court thought this testimony was sufficient to take the case to the jury, but it nonetheless vacated the plaintiff's judgment and remanded for a new trial because the trial judge refused to give the jury the following instruction on the question of "superseding" causation: "If you find that the gasoline tank in the 1962 Chevrolet station wagon was improperly located, but that the fire would have occurred even if the tank had been properly located, its location was not a substantial factor in bringing about the fire and was, therefore, not a contributing cause therefore."[45] The instruction was, as the Court of Appeals noted, correct. In order to decide the full complement of causal questions, it is necessary to know the exact speed at which the vehicle was struck, the exact point of impact, the exact way or ways in which the gasoline tank should have been positioned, and that portion of damages that could have been avoided if the proper location had been chosen in the first instance. It simply will not do for a court to allow a jury to hold for the plaintiff on the ground that the "[negligent] defect in question was a proximate cause of the plaintiff's harm."[46] This simplified form of instruction conceals the separate components of the basic design defect cause of action, and falsely treats the most complicated design defect as indistinguishable from the ordinary intersection collision.

If the old privity limitation was far too restrictive of recovery, the modern design defect cases are far too generous. There is no evidence whatsoever that they serve an intelligent function to keep manufacturers "on their toes," given the other constraints which already bind them. Design defect cases today are the source of great expense, mischief, and uncertainty. Some retreat from the extremes of possible liability is surely needed. The court in *Self* was, for example, aware of the pitfalls in design defect litigation, and said: "It also seems probable that legislatures and courts will develop techniques for summary disposition of extravagant claims of defective design so that the good in product protection against injuries resulting from abuse and misuse is not drowned in a sea of unmeritorious demands for payment of the wages of recklessness and folly."[47] Those words were written in 1974. As of 1980, relief has not been provided.

44. Id. at 9, 116 Cal. Rptr. at 580.

45. Id. at 10, 116 Cal. Rptr. at 581.

46. The Florida Courts have held this simple form of instruction sufficient. *See In re Standard Jury Instructions*, 198 So.2d. 319 (Fla. 1967).

47. 42 Cal. App. 3d 1, 8, 116 Cal. Rptr. 575, 579-80 (1974).

CHAPTER

# 8

# THE DUTY TO WARN

This chapter is devoted to the third class of modern products liability actions: those in which the plaintiff's case is predicated upon the defendant's failure to warn the product user (who may, but need not, be the plaintiff) of any product hazards or dangers. In addition to the theoretical issues it raises, this cause of action is of exceptional importance today because of its sheer versatility. It is always possible in principle to argue that any mishap could have been prevented in advance, cheaply and effectively, by some warning or instruction that the defendant might have given but did not give. Indeed, the very versatility that lends vitality to this cause of action is also the source of its potential dangers. Therefore, unless the theoretical boundaries are set out with some clarity, a ritualistic insistence upon product warnings can reverse the time-honored presumption that losses should lie where they fall. No injury will be self-inflicted, because all injuries could have been prevented by some warning. Before examining specific issues in depth, it is useful to identify the proper theoretical approach to duty to warn cases.

## THEORY

The nature and function of product warnings and instructions can be best understood by first returning to the account of product defect dispositive in both construction and design cases. In both these situations the essence of the plaintiff's cause of action, properly understood, is that the defendant's product departed in some material particular from the construction or performance standard under which it was, expressly or impliedly, manufactured and marketed. In both situations the gist of the plaintiff's case is estoppel by misrepresentation, and in both situations it is necessary in principle that the product user relied upon the belief that the product would be in one condition, when in fact it was in quite another. Where the plaintiff is a bystander, the argument is that the actions of all intermediate parties are imputed to the product manufacturer who misrepresented to those third parties the nature and quality of his product. Where the plaintiff is the product user, and his own conduct is the immediate cause of his own harm, he is allowed to impute his own actions to the defendant, who must then answer in damages, even in the absence of privity. As between the person who makes a representation of product fitness and the person who relies upon it, the loss should be, prima facie, placed on the former.

The same theory is capable of obvious extension to duty to warn cases. Again, the initial presumption is that a party who takes possession of a given product and uses it in a manner that immediately causes harm to himself or to a third party is, as against its maker or seller, responsible for the consequences of his own actions. Again it is necessary to find something in the totality of the defendant's representations that will allow the product user to shift the loss farther back in the chain of distribution. The lack of a warning, which creates the false impression of product safety, provides the necessary lever. In this context, the traditional distinction between active misrepresentation and simple nondisclosure is by no means dispositive. Even if the defendant has said nothing about his product, the product itself makes, by its very appearance, certain implied representations about both its use and its limitations. The question is always whether the initial false impressions created by the product are neutralized either by further disclosures or by other features of the product design. Where the design change is possible or effective, there may well be no need for a warning because the manufacturer has taken upon himself the discharge of all necessary precautions. Where the design change is not effective, the question then is whether the manufacturer has supplied the consumer or user with sufficient knowledge of the product to take specific precautions on his own behalf. These warnings—and the mode of their communciation—are of special importance when redesign is out of the question because the product desired—say pure sulfuric acid—is such that its beneficial properties are precisely those that make it dangerous. But these warnings may be of little assistance where the basic presentation of the product itself tends to override whatever message the separate written warnings might otherwise convey. The defendant who makes a chair with a back cannot be heard to say that he marketed the chair with a warning (whether by package insert or attached label) that the back was only for decoration and not for support: only a person who knew and was conscious of the very risk at the time he sat down would be barred from recovery. Because of the conflicting messages and impressions that can be created, the entire issue of when warnings are insufficient and design changes are required must remain one of the most vexed issues in the law of products liability. We can only identify the ultimate question, which is, given the intrinsic nature of the product, what can and should be done to alert the user to take steps to reduce the implicit hazards associated with its use.

Within this basic framework there are two possible approaches to the issue of product warnings. The first is to assume that all relevant information about the product should originate with the parties who first prepared or sold it. In effect this argument assumes that any information about the product should be tied to the product itself, instead of being generated elsewhere in the chain of distribution and use. The alternative, and preferred, assumption is that the need for and the appropriateness of warnings rest on a showing that the producer of a product is better able than other parties in the chain of distribution to generate the needed information. The first position is credible only where parties farther down the chain of distribution cannot make any sensible contributions to product safety at an acceptable cost. The second position rightly cautions against any automatic presumption that a warning is required, or that if required, it must take on encyclopedic proportions. Some circumstances require detailed and exhaustive warnings; some require none at all. With so much stated, there is yet a second step to the inquiry. The supervision of product warnings through private actions by injured parties takes both time and money. Before duties to warn are too freely created, it must be asked in every case whether the benefits they create justify the administrative costs that they impose.

The previous arguments have been stated very generally. Their power can, however, be well illustrated by examining the discrete fact patterns in which the questions of warnings arise. All products are not alike, and the operating presumptions applicable for one class of products, be it foodstuffs, drugs, chemicals, or machine tools, may well be ill suited for another. Here in the course of the analysis we shall speak first about drugs and chemicals, then about machine tools and capital equipment, and at last about the entire range of consumer products.

## DRUGS AND CHEMICALS

It is possible to specify some of the situations in which warnings or instructions about drugs and chemicals are clearly required. The first and simplest is, of course, proper labeling. The plaintiff in *Thomas v. Winchester*[1] had an ironclad case precisely because the druggist mislabeled deadly belladonna as harmless dandelion extract. No amount of knowledge about the properties of belladonna could have helped the plaintiff deal with the mislabeled drug. The wrong label on the product cuts off the plaintiff from access to the general pool of common knowledge; it should therefore cast the risk of error upon the defendant even in the absence of negligence or

1. 6 N.Y. 397 (1852), discussed in ch. 2.

privity. The same principles also apply, for example, to expiration dates on such drugs: even expert physicians have limited means of knowing when a particular batch of a given drug was prepared.

Beyond these simple minimums the case for further disclosure, at least as a matter of common law, becomes problematic. Thus, if the drug is sold in an unlabeled container, it can easily be argued that no one should use it precisely because its unknown identity itself warns of the possible dangers. Likewise, with respect to labeled drugs such as the belladonna in *Thomas v. Winchester*, it is surely reasonable to argue that the drug user who knows the nature of the product can then resort to publicly available information to determine its proper use. Indeed, such information may well be superior to that supplied by drug companies because it may come in the form of a specific comparative analysis of different drugs that might be used for the same condition.[2] With such abundant information generated by other sources, it becomes unwise to lay too much stress upon package inserts and other warnings provided by suppliers, especially as there are no obvious boundaries for disclosure once the narrow threshold of mislabeling is crossed. The entire common law development of the area might well come to a quick and easy halt. Statutory controls, such as those imposed by the Food and Drug Act, can take over where the common law leaves off. Thus the use of specific labels or inserts, complete with expiration dates, dosage limitations, and whatever else is necessary, might in so many words be demanded by the Food and Drug Administration. As with design defects, the real question, statutes apart, is whether it makes sense to extend the scope of the duty to warn cause of action at common law beyond the narrow and simple situations in which it seems clearly warranted. Let us look first at chemicals, then at drugs.

## INDUSTRIAL CHEMICALS

The different approaches to the adequacy of warnings are neatly illustrated by two cases, *Jackson v. Coast Paint & Lacquer Co.*[3] and *Martinez v. Dixie Carriers, Inc.*[4] In *Jackson* the defendant sold paint with a warning which first referred to the toxicity of the paint if ingested and then continued:

2. *See, e.g.*, in this connection any issue of The Medical Letter, which publishes detailed analyses of any given drug and information that compares the use of the drug to alternative treatments (including other drugs and no drugs) that might be available. Such sources of information are impeccable in their origin and up-to-date in their content. Where available, they weaken the case for complete (and perhaps even dominant) reliance upon drug inserts as the best means of communicating the relevant information to physicians.

3. 499 F.2d 809 (9th Cir. 1974).

4. 529 F.2d 457 (5th Cir. 1976).

Keep away from heat, sparks, and open flame. USE WITH ADEQUATE VENTILATION. Avoid prolonged contact with skin and breathing of spray mist. Close container after each use. KEEP OUT OF REACH OF CHILDREN.

The plaintiff used the paint inside a closed tank car, while wearing a makeshift tube and mask of his own design which allowed him to breathe air from outside the car. He did so, he testified, because he (and his fellow workers) thought the caution about adequate ventilation referred to the inhalation but not to the fire hazard. The plaintiff's employer knew of the fire hazards involved, even though he had not communicated that knowledge to the plaintiff. The paint fumes triggered an explosion, resulting in serious burns to the plaintiff. The Court of Appeals held that the plaintiff made a case for the jury and reversed the directed verdict entered for the defendant in the lower court.

In *Martinez*, the decedent, an employee of the Wilsco Company, was responsible for cleaning the inside of a barge that had previously carried dripoline, a common toxic industrial compound made and marketed by the codefendant, DuPont Company. The barge shipment was covered with ubstances in commerce. In this environment, statues apart, the manufacturer only where the information in question was directed to technicians and engi- it contained special warnings in a designated compartment that indicated that the product was "MODERATELY TOXIC ON SHORT EXPOSURE TO HIGH CONCENTRATION. SEVERELY TOXIC ON REPEATED EXPOSURES."

Martinez' employer failed to follow normal safety procedures. He did not test the barges for oxygen content and toxicity, either before Martinez began the cleaning up process or intermittently while it was carried on. In the midst of cleaning his fifth tank, Martinez began to experience the harmful effects of the fumes; he collapsed inside the barge in his desperate effort to climb out. He could not be saved partly because the other workmen did not have ready adequate respiratory devices that might have enabled them to enter the tanks. The decedent's employer was well aware of the toxic nature of the cargo, and the decedent, although new to cleaning barges, had for eight years cleaned shore tanks for the same employer. The District Court found that DuPont's warnings in question were not adequate and charged DuPont for part of the loss. The Circuit Court reversed and exonerated DuPont, although it held a second defendant responsible for the loss on an unseaworthiness theory.

These two cases illustrate two divergent approaches to the problem of industrial warnings. Both raise the issue of whether the knowledge of the employer, no matter how derived, should be taken into account in determining the scope of the manufacturer's duty to warn. Both raise the further issue of what warnings are adequate, given that the manufacturer must make some "direct" warning to the employee. On each of these issues the approach in *Martinez* is to be preferred to that in *Jackson*.

In virtually all circumstances it seems proper to conclude that the employer has the *sole* duty to warn his employees about, or otherwise protect employees from, the possible dangerous effects of the chemicals (or other dangerous substances) in question.[5] In addition to his general knowledge of the hazardous nature of the chemicals in question, only the employer can consider the residual concentration of the chemical in the particular locations, the previous exposure levels of employees, the availability of additional safety devices (such as the respirators in *Martinez*), the possible interactions of different chemicals, and the dangers of the chemical when removed from its original container. Well-established industry customs, as in *Martinez*, govern procedures for handling, loading, and cleaning up after dangerous cargoes at the operational level; and direct safety obligations, both under Occupational Safety and Health Act (OSHA) regulations and other specific statutory schemes, govern the movement of dangerous chemicals and other substances in commerce. In this environment, statutes apart, the manufacturer who properly packages and identifies, if only by generic or common name, the goods shipped in commerce may well be regarded as having discharged whatever common law duty he owes to persons farther down in the chain of distribution. He should surely be regarded as having discharged his common law duties if the goods are identified as hazardous, instructions are given about proper handling, and mention is made of the proper first-aid techniques associated with the different forms of contact—ingestion, touching, breathing.

This position has the desirable efficiency consequences of reducing the considerable administrative costs of third-party actions and of preserving the incentive and safety effects created by workers' compensation and other direct statutory schemes. The general arguments about loss control made in the previous discussion of *Escola*[6] and *Greenman*[7] militate against the creation of any direct duty to warn where there is a responsible intermediary, and this position appears to be supported, though with far from perfect clarity, in the comments of the Second Restatement, and, with some greater

5. For a case so holding in an analogous situation, *see Jones v. Hittle Service, Inc.*, 219 Kan. 627, 549 P.2d 1383 (1976), where the court insulated the manufacturer of propane gas from any duty to supply special warnings (beyond odorizing the gas as required by statute) to the ultimate consumers of such gas, when he has adequately informed his distributors about the dangers in the product. The question of the retailer's liability for failure to issue appropriate warnings was left to the jury. Note that this situation reverses the usual position in that the manufacturer here is not in the better position to avoid the risks.

6. 24 Cal. 2d 453, 150 P. 2d 436 (1944).

7. 59 Cal. 2d 57, 377 P. 2d 897, 27 Cal. Rptr. 697 (1963).

confidence, in the recent Model Uniform Products Liability Act.[8] The breach of the employer's duty to warn should fall upon the employer, but it should not create any liability upon a third party. The insistence that a duty falls upon the manufacturer, and that it is "non-delegable" to the employer, places legal pressure on the wrong part of the distribution chain.[9] The court in *Jackson* accepted much of this argument, but assumed that it applied only where the information in question was directed to technicians and engineers. Yet it is by no means clear why foremen and supervisors, if usually charged with safety obligations, should not be treated in the same fashion. As ever, it is "foreseeable" that such persons may disregard their responsibilities out of indifference, incompetence, or neglect. A simple foresight test, however, precludes any sensible division of labor by invariably mandating direct warnings, however costly and inappropriate. The real question is not one of foresight but rather of entitlement, with the understanding being that the original supplier has the *right* to assume others will do their job, at least in the absence of specific knowledge that they will not. It is

8. *See* Restatement (Second) of Torts, §388, comment *n*, where there is a noticeable reluctance to lay down any clear rules of decision. At several places (*see* pp. 309-10), the comment indicates that the exposure to liability will be greater if there is reason to doubt the reliability and trustworthiness of the intermediate party. The converse proposition, that the duty is not imposed where there are strong institutional constraints upon the conduct of intermediates, is not discussed.

The Model Act provides in § 104(C) (5)

> A manufacturer is under an obligation to provide adequate warnings or instructions to the actual product user unless the manufacturer provided such warnings to a person who may be reasonably expected to assure that action is taken to avoid the harm, or that the risk of the harm is explained to the actual product user.
>
> For products that may be legally used only by or under the supervision of a class of experts, warnings or instructions may be provided to the using or supervisory expert.

9. The development of these nondelegable duties, especially in connection with machine tool cases, marks one of the great, if unheralded, revolutions in products liability. Under the traditional doctrines the maker of a machine tool could not be sued if the product was sold with the understanding that the immediate purchaser (or for that matter subsequent purchasers) would customize it for the particular purposes of his own plant. The justification for this procedure was twofold. First, the immediate user of the product had better information about the particular tasks for which it was to be used, and hence could make not only the original safety adjustments but also whatever future adjustments were required by changing plant needs or changing technology. Second, there was in place a scheme of direct statutory regulation that could pick up whatever slack was left by private initiatives. In more recent years, however, it has been held that the manufacturer has a non-delegable duty to make the machine fit for its whole range of intended purposes, raising a jury question in all cases as to whether that duty has been discharged. *See, e.g. Finnegan v. Havir Manufacturing Corp.*, 60 N.J. 413, 290 A.2d 286 (1972); *Balido v. Improved Machinery, Inc.*, 29 Cal. App. 3d 633, 105 Cal. Rptr. 890 (1972). The change seems unwise on general grounds, and for the reasons stated, it is especially unfair to those manufacturers who are sued for placing defective products into the stream of commerce long before the courts developed their new doctrine of non-delegable duties.

necessary to concentrate not on the mishaps of the given case, but on the required conduct of intermediate parties.

*Martinez* is also superior to *Jackson* on the second issue, the nature of the warnings required. Assume for this purpose that warnings must be made directly to the injured party. In *Martinez*, the circuit court took into account the general knowledge which the decedent and those in his profession had of the substances in question. It refused to treat him as incapable of taking steps for his own protection. Here, of course, it is common knowledge that many chemicals are toxic and must be treated with great care. Any ignorance about the possible extent and type of damage is immaterial in the face of information that, on the bottom line, warns of the certainty and gravity of harm, if not its form.

Common knowledge should also be a decisive defense in *Jackson*. Yet even if it is not, *Jackson* remains an especially weak case for the plaintiff, given that the warnings in question did, on any reasonable construction, link the dangers of "heat, sparks, and open flame" with the need for adequate ventilation. While the plaintiff may have testified that he thought the ventilation was required only for inhalation, the very organization of the warning cuts, if anything, in the opposite direction: the cautions about ventilation are juxtaposed not to the inhalation hazard but to the fire hazard. The Restatement provisions take the correct position that warnings should be presumed to be both read and heeded.[10] The position in *Jackson*, to the contrary, brings the eye of a grammarian to a proposition that was both understood and disregarded. The older position is consistent with the sensible distribution of responsibility throughout the chain of product use. *Jackson* comes all too close to the proposition that recitation of the elements of a duty to warn cause of action is always sufficient to take a case to the jury.

## DRUG CASES

The drug cases, too, illustrate many of the problems with all the elements of the modern duty to warn cause of action. In this connection it is useful to consider two separate situations. The first, exemplified by *Incollingo v. Ewing*,[11] involves prescription drugs administered by a physician in the ordinary course of treatment to an individual patient. The second, illustrated by both *Reyes v. Wyeth Laboratories, Inc.*,[12] and *Davis v. Wyeth Laboratories, Inc.*,[13] involves the role of duty to warn actions in the context of mass public immunizations. In both situations, the acceptance of the expanded duty to warn cause of action has worked an injustice to the defendants charged with liability and a disservice to the public at large.

10. Restatement (Second) of Torts, §402A, comment *j*.
11. 444 Pa. 263, 282 A.2d 206 (1971).
12. 498 F.2d 1264 (5th Cir. 1974).
13. 399 F.2d 121 (9th Cir. 1968).

*Individual Cases*

In *Incollingo v. Ewing*, the defendant, Parke, Davis, manufactured and distributed the drug chloromycetin, a broad-spectrum antibiotic widely used by the medical profession. At all material times, the drug was distributed with an insert which said in full:

> WARNING—Blood dyscrasias (disorders) may be associated with intermittent or prolonged use. It is essential that adequate blood studies be made.

The literature generally distributed by Parke, Davis about the drug also warned that it "is a potent therapeutic agent and, because certain blood dyscrasias have been associated with its administration, it should not be used indiscriminately or for minor infections."[14] In accordance with standard practice these warnings were made, not to the individual user of the drug, but to the physicians who dispensed the drug under prescription, for again the presence of a responsible intermediary eliminates any direct duty to warn.

Mary Ann Incollingo was brought by her mother to Dr. Cucinotta for several visits between October 1958 and January 1960. On each occasion the doctor prescribed limited dosages of chloromycetin to control Mary Ann's illness, diagnosed as acute tonsillitis complicated perhaps by some stomach disorder. Mary Ann's mother, the plaintiff in this action, asked her druggist to refill the prescription, which he refused to do unless so instructed by Dr. Cucinotta. The plaintiff then phoned her own physician, Dr. Levin, and told him that Dr. Cucinotta was not available to renew the prescription. Dr. Levin then ordered the druggist to refill the prescription on several occasions, even though he had never examined the child and had never consulted with Dr. Cucinotta on the case. In addition, Dr. Levin never read the warnings on the packet; he also testified that the "detail men" (salesmen), charged with promoting the drug, had in conversation played down its dangerous side effects. The plaintiff spoonfed the drug to her daughter notwithstanding the warnings contained in the packet. Mary Ann was treated by Dr. Cucinotta until her death, some months later, of aplastic anemia brought on by the drug.

The Pennsylvania Supreme Court held that the plaintiff stated a cause of action not only against the two doctors[15] but also against the drug company, the last solely on a duty to warn theory. The weakness of that duty to warn cause of action against Parke, Davis illustrates much of what is wrong with modern drug litigation.

The threshold question in *Incollingo* concerned the adequacy of warnings

14. 444 Pa. 263, 272, 282 A. 2d 206, 212.

15. The cause of action against Dr. Levin seems plain enough, however complicated by the subsequent actions of Mrs. Incollingo. The action against Dr. Cucinotta, based on the theory that it was improper to prescribe the drug in the first instance, was far more dubious, given that he both followed the then standard practice within the profession and monitored the use of the drug to guard against precisely the contingency that occurred.

issued by Parke, Davis. The issue is by no means clear as a common law matter. The serious risk of aplastic anemia suggests the desirability of a package warning that will alert physicians to the need of frequent and detailed blood testing. Measured against this standard, it could be urged that the vice of the warning as given was that it could mislead physicians by stating, and then understating, the risks of blood disorders associated with the use of chloromycetin. On balance, however, it seems preferable to argue that the warnings are indeed adequate (even if not perfect) because they put the physician on notice of the possible peril so as to enable him to exercise an independent judgment to determine what procedures are suitable in each case. The warning in *Incollingo* did just that: it mentioned that blood disorders could arise from "intermittent or prolonged" use of the drug and that tests should be taken to see that these did not develop. At this point the burden of patient protection shifts to the physician, who can combine that information with other information about the patient's condition received from independent sources.

A second aspect of the adequacy issue in *Incollingo* also highlights the possible extensions of the duty to warn cause of action. Thus the court held that, even if the insert warnings were adequate in themselves (a point on which there was no separate jury finding), the plaintiff could still recover on the ground that the "overpromotion" of the drug by the detail man nullified the effect of the written warnings. The merits of the overpromotion theory are difficult to assess. As an initial point, there is a great variation in the way in which different detail men behave and different physicians respond to their overtures. In some instances, a detail man may exert a dominant influence upon physicians too busy or too indifferent to think for themselves. In other cases the physician will have little time or patience with a detail man, and will use him, if at all, as just another valuable tool to gain needed information about the possible merits of available drugs. The use of the overpromotion theory has attractions in some circumstances but great perils in others. The problem is made all the more pressing because there seems to be no practicable way to limit the strong impact of the overpromotion theory to those cases in which its application appears warranted. It is, of course, difficult to reject the theory on conceptual grounds because it goes to the transmission of product-related information which lies at the very core of any sound conception of product liability law. It may, therefore, be appropriate to allow the plaintiff to proceed on this basis, provided, of course, that the burden is placed squarely on the plaintiff to show that the oral representations dissipated the beneficial effects which the written warnings had upon the physician.

Within this framework the decision of the Pennsylvania court in *Incollingo* is especially troublesome, not because it accepted the overpromotion theory, but because of its treatment of the evidentiary issues. The direct evidence of Cucinotta, that he was uninfluenced by the detail men, was borne out by his limited prescription of the drug, and was, of course, properly admitted. Likewise, the court properly permitted Levin to say that the detail men oversold the drug to him at all material times. The crucial part of the case lies in one of the many minor skirmishes that have altered the shape of the products liability law. The court, in addition to this self-serving direct evidence, allowed the plaintiff to introduce evidence about the representations made by detail men in general to the entire *medical profession.* Such evidence vastly expands the dimensions of the trial (especially if the drug company can counter with similar evidence of its own), and makes it necessary to go, not only beyond the paper record, but beyond the participants in the particular case as well. The evidence also carries the badge of its own irrelevance because, owing to the wide variation in medical practice, it provides almost no clue to what, if anything, was said to *these* doctors, by *these* detail men, about *this* drug. The court justified the use of evidence of such dubious pedigree by noting that, "[a]s a practical matter, it would have been difficult, if not impossible, to show how the promotional efforts of the manufacturer bore on the judgments of these codefendants without demonstrating that the efforts were directed to the entire class or group of which they were members."[16] The difficulty of the plaintiff's task is evident enough, but it does not follow that the evidence should be admitted. If, as seems likely, the errors from using the evidence exceed those of keeping it out, then the proper course is to force the plaintiff to develop other evidence if he wants to pursue this theory further. The initial shakiness of the basic theory should not be compounded by faulty evidentiary rules.

The problems with the overpromotion theory illustrate only one set of difficulties that arise in connection with the aggressive use of the duty to warn cause of action. In many ways the problems with this cause of action parallel those in the design defect cases, for at every point the basic cause of action gives rise to difficult questions whose combined effect only saps the strength and vitality of the plaintiff's case. We have already commented upon the problems associated with the adequacy issue and some of the problems associated with proof of the causal elements of the basic case The causal problems associated with the cause of action need further attention, but only after some discussion on the recurrent tension between negligence and strict liability theories.

The discussion of negligence and strict liability at this juncture is confined to the question of whether the defendant should be excused from issuing an adequate warning for a *known* product hazard solely because he has taken all reasonable precautions to prepare the proper warnings.[17] Within this

16. 444 Pa. 263, 282, 292, A. 2d 206, 221-22.

17. The question discussed in the text should of course be sharply distinguished from the wholly separate inquiry about whether the manufacturer should take the risk of unknown and undiscoverable defects associated with his products. By definition no warnings can be issued with respect to these defects, and the question of their proper treatment is reserved for ch. 9.

context, the debate assumes the familiar form that it took in connection with construction and design defect cases. The strict liability rule removes one extraneous issue from the entire case at no cost in comparative equity. The high standard of care expected of specialist pharmaceutical houses denies them any practical escape on the ground that although the warnings about known hazards were inadequate, they did their best to comply with the common law standards imposed upon them.[18] The convergence of strict liability and negligence has already been commented upon in the historical account of products liability law, and in the analysis of the modern design defect cases.[19] The same observations apply with equal force in this context.

The treatment of the causal issues is somewhat more difficult, given the complicated structure of the duty to warn cause of action. As an initial point, the case depends upon the proof of two separate causal links.[20] First, it must be shown that the drug in question is the physical cause of the plaintiff's harm, for otherwise the absence of any warning about its proper use cannot be said to bring about the injury. Second, it must be shown that the conduct of the physician or the patient, as the case may be, would have been influenced by the receipt of an adequate warning from the drug manufacturer. Where matters are simple, as with *Thomas v. Winchester*, these two elements are easily satisfied. The chemical consequences of taking belladonna are easily identifiable, and nothing in the facts of *Thomas v. Winchester* suggests that the plaintiff was intent upon suicide.

These twin causal issues—physical and interpersonal—assume more troublesome proportions in modern cases like *Jackson, Martinez*, and especially *Incollingo. Jackson* and *Martinez* present no special difficulties on the matter of physical causation, but they do raise considerable uncertainty on the issue of interpersonal causation: there is simply no good evidence available to tell how each plaintiff would have responded to a hypothetically adequate warning. *Incollingo* is even more difficult, as it raises intractable issues on both halves of the causal argument. With causation it becomes necessary to decide which dosages of chloromycetin contributed to Mary Ann's death. If the initial dosages prescribed by Cucinotta were sufficient, then the conduct of Levin and Mrs. Incollingo, no matter how disgraceful, is of no consequence, and Parke, Davis' omissions, if any, in the insert warnings are irrelevant. Even if the initial dosages were insufficient to cause the harm, Parke, Davis arguably should still be exonerated. Cucinotta was aware of all the relevant risks and, no matter what the warnings, the wrongful, indeed reckless, conduct of either Levin or Mrs. Incollingo,

18. For an example of the high standards that can be imposed upon pharmaceutical houses, *see, McEwen v. Ortho Pharmaceutical Corp.*, 270 Or. 375, 528 P.2d 522 (1974).

19. *See* chs. 4 and 7.

20. The precise parallel to these two issues is raised in connection with the informed consent actions brought against physicians. *See* Epstein, *Medical Malpractice: The Case for Contract*, 1976 Am. Bar Foundation Research J. 87 (1976) for an analysis of these questions in connection with the important case of *Canterbury v. Spence*, 464 F.2d 772 (D.C. Cir. 1972).

or both, supervened between the original drug distribution and Mary Ann's death. On these last issues, evidence that chloromycetin causes aplastic anemia is quite insufficient for the task at hand, because propositions about generic drugs cannot apportion causal efficiency between different dosages of the same product. The problems with physical causation in this case do not, moreover, depend exclusively upon the reprehensible aspects of the entire situation. Even in cases of medically supervised use, the injured patient may be treated with the same drug furnished by several different drug companies, perhaps to several different doctors. Alternatively, many patients are treated with many different drugs for a whole host of serious ailments. The causal segregation necessary to associate each segment of the harm with each drug dosage is, therefore, a necessity in many cases of this sort; it is also a determination that can be made with only a very low probability of success in an adversary setting, given the substantial gaps between treatment and manifestation of harm, and between manifestation and litigation.

Parallel complications on causation arise as well with the interpersonal aspect of the case. It is clear that warnings against poisoning and overdoses will normally have their desired effect. Yet, it is not clear that adequate warnings could have had their desired effect upon the two physicians in *Incollingo.* Cucinotta testified that the warnings had been sufficient with respect to him; and even if it had been decided that they were inadequate in some particular respect, it would be necessary to determine what, if any, changes in conduct would have been generated had the warnings been properly strengthened.[21] And the entire question of the response to adequate warnings becomes purely conjectural in the case of Levin, who admitted that he had never read the insert warnings to begin with.

There are two possible techniques for controlling the evident causal problems in particular cases, but both only evade the central challenges. The courts in *Incollingo* applied the common legal rule that causation issues in duty to warn cases are left to the jury in precisely the same manner as, say, in highway accidents. Yet no comfort can be taken from this all-too-common strategem unless and until it is determined what the jury can and should do with its broad discretionary powers. We can trust a jury to decide whether a car is driven in excess of the speed limit or whether a drug is mislabeled

21. On the extremes to which the law has been taken on the question of the adequacy of warnings on physician's behavior, *see Dalke v. Upjohn Co.*, 555 F.2d 245 (9th Cir. 1977). The plaintiff was allowed to reach the jury in a duty to warn case involving teeth discloration caused by the tetracycline-based prescription drugs administered to the plaintiff by her physician. The drugs in question were provided with explicit F.D.A. warnings about teeth discolorations; nonetheless, the plaintiff's physician's affidavit, to the effect that he would "in all likelihood" have chosen a different drug if more "stringent" warnings were provided, was held sufficient on appeal to withstand a summary judgment, even though his affidavit was regarded "questionable" in light of his own practice. If this case does not give a summary judgment for the defendant, then what case will?

because we—as judges, experts, and even ordinary citizens—know what evidence works to validate or falsify such claims. Yet with the causation issues lurking in *Incollingo*, the gist of the problem is that no one, no matter how detached, knows how to decide them. Judicial deference to the jury does not solve the proof problems lurking in the causation issue; it only removes them from public view.

The second approach to the general problem is to erect a set of presumptions on the causation issue. Thus whenever the plaintiff shows the defendant in breach of the duty to warn, a rebuttable presumption could arise that the plaintiff would have responded to the proper warnings if they had been given. This approach makes good sense in a simple case like *Thomas v. Winchester* because there is an enormous gap between what the plaintiff was told and what he should have been told. The soundness of inference from the inadequate warnings to their causal consequences is far more dubious, however, in the modern cases like *Incollingo*. Here the gap, if any, between the information provided and the information required is so narrow, that the safer bet by far is to assume that any change in emphasis and tone in all likelihood would have had only negligible influence on physician attitude and behavior. The presumptions that adequate warnings would have been causally efficacious surely aids the plaintiff by easing his problem of proof, but it does so only at the cost of substantial error. This position might be justified on the ground that, once it is established that the defendant is a wrongdoer, the burden of proof on causal issues should be against, and not with him.[22] Yet here the original conception of wrong is so tenuous that use of this presumption requires the piling of indulgence upon dubious indulgence. Where the causal question is not susceptible to any reliable proof whether direct or circumstantial, the proper response seems to be to deny the action in its entirety.

Parallel arguments apply, moreover, to a similar strategy that might create a rebuttable presumption for the plaintiff on the interpersonal causal issue once the plaintiff has made out a prima facie case on the physical causation question. Yet here too there is no organic connection between the proof of the two distinct causal issues, such that the proposed presumption is likely to be productive of systematic error even if it lightens the burdens upon the plaintiff. The artful use of these presumptions may be decisive in the individual case, but it leaves utterly unanswered the larger social challenges to their use.

22. Precisely this line of argument was adopted in *Haft v. Lone Palm Hotel*, 3 Cal. 3d 756, 478 P.2d 465, 91 Cal. Rptr. 745 (1970), where the question was whether the admitted negligence of the defendant in failing to provide a lifeguard at the pool or post a sign to the effect that no lifeguard was on duty created the presumption that the absence of said sign or lifeguard was the proximate cause of the death of the father and son who drowned in the pool. The argument has been carried over to the products liability area in the curious case of *Dimond v. Caterpillar Tractor Co.*, 65 Cal. App. 3d 173, 134 Cal. Rptr. 895 (1976), in which the plaintiff argued that the defendant's warnings were *too strong*.

The examination of the inner workings of the modern duty to warn cases in connection with single identifiable harms is therefore instructive because it shows that whatever good is promised by the ideals of the new duty to warn cases is overwhelmed by practical difficulties of administration and enforcement. It is one thing to note that a failure to warn properly may cause harm in certain instances; it is quite another to show that a specific failure in a specific case caused the specific harm for which the plaintiff seeks to recover. The weaknesses implicit in each separate element of the modern duty to warn case are, moreover, heightened when placed in the context of the overall cause of action. The plaintiff must prove his case by a preponderance of the evidence. Under this standard, it is not enough for a jury to think that it was likely that this drug caused the damage, that it was likely that the warning was inadequate, and that it was likely that a proper warning would have been heeded. Proof of the cause of action requires that *all* of these be true at once, not just that any one of them be true. If each independent element is "likely" to be true, then the cause of action is "likely" to be false because the fractional probabilities of the constituent events must be multiplied by each other to calculate the probability of their simultaneous occurrence.[23]

*Mass Immunization*

What has been said about drugs and chemicals makes it much easier to approach and analyze the mass immunization cases. In *Reyes*, oral live virus Sabin vaccine was administered to the plaintiff, an infant, by a public health nurse in a country health clinic; in *Davis* the vaccine was administered by the local pharmacist, directly supplied by the defendant, who was then reimbursed by the local medical association for his expenses. The gist of the action in both cases was that the vaccine that brought on the polio was taken only because of the absence of a warning of the one chance in a million that the vaccine, even when properly prepared and administered, could cause polio. In the normal case of prescription drugs, the manufacturer is under no duty to issue a direct warning about the product's hazards and side effects to the user, as the physician, a responsible intermediary bound to make appropriate disclosures under the doctrine of informed consent, has the exclusive duty of directly informing the patients of the relevant risks. Both *Reyes* and *Davis* raise special questions because in neither was a physician in control of the case. The court, therefore, decided that a direct duty to warn was owed to each participant in the mass immunization program. It further decided that the jury could determine, first, whether a warning was required in this case, in spite of the low probability of the harm, because of

23. Thus if there are three disputed issues and the plaintiff's version of the facts is likely to be true 50 percent of the time on each issue, then (assuming the independence of each separate assertion), the probability that the plaintiff has made out his entire case is 12½ percent.

the expected gravity of the loss; and second, the twin questions of physical and interpersonal causation.

The mistakes in *Reyes* and *Davis* parallel in their logic those made in *Incollingo.* First, as a general matter it is far from clear that any direct warning should be required, notwithstanding the absence of an individual physician in the case. The United States government decided—whether correctly or not is beside the point—to institute these programs, and its health experts thought that the slight risk of taking the vaccine was more than offset by the greater risks of doing without protection. The collective and independent judgment of the government should be regarded as an adequate substitute for the physician in the individual case. The sensible distribution of risks leaves manufacturers responsible for the quality of their preparations and the government responsible for the warnings distributed with them.

The theoretical argument to one side, the practical difficulties still remain. Once the basic duty is imposed, it remains to be settled what the warning should say, how it should be delivered, and how its dual causal elements should be assessed. On the first of these questions, *Reyes* and *Davis* are of no particular value, as in neither did the defendant issue any warnings about the vaccines. The more recent case of *Givens v. Lederle* is, however, very illustrative of the difficulties with this aspect of the case. There the defendant's warnings provided:

> Paralytic disease following the ingestion of live polio virus vaccines has been reported in individuals receiving the vaccine, and in some instances, in persons who were in close contact with subjects who had been given live oral polio virus vaccine. Fortunately, such occurrences are rare, and it could not be definitely established that any such case was due to the vaccine strain and was not coincidental with infection due to naturally occurring poliomyelitis or other enteroviruses.[24]

The insert went on to say that if the vaccine held out any risk, it was for no more than one case of vaccine-induced polio for every three million or more doses.

The plaintiff, who did not receive the vaccine herself, contracted polio shortly after her child had been vaccinated. In spite of the warning in the case, her recovery was sustained on appeal when her doctor (who had given no warnings to the plaintiff, but who had not, at least from the record here, been sued) testified that the warning was "nebulous" because it said that no definite connection between polio and the vaccine had been established in *any* of the cases studied. The plaintiff introduced no evidence showing that the statements made in the package insert were in fact incorrect or that the studies done by Dr. Sabin and others about the possible dangers of the vaccine were in fact subject to challenge on medical or scientific

24. 556 F.2d 1341, 1343 (5th Cir. 1977).

grounds. In effect, the court held that an accurate warning may be nonetheless inadequate because it does not overstate the risks of treatment.

The move to such an extreme position may stem from the laudable desire to have issued the strongest possible warnings in order to protect the autonomy of the plaintiff, who might, as the court in *Givens* suggested, have declined to have the vaccine administered to her child at that time, perhaps waiting until her child had become older. Yet this argument ignores what is perhaps the greater peril in the case, that the warnings will induce intended beneficiaries of the program *not* to submit to vaccination because the drug company is, under the common law rule, obliged to mislead individual citizens about the relative hazards of taking and not taking the drug. The central purpose of such warnings is surely not to limit drug company profits, but to help the general public make a balanced assessment of the risks. The warning provided by Lederle bent over backward to achieve that result. And if there is any suspicion whatsoever about Lederle's motives or behavior, then the sensible approach is for the government, after appropriate administrative hearings, to write the very warnings that it wants to issue in mass immunization cases. The government should say that it thinks that vaccination is called for even though it is not without risk, and that individuals who are concerned about the uncertainties of their own personal position should seek whatever advice they choose (including government reports) before they come for the vaccine. The warnings that are to be distributed should be sanctioned in *advance* by legislation, so that their "adequacy" is not left to the vagaries of jury sentiment on a case-by-case basis.

Still other problems should be enough to warn courts away from judicial control of immunization decisions. The overpromotion problem confronted in *Incollingo* provides but a small taste of the comparable problem in connection with mass immunization programs. Thus it must certainly be permissible to allow into evidence whatever radio announcements, circulars, or speeches were used to encourage people to come into the immunization centers in the first place, as well as all assurances, whether by word or gesture, made by program personnel. These, of course, are matters about which testimony can be carefully rehearsed on the plaintiff's side, which are impossible to counter with specific testimony by program personnel who have dealt with tens or hundreds of patients. The preparation of the adequate warning in the corporate or government headquarters is scant assurance of its *communication* to the persons who are vaccinated under any mass immunization programs. The courts in *Davis* and *Reyes* said that discharge of the duty to warn was easy enough. In this they underestimated the technical dimensions of the problem and the devastating effects of their own legal doctrines.

Last, of course, is the problem with the two causal elements of the case. Should a jury decide whether this vaccine caused this injury when the odds are ten to one (a hundred to one?) that the illness was caused by natural viruses? Here it can be done, but only with flights of judicial invention. Sabin, testifying in *Givens* as an expert witness for the defendant, stated that the vaccine could not cause polio, and Lederle organized much of its defense around this proposition. The plaintiff's case, as summarized on appeal, rested on two propositions. First, that the warnings, however inadequate, admitted the possibility that such cases could occur. Second, that juries, in separate actions brought by other parties, had determined that polio could be so caused. The first proposition takes a warning, designed to guard against liability, and converts it into a source of scientific truth. The second allows one jury to take refuge in the errors and speculation of its predecessors. These methods are, of course, compounded by the errors on the interpersonal causal question. There may be some persons who would hesitate to take the drug because of the overly pessimistic account of the risks seemingly required by the courts. Yet, it is difficult to know how proof of this decision could be generated in any particular case, and unwise to presume it, given that taking the vaccine is by all odds the more prudent course of action. Here the presumption should be set against the plaintiff, and not, as the court in *Reyes* suggested, with him.

Only unthinking deference to the jury can salvage these causes of action. It may well be desirable to establish some collective program for the compensation of polio victims, but if so this is surely a matter for legislative and not judicial decision.[25] The courts should not introduce cumbersome compensation schemes cloaked in the traditional corrective justice language of defect, causation, and wrong. It would be tragic indeed if a misguided judicial insistence upon excessive warnings helped contribute to an increase in polio by inducing parents to keep their children from being vaccinated.

### *Statute and Common Practice*

The unsatisfactory state of the common law duty to warn actions, especially in drug-related cases, makes it urgent to search for some safeguards against the excesses of the new common law rules. Here the common industry practice on the warning issue seems to provide little help, as the standard admits too great a variation to have much predictive value. With drugs, however, it should be possible to rely upon the statutory framework of the Food and Drug Administration (F.D.A.) to determine adequacy of warnings. Here the F.D.A. regulations require that both package inserts and the Physician Desk Reference list "indications, effects, dosages, routes, methods, and frequency and duration of administration and side effects, and any relevant warnings, hazards, contraindications, side effects and precautions." The list is surely exhaustive. What is more, the supervision of the F.D.A. does not cease with the promulgation of the general standards

25. *See* Franklin and Mai, *Tort Law and Mass Immunization Programs: Lessons From the Polio and Flu Episodes*, 65 Calif. L. Rev. 754 (1977).

for approved drugs. Instead, the agency assumes responsibility for evaluating the clinical and laboratory tests about drug usage and in many instances demands that certain language be added or dropped from standard product inserts. This type of comprehensive administrative scheme makes it proper to use the standards of warning and labeling of the F.D.A., whatever their own internal uncertainty, as *both the minimum and maximum* requirements. While it can be objected that the warnings required by the F.D.A. are often only "minimal" in nature,[26] this objection is not of itself sufficient, given the comprehensive and continuing nature of the administrative review.[27]

The major criticism today of the F.D.A. is that its restriction upon the use of new drugs, far from being too lax, is too stringent.[28] This criticism is largely directed against the agency's refusal to permit the use of new drugs until they have been demonstrated to be "safe and effective" under very exacting standards of proof. But similar criticism may also be directed to F.D.A. policies on drug inserts. It takes little evidence for the F.D.A. to require that contraindications be listed or that favorable indications be suppressed. Indeed the F.D.A. is so active in the warning area that it may even prohibit the inclusion of additional warnings on products for fear that they will amount to an implied authorization to use the product in ways that had not been previously sanctioned by the F.D.A. Given this strong regulatory bias, what if anything is to be gained by allowing juries to decide on an ad hoc and ex post basis that the warnings in fact given were inadequate, say, in matters of tone and emphasis, when it can lead to the judicial response to Lederle's warnings in *Givens*? And is there any reason to fear government laxity today, even if there was some doubt about the diligence of the F.D.A. in years past? Even if the original warning for chloromycetin in *Incollingo* is regarded as suspect, the same charges cannot be made against the revised warning that begins with a stern warning painted in a black box:

26. *See, e.g., Stevens v. Parke, Davis & Co.*, 9 Cal. 3d 51, 507 P.2d 653, 107 Cal. Rptr. 45 (1973). In a similar vein *see, Burch v. Amsterdam Corp.*, 366 A.2d 1079 (D.C. Ct. App. 1976), where the defendant's motion for summary judgment was denied when the court decided that the Hazardous Substances Act, 15 U.S.C. § 1261, only prescribed minimum standards for labeling hazardous substances. The gist of the plaintiff's case was that specific mention should have been made of the special hazard posed by pilot lights in ovens, to which the dissent's response was that "it would seem equally incumbent upon the vendors to devise a label warning against lighted pipes, cigars and cigarettes, vigil lights, candles, sparks from an electric lamp switch, a running fan or motor, and the other myriad of things which could possibly ignite vapors." Id. at 1089.

In spite of the arguments to the contrary, the proposed Model Uniform Product Liability Act, Section 107, does not give conclusive weight to compliance with statutes, even those as detailed as the Hazardous Substances Act.

27. For a discussion of the procedures used by the Food and Drug Administration (F.D.A.) to evaluate proposed drug warnings, *see* Comment, *Package Inserts for Prescription Drugs as Evidence in Medical Malpractice Suits*, 44 U. Chi. L. Rev. 398 (1977).

28. *See* Wardell, *Rx for Drug Regulation*, Regulation 25-33 (Sept.-Oct. 1979) for a detailed account for the regulatory barriers.

"Serious and fatal blood dyscrasias (aplastic anemia, hypoplastic anemia, thrombocytepenia, . . . ) are known to occur after the administration of chloroamphenicol," and then continues at length for five tightly packed columns of fine print.

The basic rule here should be subject to an exception in those cases in which the defendant drug company has deliberately withheld from the F.D.A. information that is relevant to the marketing of the drug,[29] and it might be subject to further exception where the company has new and relevant information that has not yet been acted upon by the F.D.A. Admit these qualifications and the standard should be given conclusive weight. A few deserving cases may be denied recovery; but a vast number of dubious actions will by the same token be weeded out. This sharp contraction of the duty to warn action in drug contexts should, moreover, be greeted with relief, not concern. It is socially desirable that these firms continue to produce goods we all need and consume. To that end it is vital to set for drug companies a standard with which advance compliance is possible. A clear specification of what counts as adequacy will remove the pressure from the other elements of the complete cause of action with little, if any, loss in consumer protection.

## MACHINE TOOLS AND KINDRED PRODUCTS

While the duty to warn cause of action is of special concern in connection with drugs and chemicals, it also has an important role to play in modern cases involving machine tools and other capital equipment. In many cases the effective and safe use of a product requires that some inescapable hazard be built into it. Many band saws, for example, cannot function with guards; an appropriate warning, properly communicated or displayed, might be a cheap and effective means to avoid personal injury or property damage. As with the drugs and chemicals, the central issue is not whether there should be some duty to warn cause of action, but rather, what should be its precise form.

The basic theory of the cause of action remains unchanged. The essential task of the manufacturer is still to supply that information about his product which he can generate more cheaply and effectively than persons downstream in the chain of distribution, except where the administrative costs of such actions render social control impractical through the tort law. Yet, these individualized warnings, particularly instructions, may assume a unique importance in machine tool cases. Knowledge about the dangers and hazards of generic goods, such as drugs and chemicals, is essentially available to all

29. *McDaniel v. McNeil Laboratories, Inc.*, 196 Neb. 190, 241 N.W.2d 822 (1976).

persons within the chain of distribution, and the required warnings are in any event as often as not subject to detailed statutory standards. Patterns of access to knowledge about machine tools are apt to be very different, for machines are not generic goods susceptible to direct statutory controls, and it is quite likely that the party that designed and manufactured them will have special information about their hidden strengths and limitations. The range of relevant issues extends to the operating instructions of a given machine, its maintenance and repair schedules, its capacity, the common pitfalls in its operations, the danger signs of greater troubles, and the like. The sense that a product could be sold and used without this information runs contrary to the common practice and shared expectations of virtually all industries. The only question that matters concerns the precise dimensions of the duty.

There is, in principle, no clear answer to this question, but it is possible to find, at least in the better-decided cases, some guidance as to the appropriate definition and limitation of the manufacturer's duty to warn and instruct. The central element that works in favor of the plaintiff is, of course, the existence of a *latent* defect that will work harm in ordinary product use. The stress on latent dangers in ordinary use returns us to the basic misrepresentation theory of product defect so common in the earlier cases and precludes recovery on a warning—statutes apart—for conditions that are open and obvious to the plaintiff in the normal course of the work. The emphasis upon latent dangers accounts for proper *plaintiff's* verdicts in many modern cases as well.

Consider only the Oregon case of *Fulbright v. Klamath Gas Company*[30] The plaintiff was burned while using a potato-vine burner manufactured by the defendant. The purpose of the burner was to destroy undergrowth that might interfere with harvesting potatoes by mechanical diggers. As designed, the burner was a portable unit with two propane tanks; the tanks were connected to four large torches, each of which directed a flame toward the earth. The tanks were separated from the burners by a galvanized metal shield, and were also equipped with pressure valves that released propane gas into the atmosphere whenever excessive pressure built up inside the tank. While the device was being towed by tractor, the excessive pressure buildup released gas into the air that was in turn ignited by the burners, and the plaintiff was severely burned in the ensuing flames. The parties agreed that there was no effective alternative design for the burner which would permit it to perform its intended function, and the question was whether some warning, preferably one attached to the machine itself, should have directed the operator's attention to the possibility of a flare-up when

30. 271 Or. 449, 533 P.2d 316 (1975).

the machine was operated under windy conditions. Here even though the operator must have known that there was some possible danger associated with the use of any burning device, it seems proper to argue that a warning of this recurrent hazard could have and should have been communicated to its user.

A similar case, somewhat closer to the line, is *Outboard Marine v. Schupach.*[31] The plaintiff was injured by an explosion that took place when a cart of defendant's manufacture, while in motion, produced sparks which set off chemical vapors in the plaintiff's place of work. The cart was not normally intended for use in that particular plant environment, but to all outward appearance was suited for the work to which it had been put. The court allowed—and the result is surely defensible—the case to go to the jury on a duty to warn theory. "Although employees at the plant knew that the cart sparked, they did not know that the sparking was of such intensity as to cause an explosion in a chemical atmosphere."[32]

The very theory that creates liability on duty to warn grounds also limits the recovery that can be had upon that theory. Thus, the plaintiff has no cause of action where the hazards against which he demands warning were not created by the manufacturer at the time of the original sale of the product. As has been well stated, "[t]he manufacturer of a chattel can hardly be expected to warn of every conceivable danger that might arise from misuse of the chattel or failure to maintain it after it breaks down."[33]

In *Rodiguez v. Besser Co.*,[34] the plaintiff was injured when his head was crushed against the side of a machine by a moving paddle. The plaintiff was standing on a special platform, erected by the employer, which put him in a position where the paddle could strike his head if he leaned forward. If the machine had been left in its original condition, such an accident could not have occurred. The court held that the defendant was not accountable for the loss even though it knew that the plaintiff's employer had made modifications in the platform of the machine. Although the court noted its general acceptance of the proposition that the duty to warn rests upon the "foreseeability" of harm, it appreciated the proper scope and limitations of the maxim. Thus the court decided that the manufacturer is under no duty to correct a condition created by the employer, noting that the alternative rule would impose an "intolerable burden" on the manufacturer to prevent not only defects of its own creation, but also defects made and im-

31. 93 Nev. 158, 561 P.2d 450 (1977).

32. 93 Nev. 158 at 161-62, 561 P.2d 450 at 452.

33. *Westerberg v. School District No. 792,* 276 Minn. 1, 6, 148 N.W. 2d 312, 315 (1967): the case is cited in *Rogers v. Unimac*, 115 Ariz. 304, 309-10, 565 P.2d 181 at 186-87 (1977).

34. 115 Ariz. 454, 565 P.2d 1315 (1977).

posed by others. In effect the decision states that the manufacturer is responsible for his own conduct and not for the misconduct of others.[35]

## CONSUMER GOODS

The previous three sections of this chapter have considered the duty to warn in connection with various types of products intended for professional use. The principles derived in these contexts do have broad application to various types of consumer goods but with some crucial differences in emphasis. As before the general theory is unchanged, in that the office of warnings remains to provide individuals farther down in the chain of distribution the relevant information that they cannot cheaply and reliably acquire from other sources. What is different about the situation is that here it can no longer be expected that the goods in question will often be controlled and supervised by intermediaries who have access to independent information that is equal to or better than that which may be provided by the original product manufacturer. The warnings and instructions that are to be provided should, therefore, unless administrative constraints interfere, take into account the different status of the expected user of the good by providing some additional information. Accordingly, the role of warnings should be expected to have special importance in dealing with consumer goods that have dangerous or toxic properties that may not be understood by the individuals who use them. It would, for example, be almost incomprehensible to see strong toxic materials, such as those used to remove debris from drains and toilets, marketed without some prominent mention that the product is poisonous, some instructions on the proper use of the product, some list of the common hazards to be avoided, and some statement of the proper first-aid remedies to be applied if a mishap does occur.

Yet even though these consumer cases rightly require warnings and in-

35. Note that the result in this case would be codified by the legislation that provides in substance that a manufacturer is not responsible for injuries which would have occurred but for the modification or alteration of the original product, except in accordance with the original product instructions or specifications or with the consent of the manufacturer.

*See, e.g.*, Ariz. Rev. Stat. Ann § 12-683 (2) (Supp. 1979); and Model Uniform Product Liability Act, § 112(D). Both the Arizona statute and the model bill have a further provision that holds the manufacturer responsible for such alterations and modifications if they could have been "reasonably anticipated." These words should not be read to embrace any and all changes but only those which are prudently made by persons other than original manufacturer. The Arizona statute reaches that result by special definition: " 'Reasonably foreseeable alteration, modification, use of consumption' means an alteration, modification, use or consumption of the product which would be expected of an ordinary and prudent purchaser, user or consumer and which an ordinary and prudent manufacturer should have anticipated." § 12-681(4).

structions, certain limitations must be observed, for even in consumer contexts there are expected hazards so obvious to all that no mention need be made of them. Thus, it is quite possible today to find perfume bottles with warnings that their contents are inflammable, or phonograph sets with column instructions not to use while submerged in water, or kitchen equipment with warnings to use only after reading instruction booklets, or infant seats that say the children should be buckled up and never left unattended, or air conditioners with warnings not be dropped out of windows. The wisdom of such warnings is open to serious doubt, not because they may be made stronger, but because they convey only information that is already known to the vast number of product users to whom the warnings are directed. Those who cannot understand the hazards of certain products that are before their eyes will not respond to the more subtle messages contained in written warnings or even in pictures. Here, as in so many other areas, there is a limit to what the law can and should do to make one person protect another person from himself. The proliferation of endless warnings about all things great and small may, moreover, even be destructive solely from the point of view of product safety as individuals are anesthetized by a constant refrain of trivial cautions. Saccharin is not cyanide. Both courts and legislatures should proceed with caution lest warnings assume a decisively ritualistic function at trial, even if they have no influence whatsoever upon the primary conduct of the parties to whom they are directed.

One amazing case shows well the lengths to which courts can go to conjure up the need for product warnings. In *Moran v. Faberge*[36] the Maryland Supreme Court upheld a jury verdict against the defendant manufacturer on behalf of a teenage girl who was injured after her friend poured the manufacturer's cologne upon a Christmas candle in order to "make it scented." No similar instance had ever been reported in the twenty-eight years that the cologne had been the market. The court noted that it was possible (what is not possible?) that some woman at her vanity table just might heed a warning about inflammability if tempted to flick a cigarette ash near the bottle, where the ash might just squeeze through its tiny opening. The jury therefore could conclude that the warning was required for the wholly different circumstances of this particular case, even though it was far from clear that any warning, if printed, would have been read or heeded by the plaintiff's overly eager friend. Today these warnings routinely appear on toiletries. They are accompanied by others that say that toiletries should

36. 273 Md. 538, 332 A.2d 11 (1975). *Moran* was rejected in *Thibault v. Sears, Roebuck & Co.*, 118 N.H. 802, 395 A.2d 843 (1978). *Thibault* also rejected the earliest of the extended duty to warn cases, *Spruill v. Boyle-Midway, Inc.*, 308 F.2d 79 (4th Cir. 1962), in which the defendant was held liable for the death of a child who drank the furniture polish which was being used by its mother.

not be stored in hot places or rubbed into eyes. Is there liability if an infant drinks the cologne after its mother places it on the kitchen table?

A similar tendency to overstate the importance of warnings is found in *Greiner v. Volkswagenwerk Aktiengeselleschaft.*[37] There the plaintiff, a passenger in a Volkswagen, was injured in a serious crash. While speeding, the driver lost control of her car. It swerved toward the wall of a narrow bridge after crossing the oncoming lanes. Eventually the car rolled on its side, the roof against the front of another car. Again we have a situation in which the prominent causal components of the accident rest within the control of the driver, not the manufacturer of the vehicle. Nonetheless, the Court of Appeals, in reversing the defendant's directed verdict in the lower court, remanded the case to determine whether the plaintiff could recover on a duty to warn theory. On remand the trial judge again entered a summary judgment for the defendant, holding that even if any warnings were required, the plaintiff's driver could not possibly have heeded them in the few seconds between the time she lost control and the time that she crashed.

This causal argument neatly disposed of the particular case but only by avoiding the fundamental problems of the entire area. As the plaintiff urged, the relevant moment at which to consider the potential impact of the warnings was either at the point of purchase or alternatively just before the car approached the bridge. A stronger warning "might" have influenced the decision whether to purchase or the decision on how to drive, and in either event, the accident in question might have been avoided. The case points up the universal trend in products liability actions toward shifting responsibility from immediate actions to remote causal antecedents.

The shift in time, however, complicates every feature of the case. No longer is it possible to limit warnings to those which involve the possibility of one kind of crash. Instead, it will be necessary either to give very broad warnings about the relative dangers of small cars—information that is common knowledge in any event—or to give a detailed list of dangers associated with all possible accidents. Do we want to mandate disquisitions that could never serve as the foundation for action? Then, too, the causal arguments are incapable of direct or inferential proof. The only evidence that could be obtained ex post is of a probabilistic, not to say speculative, kind that suggests some stronger warning might have had some effect on some portion of the purchasers; from this evidence it is impossible to draw sensible inferences in individual cases. What is more, this extended theory of warning opens up every automobile accident to a warning theory. If the stronger warnings had been given, some plaintiff might not have driven the car on

37. 540 F.2d 85 (3rd Cir. 1976), *remanded* 429 F. Supp. 495 (E.D. Pa. 1977).

the freeways where he could be struck by a truck or on back roads where he could land in a ditch, all through no fault of his own. The causal approach taken in *Greiner* on remand might blunt the use of warning theories in one case, but it is far inferior to a "no-duty" approach that renders issues of causation irrelevant in cases in which common knowledge utterly negates any warning requirement.

Our discussion of *Greiner*, therefore, leads to a repetition of the dominant theme. It is one thing to talk in general about the desirability of warnings, and it is quite another to implement that desire through private damage actions. Confined to cases of latent defects or statutory commands, the duty to warn cause of action represents a useful and valuable approach to the problems of product safety. Extended beyond these limits, the cause of action is both expensive and unreliable, and in all probability productive of undesirable, but foreseeable, social consequences.

CHAPTER

# 9

# PLAINTIFF'S CONDUCT*

Every products liability action has two sides. The first, already the subject of extensive discussion, concerns the defendant's initial exposure for product defects, whether under a theory of negligence or of strict liability. The second, the subject of this chapter, concerns the defenses based upon plaintiff's conduct made available to a defendant against whom some basic cause of action has already been established. These defenses in most products liability actions number three: contributory negligence, product misuse, and assumption of risk. All have been exhaustively studied and debated as part of the general tort law, and nowhere has the debate been more intense than in the area of products liability. The narrow focus of this chapter will be on products liability actions. Yet its analysis will invariably take us farther afield. While the material in this chapter will break some new ground, it will perforce review from a different vantage point themes that have been once pursued: What is the proper account of product defect? What is the importance of a distinction between actions brought by users and consumers, as opposed to actions brought by bystanders? What is the importance of the distinction between negligence and strict liability? These questions help illumine the law governing plaintiff's conduct and are in turn illuminated by it.

## BACKGROUND AND HISTORY

In the formative years of products liability law little attention was paid to affirmative defenses based upon plaintiff's conduct. At first blush, this conclusion seems odd because the vast bulk of products liability actions involved injuries to users or consumers. In these cases the simple temporal

*Sections of this chapter were published in slightly different form in Richard Epstein, *Plaintiff's Conduct in Products Liability Actions: Comparative Negligence, Automatic Division and Multiple Parties*, 45 J. Air L. & Comm. 87 (1979).

progression of events makes the plaintiff's conduct a link in the chain between original defect and ultimate injury. How then can his conduct not be an issue? The puzzle, however, is resolved by noting that the original products liability actions were limited to cases in which a concealed defect caused harm while the product was being used in the ordinary and proper way. The ordinary and proper use requirement (as part of the basic cause of action) negated recovery whenever any plaintiff's misconduct was found. It also eliminated the need to attach independent status to the defenses concerned with plaintiff's conduct.

This basic account of the original products cause of action also helps explain why assumption of risk, often disfavored in other areas of the law, paradoxically emerged as the first of the products liability defenses. Typical of the early cases that coupled assumption of risk with the narrow conception of product defect is *Kassouf v. Lee Brothers, Inc.*[1] In that case the plaintiff suffered severe internal disorders when she ate a chocolate bar that contained worms and maggots. The first bite tasted "funny," but only too late did she discover its contamination. The defect, of course, was latent and unknown; the consumption of the bar was normal and proper. If the plaintiff had known of the defect, the injury would have been self-inflicted and the action properly barred. The importance of knowledge and assumption of risk is highlighted, moreover, if the plaintiff's action is regarded as based upon an implied representation that the defendant's chocolate was fit for human consumption.[2] Reliance is one of the essential elements of that claim, and such could not be established if the plaintiff had in fact known of the chocolate's dangerous condition.

The real question is whether the facts in *Kassouf* admit a contributory negligence type of defense. Here the court quite properly held that they did not. The shared expectations of buyers and sellers of food and drink are that the buyer is *entitled* to trust the seller to package it correctly and need not make any independent investigations of product fitness. The result reached depends solely upon the sense of the bargain between the two parties, who, with the passing of the privity limitation, are treated as if they had entered into a direct contract of sale. The very misrepresentation theory that makes short shrift of cases like *Kassouf* also lends support for the treatment of plaintiff's conduct in comment *n* to Section 402A of the Restatement (Second) of Torts. This comment, widely accepted as the basis for the modern law, reads in full as follows:

> Since the liability with which this section deals is not based upon negligence of the seller, but is strict liability, the rule applied to strict liability cases (*see* § 524) applies.

1. 209 Cal. App. 2d 568, 26 Cal. Rptr. 276 (1962).
2. *See* the discussion of *Greenman v. Yuba Power Products, Inc.*, 59 Cal. 2d 57, 377 P.2d 897, 27 Cal. Rptr. 697 (1963) in ch. 4.

Contributory negligence of the plaintiff is not a defense when such negligence consists merely in a failure to discover the defect in the product, or to guard against the possibility of its existence. On the other hand the form of contributory negligence which consists in voluntarily and unreasonably proceeding to encounter a known danger, and commonly passes under the name of assumption of risk, is a defense under this section as in other cases of strict liability. If the user or consumer discovers the defect and is aware of the danger, and nevertheless proceeds unreasonably to make use of the product and is injured by it, he is barred from recovery.[3]

The comment, of vast importance to the modern law, serves as the focal point for our subsequent analysis of contributory negligence, assumption of risk, and product misuse.

## CONTRIBUTORY NEGLIGENCE

### IN MODERN PRODUCTS LIABILITY ACTIONS

*Kassouf* and kindred cases illustrate the wisdom of rejecting the contributory negligence defense for harms caused by latent defects in food and drink. After publication of the Restatement (Second) of Torts, the central analytical problem relating to defenses was whether to preserve comment *n* in the face of the unprecedented expansion of the basic defect concept.[4] Most courts, not fully cognizant of the revolution on the defect issue, either blandly adopted the Restatement position or announced the even broader proposition that all contributory negligence defenses were incompatible with the strict liability theories of Restatement Section 402A. These extensions are misconceived. *Kassouf* does not rest upon the immateriality of contributory negligence to products liability causes of action; it rests instead upon the narrower proposition that *in this particular context* the shared expectations are that this consumer has *no duty* to seek out product defects. Change the product or the circumstances under which it is distributed and the web of obligations that governs its use will change as well. While comment *n* reads as though it were a first principle of tort law, it should be construed as a statement of the implied terms of a bargain about a narrow, if important, class of products. Food and drink, to which the early versions of Section 402A were in fact limited, conjure very different expectations than do airplanes, machine tools, or automobiles.[5]

The pressure that the broad definition of defect places upon the rules for

3. Restatement (Second) of Torts, § 402A, comment *n* (1965).

4. *See* chs. 7 and 8.

5. *See* Restatement (Second) of Torts (Tent. Draft No. 6, 1961), which was limited to food products, and Restatement (Second) of Torts (Tent. Draft No. 7, 1962), which was extended to products intended for "intimate body use." The development of the case law within the area was so fast on the strict liability question that by 1965 the section was extended to cover all products.

plaintiff's conduct is well revealed by *Melia v. Ford Motor Co.*[6] The decedent was killed in an intersection collision when she was thrown out of her car through the unlocked door on the driver's side. The plaintiff contended that the door was defective in design in that it was not fail-safe against certain horizontal forces that could open it while shut but unlocked. This question of design defect was difficult and controversial, and the dissenting judge thought the plaintiff's case should not even reach the jury. At issue were three facets of the plaintiff's conduct: (1) she entered the intersection against the red light; (2) she left her door unlocked; and (3) she had not buckled her seat belt. By a divided vote the court held, on its view of Nebraska law, that these issues were of no concern in a products liability action, citing Restatement comment *n* in support of that position.[7] In the absence of plaintiff's knowledge of the particular defects in the door-locking mechanism, the comment *n* defense was not established.

Again the court flounders on the issue of shared expectations. The elimination of the privity requirement forces the court to treat the parties as immediate buyer to immediate seller. It staggers the imagination to assume that any implicit agreement between them contemplated that the buyer could drive as he pleased, thereby exposing the defendant to costly and uncertain litigation. Simply because the plaintiff in *Kassouf* did not have to pick her way through a wormy bar of chocolate does not mean that the decedent in *Melia* could drive like a fool. Knowledge that the chocolate has turned in one case may be a precondition for intelligent action by the user of the product, but knowledge of a minute design defect in a car door is not required in order to make safe driving necessary. Running red lights is a violation of statute, regardless of the condition of the automobile; it is not wrongful or risky solely because of an alleged design defect. Wearing seat belts and locking doors are common precautions that protect against a host of injuries; the decedent's was but one. *Greenman v. Yuba Power Products, Inc.* evokes the image of a plaintiff "powerless" to protect himself against an array of awesome and unknown hazards. Its message should be established in each individual case. The plaintiff's conduct in *Melia* barred her action against the driver of the other car.[8] It is difficult to see why a defense of contributory negligence, clearly applicable in the one context, should not be applicable to the other.

Still another illustration of the same basic problem arises in connection with aviation accidents, where contributory negligence in products cases has been greeted with the same chilly reception. In *Rudisaile v. Hawk Avia-*

6. 534 F.2d 795 (8th Cir. 1976).

7. The Nebraska statute on the subject involves a slight-gross rule whereby the comparative approach is invoked when the plaintiff's negligence is "slight" and the defendant's negligence, in comparison with it, is "gross." Neb. Rev. Stat. § 25-1151 (1975).

8. *Melia v. Svoboda*, 191 Neb. 150, 214 N.W.2d 476 (1974).

*tion, Inc.*,[9] the New Mexico court allowed the plaintiff to recover when her husband, a qualified pilot, crashed after taking off in a Piper Cherokee 140 E. The plane had been drained mistakenly of all its oil before flight, and it had not been replaced. The decedent did not undertake the customary preflight check of the aircraft before he took off. Here there is no question but that the defendant's conduct is inexcusable; yet the same can be said about the plaintiff's. If the plane had crashed into a farmhouse, the decedent's estate would have been held jointly responsible with the defendant, precisely because the decedent's duty was so clear. Given this web of shared expectations within a highly structured institutional framework, there is no reason why the plaintiff's contributory negligence should not be regarded as a defense, simply because his action is brought under a products liability theory.

*Melia* and *Rudisaile* represent one side of an issue on which legal opinion is divided.[10] In a stunning reversal, the California Supreme Court, long a leader in the expansion of products liability, adopted comparative negligence type principles by a four-to-three vote in *Daly v. General Motors Corp.*[11] The matter is one on which present division of opinion invites a closer examination of the arguments both for and against the contributory negligence defense. The case for accepting some form of contributory negligence is best made by looking at the reasons that are used for its rejection. These are clearly expressed in the impassioned dissent of Justice Mosk in *Daly*:

> This court has emphasized over and over again that strict products liability is an independent tort species wholly distinct from contract warranties . . . and from negligence. . . . Indeed, in *Cronin* we stressed that "the very purpose of our pioneering efforts in this field was to relieve the plaintiff from problems of proof inherent in pursuing negligence." . . . And in *Luque v. McLean*, . . . this court unanimously declared that "contributory negligence does not bar recovery in a strict liability action." . . .
>
> The bench and bar have abided by this elementary rule. They have learned to avoid injecting negligence—whether of the defendant or the plaintiff—into a products liability case. And they have understood the reason behind the distinction between negligence of any party and products liability. . . .
>
> Transferring the liability, or part of the liability, from the party responsible for putting the article in the stream of commerce to the consumer is precisely what the majority propose to do. They do this by employing a euphemism: the victim's recovery is to be "proportionately reduced." The result, however delicately described, is to dilute the defect of the article by elevating the conduct of the wounded consumer to an issue of equal significance. We can be as certain as tomorrow's daylight that every defendant charged with marketing a defective product will hereafter assert that the injured plaintiff did something, anything, that conceivably could be deemed

9. 92 N.M. 575, 592 P.2d 175 (1979).

10. For a collection of the relevant cases on both sides of the line, *see generally*, Annot., 46 A.L.R.3d 240 (1972).

11. 20 Cal. 3d 725, 575 P.2d 1162, 144 Cal. Rptr. 380 (1978).

contributorily negligent: he drove the vehicle with a defective steering mechanism 56 miles an hour instead of 54; or he should have discovered a latent defect hidden in the machinery; or perhaps he should not have succumbed to the salesman's persuasion and purchased the defective object in the first instance. I need no crystal ball to foresee that the pleading of affirmative defenses alleging contributory negligence—or the currently approved substitute terminology—will now become boilerplate.[12]

As stated the opinion of Justice Mosk raises both fairness and incentive issues. We consider these in turn.

## FAIRNESS ARGUMENTS

Notwithstanding Justice Mosk's strong plea, the case for retaining contributory negligence remains secure. The point of departure is that courts have always treated the plaintiff's conduct as a proper source of inquiry in all manner of torts actions, no matter what the substance of the plaintiff's original cause of action. Not only is contributory negligence regarded as an appropriate defense in the typical highway accident case, but analogous defenses based upon plaintiff's conduct are viable in traditional causes of action based explicitly upon strict liability principles. Provocation is available as a defense in strict liability actions brought against the owner of a wild animal.[13] The default of the plaintiff, however defined, is a defense to actions patterned upon *Rylands v. Fletcher* for the escape of hazardous substances collected and stored on the defendant's premises.[14] Both contexts exhibit the same theme: the plaintiff has engaged in conduct that would expose him to liability if it injured a third person. There is no obvious reason, therefore, why that conduct should be ignored because the plaintiff has helped to injure himself instead. It is true that no person can sue himself; nonetheless, his conduct can be taken into account in actions that might otherwise promise full relief. The plaintiff who shares in the production of his own harm can raise no obvious moral claim against being required to shoulder a part of his own loss.[15] Within this framework, strict liability does

12. Id. at 758-60, 575 P.2d at 1182-83, 144 Cal. Rptr. at 400-01. (Citations and footnotes omitted.)

13. *See* W. Prosser, *Handbook of the Law of Torts* 523 (rth ed. 1971).

14. *Fletcher v. Rylands*, L.R. 1 Ex. 265 (1866) aff'd in *Rylands v. Fletcher*, L. R. 3 E. & I. 330 (1868), where it is noted that the defendant "can excuse himself by showing that the escape was owing to the plaintiff's default."

15. "It is unnecessary for us to catalogue the enormous amount of critical comment that has been directed over the years against the 'all-or-nothing' approach of the doctrine of contributory negligence. The essence of that criticism has been constant and clear: the doctrine is inequitable in its operation because it fails to distribute responsibility in proportion to fault." *Li v. Yellow Cab Co.*, 13 Cal. 3d 804, 810, 532 P. 2d 1226, 1230, 119 Cal. Rptr. 858, 860 (1975). The classic article in favor of comparative negligence is still Prosser, *Comparative Negligence*, 41 Calif. L. Rev. 1 (1953). For a thoughtful modern defense of the comparative negligence rule, see Schwartz, *Contributory and Comparative Negligence: A Reappraisal*, 87 Yale L. J. 697 (1978).For criticism of the pure comparative negligence approach adopted in *Li*, see infra, at 135-41.

not preclude an examination into plaintiff's conduct; to the contrary, it invites it.

The basic equities of the situation are unchanged, moreover, even when applied to products liability actions. Justice Mosk's arguments of "*symmetry*," echoing those of comment *n*, are designed to give some a priori credibility to the argument that as negligence is no part of the prima facie case, it should be no part of the defense. A closer examination of the situation demonstrates, however, that no single conceptual refinement can bear the immense burden of undoing all contributory negligence defenses. Justice Mosk is on sound ground when he notes the administrative advantages of strict liability compared to negligence. He fails to note, however, the small cash value of the doctrinal change, given the extensive use of res ipsa loquitur, and the repeated insistence on a very high standard of care. The tiny change brought about by the movement from negligence to strict liability as the basic cause of action provides no warrant for a massive revolution in the law of affirmative defenses. If anything, one expansion of plaintiff's rights should caution against any further, independent shift in the same direction. Courts that relax one requirement—defendant's negligence—in the plaintiff's case for administrative ease need not dismantle another barrier to recovery—contributory negligence—which has its own independent justifications.

Suppose for the moment, however, that the changes in the basic cause of action do justify symmetrical changes in the law of affirmative defenses. What follows from this premise is not that contributory negligence should be eliminated, but rather that it should be strengthened.[16] The point becomes clear by noting the two separate elements which together form the contributory negligence defense. The first is the identification of the plaintiff's conduct which is in fact wrongful. The emphasis here is on the causal element that *contributes* to the harm. In *Melia*, for example, that conduct was the running of a red light. In *Daly*, it was speeding down a freeway and crashing into a guardrail. The second element—the *negligence* part of the defense—is the requirement that the plaintiff who engaged in this wrongful conduct could have avoided the harm by the exercise of reasonable care. Proof of this second element is often trivial, but it is easy to give instances in which it is not. The plaintiff in *Melia*, for example, might have run the red light in order to escape from a gangster who had threatened her life. The plaintiff in *Daly* might have hit the guardrail not because he was drunk, but while hurrying to take a sick child to the hospital.

As contributory negligence involves both causation and a want of reasonable care, it then becomes crucial to ask what becomes of each element in

16. I have made the parallel arguments with respect to the treatment of plaintiff's conduct in nuisance actions. Epstein, *Nuisance Law: Corrective Justice and Its Utilitarian Constraints*, 8 J. Legal Stud. 49, 70-72 (1979).

the application of symmetry principles to a strict liability cause of action. The shift from negligence to strict liability strengthens the prima facie case; it does not insulate the defendant from all liability. So too a shift from contributory negligence to contributory causation should make the plaintiff's conduct more central to the disposition of the case. It should not insulate him from all the consequences of his own conduct. Indeed once the strengthened defense is incorporated into the law, the defendant should be able to prevail by showing that the plaintiff did some wrongful conduct, because the plaintiff's possible excuses will all be irrelevant. Under symmetrical principles the plaintiff could not use the gangster chase or the child's sickness as an excuse to escape from the basic defense, which now assumes broader proportions than before.

The basic point is unchanged even if Justice Mosk was right in dwelling on the administrative workability of the defense. The defendant has little or no access to the information about the plaintiff's conduct. The very same problem that motivated the shift to strict liability in dealing with the defendant's conduct works in favor of a shift from contributory causation in dealing with the plaintiff's conduct. "Symmetry" then leads to the elimination of negligence from the affirmative defenses, but not to the elimination of affirmative defenses from the entire lawsuit.

The real question in this entire area, however, is not what symmetry does, but whether there should be any need to satisfy symmetry constraints at all. The crucial point in products liability actions, at least those involving users and consumers of products, is that there is no initial symmetry between the roles of the two parties. Thus, there is no reason to assume that the standards of conduct applicable to the one must perforce be applicable to the other. In the simple food case it is, of course, appropriate to bar the plaintiff only where there is knowledge of the contaminated condition of the product about to be consumed.[17] Yet reasons of symmetry do not allow the plaintiff recovery only when the defendant's employees also had actual knowledge of the particular defect that caused the harm. The same principles apply to other cases. The web of shared expectations may not require the injured party to reach the level of performance expected of a manufacturer. They may make allowances for workers who do not follow every petty workplace rule, every idle statutory regulation, every detailed manufacturer's instruction, no matter how unwise or uncertain. Yet these problems can be handled

17. So Justice Mosk seems to agree. "If a consumer elects to use a product patently defective when other alternatives are available, or to use a product in a manner clearly not intended or foreseeable, he assumes the risk inherent in his improper utilization and should not be heard to complain about the condition of the object." *Daly v. General Motors Corp.*, 20 Cal. 3d 725, 763, 575 P.2d 1162, 1185, 144 Cal. Rptr. 380, 403 (1978). Although the remark was made in connection with a power saw used to trim fingernails, it applies equally well to the food cases.

as in other contexts: thus the contributory negligence provisions of the Restatement set out a workable set of excuses that can override the contributory negligence defense.[18] They do not, by any stretch of the imagination, require the abandonment of the defense in its entirety. Traditional tort principles require that some plaintiff's conduct be excused, and they allow a wide variation in the exact standards for such excusable conduct.

Before turning to other aspects of Justice Mosk's opinion, it is useful to consider another conceptual rationale that from time to time has been used to justify the abrogation of contributory negligence in product liability cases: the duty of the defendant is to guard the plaintiff against his own negligence, which cannot, as if by definition, serve as an independent affirmative defense. The basic argument was perhaps most forcefully set out by Justice Proctor in *Bexiga v. Havir Manufacturing Corp.*[19] In that case, the plaintiff, an eighteen-year-old youth on his first day of work, had his hand caught and smashed in a punch press manufactured by the defendant. The press was equipped with a foot treadle and was without any special hand safety guards. The court first decided that the plaintiff could make out a design defect case even though the defendant had followed the standard industry practice that called for the press purchaser to install whatever safety devices it regarded as suitable for its own particular end use. It then turned to the contributory negligence defense, which it rejected in the following words:

> The asserted negligence of plaintiff—placing his hand under the ram while at the same time depressing the foot pedal—was the very eventuality the safety devices were designed to guard against. It would be anomalous to hold that defendant has a duty to install safety devices but that a breach of that duty results in no liability for the very injury that duty was meant to protect against. . . . We hold that under the facts presented . . . the defense of contributory negligence is unavailable.[20]

18. Restatement (Second) of Torts § 288A (1965) sets out the plaintiff's excuses for his breach of statutory obligation as follows:

> (1) An excused violation of a legislative enactment or an administrative regulation is not negligence.
>
> (2) Unless the enactment or regulation is construed not to permit such excuse, its violation is excused when
>
> (a) the violation is reasonable because of the actor's incapacity;
> (b) he neither knows nor should know of the occasion for compliance;
> (c) he is unable after reasonable diligence or care to comply;
> (d) he is confronted by an emergency not due to his own misconduct;
> (e) compliance would involve a greater risk of harm to the actor or to others.

Objection can be taken to the details of this formulation, yet, notwithstanding, there is no reason why these excuses cannot be applied with equal force to the plaintiff's conduct in a products liability situation, whether in a regime of comparative or contributory negligence.

19. 60 N.J. 402, 290 A.2d 281 (1972).

20. Id. at 412, 290 A.2d at 286 (1972).

This passage is subject to two independent lines of criticism. First, the soundness of its conclusion rests upon the soundness of its premise. If the defendant's "duty" in design defect cases requires the protection of the plaintiff from all foreseeable misuses, then it is sensible to maintain that such misconduct by the plaintiff ought not to eliminate that responsibility by the back door. Narrower standards of design defects, however, are not only possible, but preferable. When attention shifts to "normal and proper use," or to the commands of statute or common practice, the particular conclusion reached in *Bexiga* fails along with its underlying premise. To the extent that defendant is *not* obliged to protect the plaintiff against his own misconduct or error, contributory negligence remains a defense. This assumes, of course, that the plaintiff has already surmounted the defect hurdle by showing, for instance, that the defendant's machine was not safe in ordinary use. As both the defendant's product and the plaintiff's conduct jointly cause the plaintiff's injury, it becomes only appropriate to apportion the losses between the parties under the rules applicable to other cases of joint responsibility.

The second criticism quickly follows from the first. One difficulty with the opinion in *Bexiga* (as the last sentence quoted intimates) is that it does not specify the scope of its own application. Ostensibly, the opinion is limited to design defect cases, but it is difficult to see how such a limitation can in fact be defended. Thus, under the argument in *Bexiga*, what reply can be made to the plaintiff in an ordinary traffic accident who says that his misconduct should be excused because the defendant was required to follow the rules of the road in order to protect those (if it matters, foreseeable) persons who might be driving in violation of the highway rules? All the elements of the *Bexiga* rule are there. The plaintiff's conduct is clearly substandard; yet, for that reason alone it is not unforeseeable. With negligence as a bar, a defendant's verdict will negate this duty to this plaintiff, if not to others. Notwithstanding, the contributory negligence rule persists. The defendant's liability in highway accidents may be conditioned upon the plaintiff's normal and proper driving, even when the defendant himself has violated a legal norm. The same conclusion is no less "anomalous" in products liability contexts.

All this is not to say that a total bar is itself just. Comparative negligence (or responsibility) may be in order for all products actions. The scope of these principles will be discussed in greater detail later, but one point is clear now: if the plaintiff's recovery in cases like *Bexiga* is not barred but reduced, then all mention of legal anomaly is misplaced. The defendant properly charged with a design defect—even by today's capacious standards—can *never* escape all liability once causal connection is established. The alleged duty, far from being nullified, remains the source of substantial liability. The arguments of Justice Proctor fare no better in the end than those of

Justice Mosk. There is simply no pure conceptual argument that justifies the total abrogation of contributory negligence in products liability actions.

INCENTIVE ARGUMENTS

In the course of his dissent in *Daly*, Justice Mosk also laid great stress upon the undesirable incentive effects that would be fostered by an acceptance of the contributory negligence defense in liability actions.[21] Although the point must be made with some caution, it seems in broad outline that the incentive arguments do more to support than undermine that defense. The customary justification for contributory negligence is, of couse, that it imposes upon the plaintiff those incentives that encourage cost-effective measures that help prevent his own injuries. The usual response to this argument is that a plaintiff, faced with the possibility of death or serious injuries, need not be subjected to legal sanctions in order to compel his co-operation in the loss-control process. Instead, the argument continues, the powerful incentives should be directed toward the defendant, especially in the products liability context. Defendants are typically business firms, often large, that can and do make the appropriate cost calculations. They can "design out" product error and protect the plaintiff against the hazards of systematic neglect. Plaintiffs are isolated individuals who may not even know the applicable rules governing their own conduct. It is idle to expect them to respond to the indirect pressure created by the manipulation of the liability rules. To the extent that contributory negligence either reduces or eliminates the incentives created by the prima facie case, the argument continues, the law cuts back on one of its own essential missions, that of putting the liability upon the parties best able to make and act upon the appropriate cost-benefit analysis. This argument, it should be stressed, is not wholly without force, yet it is subject to a number of important caveats.

First, there is a danger that the argument could prove too much. Airplane pilots and automobile drivers clearly risk harm to themselves when they inflict harm upon innocent third parties. Yet no one would suggest that we remove all tort sanctions against them because of the dangers they face in their activities. Why then should defenses based upon plaintiff's conduct be removed simply because the plaintiff exposes himself to injury?

Second, there is good reason to believe that many individuals will respond to the additional incentives even if faced with the possibility of personal loss. They will, in all likelihood, respond to such incentives when faced solely with property damage, especially if tort awards are fixed to make them indifferent between the property destroyed and the cash received on account of its destruction. Likewise, individuals may well respond to legal incentives even where life and limb are placed in peril. The reduction of the speed limits

21. *See* Schwartz, *Contributory and Comparative Negligence: A Reappraisal*, 87 Yale L. J. 697, 703-21 (1978), for a discussion of the basic issues in this section.

to fifty-five miles an hour is in all likelihood responsible for the sharpest drop in accident rates in the past thirty years,[22] and this is an era featuring both the extensive safety regulations under the National Highway Safety Act and the well-nigh universal adoption of the crashworthiness doctrine.[23] If individual drivers were held adequately in check by fear for their own lives, then it would be ironic to assume that the threat of a small fine, coupled with a possible increase in insurance rates, or the suspension of a license would have much influence upon their behavior. Yet the decline in death rates suggests that the marginal contribution of these additional sanctions has indeed had that effect. What is true of these statutory sanctions may well be true of the private law sanctions as well. Individual parties need not know the refinements of the tort law in order to respond to the milieu that it creates; it is quite sufficient that they know as a crude truth that they will lose all or most of their recovery if they work like fools in the shop or drive like hot-rodders on the highway. The sanctions involved may be contingent in impact and uncertain in extent, but unless all individuals are oblivious to all probabilistic facts, it seems likely that the presence of contributory negligence defenses will have some favorable influence upon their conduct, and through it upon the accident rates. Ignorance is not a fixed fact of nature. If the defense is accepted, the individuals ignorant of it today will surely be informed of it tomorrow, whether it be by a public service announcement about highway safety or from an insistent warning by a union shop steward.

22. The exact effects of the speed limit are difficult to determine because of the wide range of factors that influence the levels of accidents, including amongst others, the number of miles driven, the conditions of the roads, the use of alcohol, and the average age of the driving population. Yet it seems clear that the speed limit, especially when enforced, is a dominant factor. Thus Secretary Coleman of the Department of Transportation has reported:

> We have found that no accurate estimate can be made on the overall safety impact of the 55 mile-per-hour speed limit, but there should be high confidence that a large portion of the reduction in fatalities is due to the direct or indirect benefits of the new 55 mile-per-hour speed limit.

D.O.T. Appropriation Hearings, p. 68. Indeed major reductions in injuries and fatalities were reported between 1973 and 1974 which are in all likelihood attributable to the reduction in the speed limit.

"The flouting of the 55-mile-per-hour speed limit correlates almost exactly to the rising death rate, . . ." Chicago Tribune, April 29, 1979, § 7, at 3, col. 1-2 (quoting Lt. Robert Brandt, a spokesman for the Illinois State Police).

23. For a very skeptical account of the safety benefits of the regulations promulgated under the National Traffic and Motor Vehicle Safety Act of 1966, *see* Pelzman, *The Effects of Automobile Safety Regulations*, 83 J. Political Economy 677 (1975). In essence Pelzman's argument is that any benefits of increased safety regulation may be offset as consumers affected by such regulation change their primary conduct in ways that increase the likelihood of accidents, for example, by traveling at greater speeds in the knowledge that they are less likely to be hurt by an accident because of improved roll-bars. While Pelzman's arguments are directed toward statutory rules, they could be extended to the various tort doctrines, such as crashworthiness. *See* supra ch. 7.

Third, the conduct of private parties (to the extent that it has not been rendered futile by judicial regulation) also points to the importance of the contributory negligence defense in products liability actions brought by product users and consumers. It is commonly accepted (especially by critics of the marketplace) that, in the absence of judicial regulation, most manufacturers would require, and most consumers would accept, rules that barred misbehaving plaintiffs. As with virtually all terms between buyer and seller, there is every reason to believe that the durable distribution of risks between manufacturers and their customers represents the efficient distribution of risks between the two parties.[24] These restrictions upon recovery might be motivated in part by a commendable desire to reduce the administrative costs associated with accidents. They can also be interpreted as a market judgment that the incentives of a contributory negligence defense are worth preserving. The ultimate economic question is, of course, whether the incentives that are removed from the defendant are replaced by equal or more insistent incentives upon the plaintiff. While the result may vary from case to case and product to product, the perceived behavior of the interested parties creates a strong presumption that the incentive properties of affirmative defenses are indeed preferable to those under some alternative regime.

Fourth, the practical aspects of products liability litigation point in the same direction as the theory. The distinctive feature of these products liability actions is that the plaintiff is uniquely in the better position to prevent the harm. He typically has possession and control over the product at the time of its use and has information about the immediate environment in which it operates. The traditional negligence law allows these spatial and temporal priorities to work for the plaintiff when the defendant had "the last clear chance" to prevent harm. Recognition of the contributory negligence defense in products cases could also show the importance of the "proximate" in theories of proximate cause and ultimate tort liability in yet another context. The operator or user of a product, as in *Melia*, certainly had clear and effective means to avoid the harms in question. Incentives directed toward the elimination of their foolish conduct should not be dismissed as unnecessary or unworkable, even in a regime that seeks to create strong incentives upon manufacturers.

Fifth, the implied premise of this discussion of contributory negligence is that the rest of products liability law has already set into motion a set of ideal incentives for the control and regulation of the defendant's conduct, such that the recognition of any form of contributory negligence can only "dilute" the incentives placed upon the manufacturer "by elevating the conduct of the wounded consumer to equal significance." Yet, all is not well in the basic products liability cause of action, particularly with cases involving challenges to product warnings and design. If the incentives created

24. I develop this theme in Epstein, *Unconscionability: A Critical Reappraisal*, 18 J. L. & Econ. 293 (1975).

in these areas are indeed both perverse and undesirable, then a strong set of contributory negligence defenses has a desirable tendency to correct the imperfections that have crept into other portions of the law. The offset will be far from perfect because the contributory negligence defense will apply with equal force to the strongest construction defect case and the weakest design defect case. The guess here is that the contributory negligence defense is of greatest importance where a product is alleged defective because of its inability to prevent injuries resulting from "foreseeable misuse" or "open and obvious" defects. As these cases tend to give rise to the most strained interpretation of the defect question, it seems reasonable to believe that the contributory negligence defense will come into play precisely in those cases in which it is most needed.

The incentive arguments of Justice Mosk, then, are not without their strength, but the arguments that can be marshaled on the other side seem to have greater merit. As is so often the case with incentive arguments, the results are inconclusive without empirical evidence, and the empirical evidence that is required is, only because of the difficulty of the subject matter, never forthcoming. The original fairness arguments, as reinforced in this section, still control.

## CAUSATION AND APPORTIONMENT

The passage quoted from Justice Mosk in *Daly* requires consideration not only of the abstract arguments that can be arrayed for and against the contributory negligence defense. That passage also, if the defense is accepted, directs attention to the complicated set of causal issues spawned by the defense, and it requires some examination as to the proper *effect* of contributory negligence within the products liability context: that is, should it function as a complete defense, or only as a source of reduction of damages? We consider these two issues in turn.

### *Causal Complications*

As a matter of general tort principle, the plaintiff's misconduct is of no consequence to his lawsuit unless it can somehow be linked with the harm that he has suffered. The defendant's truck, while on a highway overpass, veers out of control because of a product defect. It crashes through the guardrail and crushes the plaintiff's car, which is speeding on the highway below.[25] The plaintiff's conduct, even if causally relevant to highway accidents with oncoming vehicles, is of no consequence here, because the plaintiff could have been exposed to the same harm in precisely the same manner even while traveling within the speed limit. The plaintiff had a right to be where he was on the highway, and his speeding did not hinder his ability to

25. Such cases are not unheard of. *See, e.g., Siegler v. Kuhlman*, 81 Wash. 2d 448, 502 P.2d 1181 (1972).

take any evasive action. This misconduct, though admitted negligence, does not bar the plaintiff's action against the owner or driver of the truck. By the same logic it cannot bar the action against the manufacturer, who stands in the same position as the other defendants, once the original defect and its causal connection to the ultimate harm is established. Whether the result in this case is reached on proximate cause grounds or on grounds that the harm suffered did not "fall within the risk" is of no moment.[26] So long as the relief itself is secure in typical torts actions, it remains secure against a products liability defendant.

In other cases, the causal issues require more specific treatment. In his dissent in *Daly*, Justice Mosk noted the case of the man who goes fifty-six miles per hour in the fifty-five-mile-per-hour zone. Although his conduct violates the basic duty, the causal elements may undercut the defendant's effort to convert this breach of duty into a viable defense. In some rare cases, it may well be that just the one extra mile of speed prevented the plaintiff from avoiding the crash. In most cases, however, there is little reason to think that any such small deviation from the speed limit could have the massive effects that a defendant would like to attribute to it. The plaintiff who concedes speeding and argues causation has every reason to expect and achieve success.

We can go further. In some special products liability contexts the speed limits have no relevance at all. Thus suppose that, instead of a crashworthiness case, we have a run-of-the-mill construction defect mishap in a car traveling on a straight residential street at forty miles per hour when the local speed limit is but fifteen. If the engine falls out of the front of the car, it makes no difference to the products liability action that the plaintiff could—and should—get a speeding ticket. The plaintiff could have driven the car at forty miles an hour on the open highway and recovered in full. The fact that the accident took place on the residential street tells us nothing about the stresses and strains to which the automobile is properly subjected. Complicated cases might arise where a car is driven seventy-five miles an hour on a curvy highway but, lest these dominate our thinking, it is important to recall that in *Daly* the facts were far removed from this theoretical balance point: the accident took place in the early hours of the morning when the decedent, while under the influence of alcohol, crashed into the guardrail on the freeway after losing control of his speeding automobile. The abuse of contributory negligence may be a problem of the future, but *Daly* furnishes no support for the proposition that it is a problem today. Yet

26. For the classical exposition of this theory, which in effect argues that causal connection is established in a way sufficient to impose liability only where the injury in question was of the type which first made the defendant's conduct culpable, *see* L. Green, *A Rationale of Proximate Cause* 40-41 (1927). For a critique, see H. L. A. Hart & A. M. Honore, *Causation in the Law* (1959), esp. ch. 9.

the importance of the defense for the basic structure of the tort law is so great that it would be a grave mistake to eliminate the defense entirely, solely as a dubious prophylactic measure.

A second set of causal complications in many products liability actions concerns the matter of causal segregation. The plaintiff in a construction defect accident suffers $100,000 worth of injuries, half of which could have been prevented by proper use of a seatbelt, in a jurisdiction that generally recognizes the seatbelt defense. Even when contributory negligence functions as a total bar, it provides but a partial defense in the case at hand; for $50,000 of harm is, on any theory, solely attributable to the defendant's wrong.

### *Automatic Apportionment*

Once it is established that the *wrongful* conduct (be it under strict liability or negligence) of both the plaintiff and defendant has jointly brought about the harm in question, the issue is how to apportion loss between them. Recent tort law has in one of its more startling innovations transformed contributory negligence from a complete bar to the source of reduction in the plaintiff's recovery: that is, comparative negligence. The earlier law regarded the administrative complications of apportioning losses as so great that courts should not burden their own facilities to aid a plaintiff who, after all, was as responsible for his own harm as the defendant.[27] The modern position on the issue downplays these administrative complications and assumes, if only as a matter of basic fairness, that an apportionment of damages is the legal corollary of joint causation. The tension between the two views of negligence runs the full length and breadth of the tort law, and it clearly applies to the products liability actions that involve the ordinary forms of contributory negligence. What should be done?

As an initial point, the debate over apportionment in products liability cases is limited by the conclusions reached in other tort contexts. Consider, for example, an action brought against both the operator of a heavy truck and its manufacturer. Where the matter concerns the conduct of the injured plaintiff, it seems difficult and unwise to have one rule for the operator and quite another for the manufacturer. This distinction *looks* unprincipled, and the use of separate rules can only complicate whatever adjustments amongst defendants are appropriate by way of contribution and indemnity. Products liability raises no distinctive apportionment issues.

The consensus of opinion today is that the "pure form" of comparative negligence best adjusts the competing equities between plaintiffs and defendants. The great advantage of this position is that it removes the possibility that any small shifts in the relative responsibility between plaintiff and

27. For a statement of this view, *see* C. F. Beach, Jr., *Contributory Negligence* 11-12 (1st ed. 1885).

defendant will have vast consequences upon the distribution of losses between them. A form of comparative negligence that permits the plaintiff to recover when found "forty-nine" percent negligent, but that bars recovery at "fifty" percent negligence places an incredible strain upon the legal system. The slightest re-evaluation of the negligence of either party can result in enormous shifts in the amount of the award.[28] The pure comparative negligence system eliminates any sharp discontinuity at the margin. In a $100,000 case, the plaintiff who is 51 percent negligent recovers $49,000. A 2 percent swing in negligence cannot result in a $100,000 swing in potential recovery.

In spite of this desirable characteristic, there are still strong objections to the pure comparative negligence system, both generally and in products liability contexts. In products cases it is often said that the formula will not work because it is impossible to compare the negligence of the plaintiff with the "strict" wrong of the defendant.[29] The argument is of little merit, and indeed leads to a delicious irony. The plaintiff brings a strict liability action to which there is a possible contributory negligence defense. Should the law insist upon a rule that induces the defendant, perhaps under the banner of negligence per se, to insist upon his own negligence in order to reduce the damages that must be paid the plaintiff? Should the law tolerate a distinction whereby the defense is inapplicable to strict liability actions for want of proper warnings or design, but not to their rough negligence equivalents that so often appear in the reports? Even if we leave these points aside, the difficulties of comparison between plaintiff's and defendant's wrongs persist even in a system of pure negligence or pure strict liability, i.e., comparative responsibility. The plaintiff may bring an action for defective design and be met with the failure to follow customary work rules. The defendant may be sued on a construction defect theory, to which a defense of statutory breach or unreasonable assumption of risk is raised. The cases are shot through with such incommensurables, as *Melia* itself indicates. The marriage of contributory negligence and strict liability adds another layer of confusion to the basic inquiry, but the system itself is beset with difficulties that antedate and overwhelm this "apples and oranges" objection.

The real source of difficulty arises even if we assume that the same standard

28. It should be noted, however, that the problems in practice may not be as acute as they are in theory, if only because so many cases are settled before trial. Where settlement takes place, the uncertainty over the percentage of plaintiff's responsibility is only one of many issues on which doubt can arise, and it is possible that the net effect of this rule on the day-to-day administration of justice is simply to reduce the settlement value of the plaintiff's case by some small degree. In any event it is interesting to note that the consensus has been clouded by the recent West Virginia decision that, as a common law matter, treats plaintiff's negligence as a bar only if it exceeds the defendant's. *See Bradley v. Appalachian Power Co.*, _____ W. Va. _____, 256 S.E. 2d 879 (1979).

29. *See, e.g., Daly v. General Motors Corp.*, 20 Cal. 3d 725, 575 P.2d 1162, 144 Cal. Rptr. 380 (1978) (Jefferson, J. concurring and dissenting; Mosk, J. dissenting).

of judgment may be brought to bear on both plaintiff's and defendant's conduct. The basic inquiry is, how does one generate *any* set of percentages about plaintiff's and defendant's responsibility from the raw data about their conduct, or their product? Whether we speak of negligence or strict liability, both parties are partly responsible for the loss in question. The defendant could not have harmed the plaintiff without the plaintiff's own cooperation; the plaintiff would not be harmed if the defendant's product was free of defect. Within this framework there is nothing about the particular pattern of factual information, even if perfectly known, that demands any unique set of percentages in any given case. All allocation of responsibility between the two parties is arbitrary, whether by a judge or by jury, whether by hunch or by computer. The claims of individual fairness are ill served by the pretense that legal principles have a degree of precision that they do not in fact possess. The economic incentives upon the parties are hardly sharpened by any shift from a fifty-fifty to a sixty-forty split. The necessary case-by-case determinations are both expensive and pointless. They may flatter the legal mind, but they do not advance the orderly administration of justice. If individual determinations must fail, then it is surely best to have a collective decision about the distribution of loss that extends to all cases of joint responsibility. The only way that such a collective decision can be made is by a fixed judicial or legislative rule that is less concerned with the false pursuit of perfect equity in the individual case and more concerned with the reduction of administrative costs and the introduction of a measure of certainty and predictability into the system.

In this connection, the best approach is still that of the older admiralty cases, however great their disrepute today.[30] Once it is settled that certain harms are jointly caused by two parties, then the loss should be apportioned between them under some fixed formula, probably one that reduces recovery for the jointly caused harms by, for example, 50 percent. The number is by no means perfect, but nothing about the facts of any particular case allows further principled refinements. *United States v. Reliable Transfer Co.*,[31] the very case which overturned the old admiralty rule, involved a ship grounding that occurred when the captain tried improperly to turn a vessel around in a narrow waterway after the Coast Guard had failed to mark the correct channel with the proper light buoy. The traditional rule required a fifty-fifty split, but only for those losses which could have been avoided by proper navigation and the proper light buoys. The court approved a division of seventy-five-twenty-five in favor of the Coast Guard, presumably under the theory that one party was "more" actively negligent than the other. In

30. For the American judicial origins of the rule, *see The Schooner Catharine v. Dickinson*, 58 U.S. (17 How.) 170 (1854). The rule was extensively criticized in G. Gilmore & C. Black, *The Law of Admiralty* 402-04 (2d ed. 1975).

31. 421 U.S. 397 (1975).

this situation, however, the relative degrees of the two negligences escape calculation. There is not only the long tradition that negligence never functions as a matter of degree,[32] there is also the admitted fact that if either party alone had caused the loss, its negligence, whether slight or great, would fasten the whole loss upon it. If the conduct of each party can hold it accountable for the full loss, then it can do so for *any* portion of it.

The artificiality of the *Reliable Transfer* solution of pure apportionment is heightened, moreover, when we consider the parallel apportionment problems in products liability cases. The negligence of the plaintiff is always closer to the injury than the wrong of defendant. The plaintiff's wrong is often active in nature, while the defendant's wrongful conduct may be only the failure to protect the plaintiff from himself. Yet cases may assign the greater weight of the loss to the defendant, on what must often be implicit "deep pocket" grounds. The possibilities for abuse are clearly evident in circumstances in which an honest person could not decide upon the proper division of losses with the criteria available for judgment. Flexible percentages, even if not misused, do not help one whit. The old contributory rule was unjust, if at all, only because of its "all-or-nothing" character. The pure comparative negligence rule avoids the all-or-nothing approach, but only at the cost of a ruinous excursion into the never-never land of flexible percentages. The fixed apportionment rule escapes the vice of the old contributory negligence rule while avoiding the routine but fruitless pursuit for illusory percentages. The rejection of the absolute bar of contributory negligence leads not to pure comparative negligence, but to automatic division. Those who think that further refinement is possible have not indicated how it can be achieved.

### *Multiple Parties*

The major problem in this area does not arise in two party suits, but in those frequent cases in which the injured party joins several defendants, each of which is arguably partially responsible for the loss. These cases create no particular problem under a contributory negligence rule because the absolute bar against the plaintiff operates for the benefit of each separate defendant. Matters are not so simple, however, under an automatic apportionment rule, for the question arises as to what principles should guide the automatic division among three or more parties.

32. Thus the famous *bon mot* of Baron Rolfe that gross negligence was the same thing as ordinary negligence "with the addition of a vituperative epithet." *Wilson v. Brett*, 152 Eng. Rep. 737 (Ex. 1843). The point may well be wrong with respect to this distinction. Yet, even if we can make functional the difference between ordinary and gross negligence, it by no means follows that we can measure the percentages of negligence causally responsible for some given harm.

The most cautious would apply the rules of automatic apportionment amongst the defendants as a class, leaving the determination of the plaintiff's percentage of the total loss to the flexible percentages in use today. Yet such a proposal is inconsistent with the notion of fixed percentages in the two-party case; and it creates an enormous discontinuity if a fifty-fifty division is imposed in two-party cases while flexible percentages are applicable to plaintiff's conduct in multiple party cases. The adding or dismissing of a party from litigation could have enormous strategic consequences that bear no relationship to the merits of the claim against the additional party.[33] As products liability actions often involve multiple-party situations, the benefits of the automatic rule will be severely circumscribed if limited to two-party cases.

Assuming that fixed rules are carried over to multiple-party cases, two possible rules of apportionment suggest themselves. By the first, some fixed percentage of the loss will be kept upon the plaintiff regardless of the number of defendants brought into the case. The advantage of this rule is that it removes any incentive from the plaintiff to increase the number of defendants in order to decrease his portion of the load. Yet this advantage is illusory and in any event appears to come at too high a cost. In the first place, the rule in question could only work if those defendants sued by the plaintiff were not allowed to bring further defendants into the case, even in situations where these additional parties bore the brunt of the responsibility. Even if this costly prohibition were granted, however, nothing could prevent a defendant from persuading the plaintiff to bring direct actions against these parties, especially if they, and not the original defendants, are solely responsible for the harm in question. A plaintiff will be faced with extensive costs of suit no matter what the rule on multiple parties. Artificial limitations on joinder seem both unwanted and unwarranted.

It seems, therefore, that the only possible rule is one that uniformly divides the loss by the number of responsible parties to the case. Where there are "n" parties, the plaintiff must keep 1/nth of the loss. To this rule there should be added an immediate qualification for an unfortunate "double counting" will arise if certain defendants are treated as separate entities in apportioning loss. In the products liability context, it is often common for the plaintiff to join both the manufacturer and retailer of a defective product. There is little to commend a rule which drops the significance of plaintiff's misconduct from a half to a third solely because of a redundant defendant, the retailer, who has in all likelihood an indemnity action against the manu-

33. One way to escape this discontinuity is to apply the pure comparative negligence rules to all cases between plaintiffs and defendants and then to use automatic apportionment among the defendants. Such a proposal in no way reduces the recovery of the plaintiff and benefits all defendants as a class by reducing the administrative costs of defending a products liability suit.

facturer.[34] All those parties who are held, whether directly or vicariously, for a single product defect should be treated as one party for the purpose of the rules. The division of responsibility amongst themselves for their share will be determined as if they were the only defendants in the case. Typically, therefore, the manufacturer will bear the full brunt of the loss, and the retailer will have to step into his shoes only if the manufacturer is insolvent or beyond the jurisdiction. The use of these apportionment rules does not, of course, do anything to abrogate the general rules on joint and several liability. If any single defendant (or group of defendants) is unable to pay its portion of the loss, then it will be borne pro rata by all other responsible parties, including, of course, the plaintiff.

The one remaining set of problems arises when the plaintiff settles with one or more of the defendants in advance of the trial. Upon plaintiff's recovery at trial, it is necessary to determine first, the effect of the plaintiff's settlement upon the amount of recovery against the remaining defendants, and second, the various rights of indemnity and contribution between settling and nonsettling codefendants. On the first of these questions, it is possible to adopt two courses of action. One approach is simply to treat the plaintiff as though he has recovered his pro rata portion of the damages from the settling defendant, no matter what the actual level of settlement.[35] A $100,000 case brought by a negligent plaintiff against four defendants, would, with the automatic 20 percent setoff, yield $20,000 from each of three nonsettling defendants, whether his settlement with the fourth defendant was for $5,000 or $150,000. This rule has been condemned because

34. The question of double counting was fairly addressed by the California legislation on the subject, Cal. Code Civ. Proc. §§ 875-879, which was gutted by the California Supreme Court in *American Motorcycle Ass'n v. Superior Court*, 20 Cal. 3d 578, 578 P.2d 899, 146 Cal. Rptr. 182 (1978). Thus section 876(b) reads:

> Where one or more persons are held liable solely for the tort of one of them or of another, as in the case of the liability of a master for the tort of his servant, they shall contribute a single pro rata share, as to which there may be indemnity between them.

While the statute does not direct its attention to the products liability context, the parallel between the master-servant case and the manufacturer-retailer case holds except perhaps where the retailer takes an active part in the preparation of the goods for sale. Indeed the argument for counting retailer and manufacturer as a single party seems especially strong. The master in employment situations has some direct contractual control over his servants so that his liability, though formerly vicarious, is often in fact based upon his primary conduct. Such is not the case with retailer's liability for the manufacturer.

35. This equal distribution was indeed contemplated in Cal. Code Civ. Proc. § 876(a): "The pro rata share of each tort feasor judgment debtor shall be determined by dividing the entire judgment equally among all of them." The California Supreme Court argued that the introduction of pure comparative negligence between plaintiff and defendant rendered the statute in effect obsolete. The position could be reversed, for the statute sets a sensible model for automatic proration amongst defendants that precludes the pure comparative negligence of *Li*. It goes almost without saying that the rules of contribution amongst joint tortfeasors are among the most shapeless of the common law.

it allows the plaintiff to recover an amount *in excess* of his full injuries.[36] Likewise, it abrogates full joint and several liability where the settling defendant escapes for less than his pro rata share. Yet, as both double and partial recovery could occur by settlement alone, it is by no means clear that the point is decisive.

The alternative rule reduces the amount of the damages owing by the amount actually paid in settlement. It avoids the problem of excessive or insufficient recovery, but it creates an incentive for a plaintiff to accept an inferior settlement from one defendant in order to finance suits against the others. The frequency of this occurrence is, however, hard to predict. It is unlikely that a plaintiff will settle cheaply with one defendant against whom he has a strong case in order to pursue the other dubious defendants into the shades of night. In any event, it might well be possible for all defendants to mount a united front against the plaintiff, so that partial settlements with single defendants may be difficult.

The exact merits of the two alternative rules are quite difficult to evaluate. On balance, however, it appears that a rule which reduces recovery by a proportionate share is preferable to one that reduces by the amount paid. Such rule in effect treats each separate defendant as independent of all others. A decision by one defendant to settle will, therefore, neither increase nor decrease the exposure of other defendants. In this case, no plaintiff has an incentive to settle cheaply with any given defendant. The fact of settlement can be introduced, it should be assumed, by other defendants in order to reduce their own proportion of the liability, so the plaintiff cannot recoup his early losses from other defendants. By the same token, the independence of each defendant's liability eliminates any need for allowing any actions between settling and nonsettling defendants. The nonsettling defendant, as is now the case,[37] should in any event be prohibited from bringing suit against a settling defendant, for only then is it possible to have any individual settlement before disposition of the entire case. In addition, given that the exposure of the settling defendant does nothing to decrease the exposure of the remaining defendants, the settling defendant should have no action against the nonsettling defendant who escapes for lesser sums. There are doubtless unforeseen complications that will cause difficulties in the administration of any particular rule; for example, what happens if the injuries become more or less severe after the settlement. These may tip the balance in favor of a rule that sets off only amounts paid from other awards. These complications, however, do not count as an argument against automatic apportionment in multiple-party cases, as they will arise with ever greater fierceness under a pure comparative negligence system. Suits among co-

36. *Jamarillo v. State*, 81 Cal. App. 3d 968, 146 Cal. Rptr. 823 (1978).

37. Such indeed was required by the California statute, Cal. Code Civ. Proc. § 877(b).

defendants (especially under pure comparative principles) have little internal structure or logic; the fewer of them that are seen, the better.

## PRODUCT MISUSE

The discussion of contributory negligence helps shape the analysis of the product misuse issue, as both defenses serve to identify those forms of conduct by the plaintiff that bar or reduce recovery. Indeed, the overlap is so great that a principled distinction between the two types of defenses becomes difficult to draw. The Oklahoma court in *Fields v. Volkswagen of America, Inc.* has, for example, held that the misuse defense covers the use of a product to an improper end, but not its "use for a proper purpose but in a careless manner."[38] This test would bar recovery where an automobile is used as a boat, but not where it is driven at excessive speeds under the influence of alcohol. Such a distinction, even if intelligible, is indefensible in principle, given the soundness of the contributory negligence defense in products liability actions. The principles of redress, economic incentives, and even loss spreading all militate against the suggested distinction between improper means and improper ends.

With this said, it is still necessary to avoid two common errors about product misuse, one which impermissibly restricts and the other which impermissibly broadens the defense. On the one hand it is incorrect to treat the manufacturer's precise intentions, express or implied, as the sole test of product misuse. Hardball bats can be used for softball; (some) chairs can be used for standing; and hair shampoo can get into a consumer's eyes.[39] Yet, bats are not hammers; chairs are not car jacks; and shampoo is not a soft drink. The precise limits of product use and the size of the margin of error about its central core will vary from case to case. This issue, like so many in the law of products liability, will often require individual adjudication. The matter is at bottom one of implied representations and shared expectations about which further precision is not possible.

The recognition that normal and proper product use has some sensible give at the margins should not, however, lead courts to the further conclusion that "abnormal" or improper product use begins only where such is not "foreseeable" by the manufacturer. Standing alone, foresight does not provide the proper limits on liability. It is of course foreseeable that a teenager might drink or sniff glue, but it hardly seems appropriate to excuse him wholly from responsibility for the ensuing brain damage. It is, of course, foreseeable that workers will use machines after they fall into disrepair, but

38. 555 P.2d 48, 56 (Okla. 1976).

39. For an instance of a struggle to maintain the proper balance between the two extremes, *see* Restatement (Second) of Torts, § 395, comments *j* and *k*, which find liability in both these cases.

their conduct is not therefore excusable. No manufacturer could escape the consequences of making defective products by showing that consumers could reasonably foresee the possibility of product defect. The unbounded foresight requirement should not work in reverse to impose such onerous obligations upon manufacturers. There is a vast difference between the foresight of possible harm and the responsibility for harm that has come to pass. Whenever plaintiff's misconduct is at issue, the better cases look both to what the manufacturer can expect and what he has a *right* to expect.[40] Properly understood, the issue of foresight is as much a question of entitlement as it is of prevision.

The last issue in this section concerns the effect of the misuse defense once its elements are established. As a first approximation, the consequences of misuse should be those of ordinary plaintiff's negligence, as the two are but variants of the single theme of plaintiff's misconduct. A jurisdiction that treats contributory negligence as a complete bar should do the same, therefore, with the misuse defense. The matter becomes more difficult, however, in a state that apportions damages in the event of plaintiff's negligence. In some instances misuse, like negligence, invites apportionment, but in others a complete bar seems appropriate on the ground that the plaintiff's product misuse is so enormous that it functions as the sole, superseding cause of injury, even where the original product was itself defective. The defendant makes a rope that should support the weight of five hundred pounds. The plaintiff uses it to lift a five-thousand-pound weight and is injured when the rope breaks under the strain. Is there any reason, given this form of misconduct, to hold the defendant partially responsible for the loss simply because this rope, in consequence of a latent defect, could lift only three hundred and not five hundred pounds? By the same token is apportionment, if generally accepted, inappropriate if the rope is used to lift a six-hundred-pound weight? The overt shift to apportionment will by no means eliminate many of the all-or-nothing issues in products liability cases. So long as the defendant is entitled to deny causal connection, a very delicate set of judgments separates cases in which recovery is totally barred from those in which it is simply reduced. Many modern cases involve products that are allegedly defective because they do not protect or warn the plaintiff against some form of product misuse. With this broad conception of defect firmly in place, running arguments will occur on the question of whether this misuse in this case is a complete bar, a partial bar, or even no bar at all. Some recognition of the misuse issue will help make the overall system workable; total disregard of the misuse issue will plunge the system into massive litigation and uncertainty.

40. *See, e.g.*, the language of the Restatement, § 395, comment *j*. "[i]n the absence of special reason to expect otherwise, the maker is *entitled* to assume that his product will be put to a normal use, for which the product is intended or appropriate." (italics added)

## ASSUMPTION OF RISK

To round out this discussion of plaintiff's conduct, it is necessary to return to the subject of assumption of risk with which this chapter began. Assumption of risk does not imply that the simple knowledge of possible harm completely bars the plaintiff's cause of action. If it did, products liability law would die before it was born, as all apparently sound products are known to be possibly defective. This possible abuse of assumption of risk, however, does not warrant its wholesale judicial abandonment. At the other extreme is the consumer who eats chocolate known to be bad; here assumption of risk is, and should be, decisive. Contributory negligence is not the issue; the conduct may be reasonable, not to say courageous, as part of an experiment to determine the effects of rotten food upon healthy people. And apportionment, however attractive in joint causation cases, is wholly inappropriate here: *all* the risk is assumed, not just some undefined portion of it.

The emphasis upon extreme cases is, however, somewhat overstated, for assumption of risk cases often do turn on reasonableness notions. Consider, for example, *Messick v. General Motors Corp.*[41] Owing to manifold construction defects, the plaintiff had constant trouble controlling the steering of his automobile. The defects were not corrected even after many trips to the dealer. In desperation, the plaintiff then took his car to an independent mechanic who told him that he risked death or serious injury if he continued to drive the car before it was repaired. In the teeth of these warnings the plaintiff used the car to commute to work some two hundred miles per day until he suffered serious bodily injuries.

As an initial matter, it is impossible to deny that the plaintiff did assume the risk of injury when he continued to drive the car. His ignorance of the particular sequence of events causing injury is (save under an unduly crabbed view of the subject) immaterial, given his full knowledge of the nature and source of the perils he chose to run. The real issue is whether the plaintiff can *excuse* his taking of the risk on the ground that the defendant forced him to that unpalatable option by not restoring the car to proper working order.[42] It is this uncertainty over the plaintiff's proper course of conduct when confronted by a wrong solely of defendant's making that qualifies assumption of risk with a "reasonableness" element. On the one hand, a

41. 460 F.2d 485 (5th Cir. 1972). For the analogous provision of the Model Uniform Product Liability Act, *see* § 112 (B) (1).

42. Additional complications arise if we consider the dealer to be a party wholly separate and apart from the manufacturer. On this view since the constraint upon the plaintiff's liberty of action was imposed only by the dealer and not the manufacturer, this excuse might be treated as unavailing against the manufacturer if acceptable against the dealer. For a defense of just this distinction as a matter of general tort theory, *see* Epstein, *Defenses and Subsequent Pleas in a System of Strict Liability*, 3 J. Legal Stud. 165, 192-93 (1974).

jury could conclude that the plaintiff should not use the car and rest content with his contractual action for out-of-pocket costs and lost profits. On the other hand, it could conclude that the plaintiff need not subject himself to the perils of litigation for the benefit of a defendant himself in the wrong. If so, he can continue to use the car. The choice is by no means clear: so much depends upon the extent of the possible danger from using the car and the degree of inconvenience from foregoing its use.

The broader question now is to what extent the issues of implicit coercion found in *Messick* can be raised in every case, given that the original product defect, when known, constrains the plaintiff's conduct. While it is not possible to give a uniform answer, it is possible to identify in broad outline the permissible areas of controversy. Thus, when a consumer eats bad food, the coercion arguments can be easily dismissed. The cash invested in the purchase of the food is trivial, and will usually be refunded by the original seller. With the exception of chocolate bars necessary for survival on a desert island, the massive social institutions for mitigating losses undercut the coercion arguments at every point. The bad food just should not be eaten.

A more difficult set of problems arises in machine tool cases where the plaintiff claims that he is forced to work with equipment known to be dangerous. That claim has great attraction where the plaintiff discovers that his equipment has just failed in midstream when it is awkward, perhaps perilous, to cease work. Yet in the typical work-place case it is far less persuasive to argue that the known defect so circumscribed the plaintiff's freedom of action as to preclude the assumption of risk defense. In *Micallef v. Miehle Co.*,[43] the plaintiff, an employee of Lincoln Graphic Arts, was operating a high-speed photo-offset press manufactured by the defendant. Just before the accident, the plaintiff noticed that a "hickie" (a foreign object) had fallen on the plates where it could ruin or blemish the printed pages. The plaintiff also knew that the press was not equipped with any safety guard at the point where the plate cylinder joined the ink-form roller; and he knew that he could catch his hand at that junction point if he "chased the hickie" without turning off the press. After consulting with his foreman, he did in fact chase the hickie, but from a place where it was impossible for him to reach the press's cut-off switch. He was severely injured when his hand was drawn up into the juncture of the plate and the ink-roller.

The elements of the assumption of risk defense are all present, and the question (assuming for the sake of argument that the machine, as designed, was defective) is whether there are enough indicia of implicit coercion by the defendant to let the jury pass upon the reasonableness of the plaintiff's conduct. The issue can be considered in two separate time frames. Im-

43. 39 N.Y. 2d 376, 348, N.E. 2d 571, 384 N.Y.S. 2d 115 (1976), overruling *Campo v. Scofield*, 301 N.Y. 468, 95 N.E. 2d 802 (1950), which had made out a strong case for the open and obvious rule.

mediately before the accident the claim of coercion is difficult to make, given the number of options open to the plaintiff. For one thing he might have requested the foreman to shut down the machine in order to make it easy to chase the hickie. If that course of conduct proved infeasible because of the lost production time involved, someone else could have manned the cut-off switch when the plaintiff positioned himself on the far side of the machine. While in some plants the employers may take a very hard-nosed attitude toward their workers, no evidence was presented here of any probable retaliation against the plaintiff if he had made that simple request for assistance.[44]

The case against implicit coercion by the manufacturer becomes even stronger if the time frame of decision is shifted further back. The defect was open and obvious, and the plaintiff knew about the hazards when he began employment and at all times thereafter. If he was unsatisfied with the conditions of labor, he might have chosen to work elsewhere. The defendant did not make him use the press. The fact that he chose to work suggests that he accepted the risks that were routinely incident to his employment in order to obtain the financial and other benefits of that employment. The various economic pressures of the labor market do not stem from the defendant manufacturer, but from the employers with whom the plaintiff does or might do business. The workers' compensation laws and the labor laws were designed to respond to those pressures, and there is no reason to modify the products liability law to make manufacturers responsible for the possible sins of employers. While there are cases in which a known defective product is one of several effective constraints placed upon the injured party, such is not the usual case. The facts in *Messick* may have rightly presented a jury question, but those in *Micallef* warranted a directed verdict for the defendant manufacturer.

### OPEN AND OBVIOUS CONDITIONS

The previous discussion was directed to situations where the plaintiff consciously and deliberately encounters a known defective condition created by the defendant. The "objective" parallel to assumption of risk bars the plaintiff's action upon encountering an open and obvious product defect, even in the absence of subjective knowledge of its dangers. The open and obvious rule functions as a workable and reliable surrogate for the assumption of risk defense which, because of its intimate connection with subjective states, is difficult to establish by reliable evidence. The removal of the subjective element not only saves costs, but it probably reduces overall error, as there are in all likelihood few cases in which an obvious risk about

44. Indeed in many situations union work rules are designed to protect workers against precisely this form of abuse. For an instance of such rules, *see Gyerman v. United States Lines Co.*, 7 Cal. 3d 488, 498 P.2d 1043, 102 Cal. Rptr. 795 (1972).

a certain product remains unknown to the person using it.[45] The traditional cases accepted the absolute status of the hard-edged open and obvious defense. The modern cases, in a major shift in orientation, tend to view the openness of the hazard as one of many features bearing upon both the reasonableness of the product design and of the plaintiff's conduct. *Micallef*, for example, endorses just this view. The question is which of these views is preferable, and this in turn rests upon the view not only of the assumption of risk defense, but also of the account of product defect.

As will be recalled, the earlier chapters isolated three possible accounts of product defect. The first emphasized the way in which the product expressly or impliedly represented itself to the user or consumer, with the defendant being held responsible only for gaps between promise and performance. The second account of product defect looked not only to the implied representations of the individual defendant, but to the web of obligations imposed upon any given defendant, both by statute and by industry custom. The third and broadest account of product defect in effect allowed the jury, by comparing relevant costs and benefits, to decide whether a product was reasonably safe or unreasonably dangerous.

Now the reception of the open and obvious rule depends upon the preferred account of product defect.[46] Where the emphasis is upon product representations, the open and obvious defense should retain its absolute status. The open and obvious nature of the condition undercuts any possible misrepresentation and with it any claim of defect. The plaintiff must lose, not so much because there is a good assumption of risk defense, but because there is no good prima facie case. By an implied-in-fact contract the manufacturer states the obvious product risks, which the user then assumes by dealing with the product with full knowledge of its condition. Freedom of contract thus extends to implicit as well as explicit bargains.

This mode of argument is not, however, decisive under the two other possible definitions of product defect. Statute and common practice limit the freedom of contract that would otherwise prevail in certain products liability cases. That restraint upon contract could not succeed if the coercive effect of public intervention were limited only to the basic cause of action: the law which allows a contractual defense to a regulatory cause of action is

45. One clear exception to the open and obvious rule covers those cases in which the defect, however obvious to one who might normally be in the position to encounter it consciously, is not obvious to a particular plaintiff who quite literally falls into the defect in question. *See, e.g., Luque v. McLean*, 8 Cal. 3d 136, 501 P.2d 1163, 104 Cal. Rptr. 443 (1972), where the plaintiff's hand slipped through an unguarded hole in the front of a lawnmower and was caught in the revolving rotary blade of the mower, after plaintiff slipped and fell while trying to remove an obstacle in front of the machine without first turning it off. While the open and obvious defect defense is not a surrogate assumption of risk in this context, the contributory negligence defense might well be available on the facts.

46. For the parallel discussion in connection with design defects, see ch. 7, supra.

in the end contractual. In a system that vacillates uneasily between the first and second accounts of product defect, the open and obvious rule will retain a great deal of sway, limited only in those cases in which either custom or statute renders illegal open and obvious conditions. Where the more expansive view of design defect and the duty to warn prevail, the defense will have little independent importance, and jury issues will predominate. The broad account of product defect anticipates the open and obvious defense and demands its limitation. The previous chapters have set out the case for caution in both design and warning cases, and little more can be done to strengthen that case here. The question in all these cases is *not* whether the plaintiff has in fact assumed the risk; he has. The question is whether he is *allowed* to assume that risk, and that is not a question of fact but a broad question of policy. Whether we speak of product defect or assumption of risk, whether in an objective or subjective form, the central issue in products liability again becomes one of private choice or public control.

### ASSUMPTION OF RISK BY CONTRACT

It is generally agreed that a plaintiff may assume by express contract the risk of certain types of injuries, even in the absence of knowledge of a specific product defect. Such assumption of risk may be vitiated by fraud, duress, incapacity, or undue influence but, subject to those exceptions, the classical common law respected those contracts as much as others not directed toward risk to life and limb. If express assumption of risk has a legitimate contractual basis, then so too has assumption of risk by an implied-in-fact contract. The use of implied-in-fact contracts always poses grave dangers, for their unwarranted extension can obliterate much of products liability law, given the ever-present knowledge of possible latent defects. Yet, even when these abuses are recognized, it is possible to identify certain well-defined situations where this implicit contractual defense does and should govern, even in a system that accepts the basic strict liability cause of action for defective products. Three illustrative cases involve (1) injury from trichinae-infested pork, (2) hepatitis contracted from blood transfusions, and (3) harms caused by unknowable and undiscoverable generic defects in drugs or, for that matter, similar products such as prosthetic devices.

### *Pork and Trichinae*

In *Scheller v. Wilson Certified Foods, Inc.*,[47] the plaintiff husband became ill with trichinosis and his wife died of the disease after they had eaten "smoked butt" pork that had been processed by and purchased from the defendant Stanley, a local meat processor-retailer. The action against

47. 114 Ariz. 159, 559 P.2d 1074 (1977).

Wilson, the original wholesaler, was brought on a theory of strict liability, with the plaintiff arguing that the pork was impliedly warranted by Wilson as fit for human consumption. The Arizona Court of Appeal dismissed the cause of action, holding in effect that the diseased pork was not an "unreasonably dangerous" product within the meaning of Restatement (Second) of Torts, Section 402A.

The decision in the case is clearly correct but not for the reason given. Diseased pork is very dangerous; it falls within the narrowest definition of product defect, as does soup with botulism. Indeed, it is only on this view of the case that the action can proceed against Stanley, who was required to kill the larvae by properly heating the meat. The decisive point is, therefore, not that of product defect, it is assumption of risk: a common precaution, cooking the meat once, was understood by all the parties to fall on Stanley. The court struck this theme when it noted that the pork was not "unreasonably dangerous" because it "was sold by Wilson, and purchased by both Stanley and the plaintiff, with the understanding by all concerned that it was to be properly cooked before it was consumed."[48] That contract point should end the discussion. The plaintiffs could not prevail on a duty to warn theory because the hazard, one of common knowledge, was known to them. And an "implied warranty" theory—the opposite side of "implied assumption of risk"—is also improper in this context because it defies the shared understandings alluded to by the court. The inescapable motif of the case remains assumption of risk, if not by express agreement, then by universal custom.

### *Hepatitis*

The tension between implied warranty and implied assumption of risk is also illustrated by actions brought for hepatitis caused by blood transfusions.[49] Until several years ago, transfused blood, even when obtained from the best of sources, presented substantial risk of infecting its recipient with hepatitis. As the blood in question was often used during or after surgery, the consequences of the disease were frequently debilitating and sometimes fatal. The past few years have produced new tests for finding the hepatitis virus, but while their standard use has substantially reduced the risk of the disease, the risk has not been eliminated altogether. The question is whether the plaintiff who gets hepatitis can shift the loss to other parties in the chain of distribution, usually the hospital or blood bank in question.

A duty to warn cause of action promises the plaintiff little by way of relief because the risks involved are known generally and are routinely

48. Id. at 162, 559 P.2d at 1077.

49. The literature on the hepatitis problem is immense. *See, e.g.*, Franklin, *Tort Liability for Hepatitis: An Analysis and a Proposal*, 24 Stan. L. Rev. 439 (1972); Kessel, *Transfused Blood, Serum Hepatitis, and The Coase Theorem*, 17 J. Law & Econ. 265 (1974).

explained to patients by physicians in advance of any transfusion. An implied warranty theory bottomed upon strict liability principles is thus a possible ground for recovery, but it can, given the web of shared understandings about risk, be maintained only under a clear preference for regulation over contract. The source of the risk in hepatitis is very different from that with trichinae, as the latter involves easily preventable risks, and the former involves risks better described as unavoidable. Yet what is crucial is not the factual patterns giving rise to the risk, but the uniform patterns of response to those risks. The implied assumption of risk is factual; the implied warranty of fitness is fictional, whatever it soundness elsewhere.

As is so often the case, the contractual arguments are more powerful than the regulatory ones. The implied warranty theory has been justified on the grounds that it will help spread the risk,[50] but this argument ignores the spreading of risks over a broader class of individuals through health, disability, or workers' compensation insurance. The principle has also been justified on familiar incentive grounds. Yet, this argument ignores the large market incentives available to any party who develops any reliable and cost-effective measure for the detection of hepatitic blood; it also ignores the possible shortages of blood if the new rule renders blood unavailable; and it ignores, too, the desirable incentive effects of limited liability, which induce patients to investigate other forms of care and treatment. What is more, implied warranty arguments tend to overlook or underestimate the administrative costs necessary to make out the full cause of action, a real concern when it is necessary to identify (where multiple transfusions are given)[51] *which* blood contained the hepatitis virus and to isolate that portion of the damages attributable to it for a person already in ill health. The legislative response, which in most cases fixed liability under a negligence standard, was closer to the original shared set of expectations, especially where negligence referred not to cost-benefit principles but to common practice.[52] The new medical tests, however, have oddly strengthened the case for strict liability, for with technological changes, undiscovered hepatitis virus in blood comes to resemble closely the undiscovered stone in a jar of peanuts. Yet in the absence of any real pressure upon the rules, it still seems that the problems of establishing cause in fact and damages, more acute here than in traumatic injury cases, justify this continued limitation of liability. Those suppliers who choose to warrant expressly the condition of their blood

50. *See, e.g., Brody v. Overlook Hospital*, 121 N.J. Super. 299, 296 A. 2d 668 (1972), *reversed on appeal*, 127 N.J. Super. 331, 317 A.2d 392 (App. Div. 1974), *aff'd per curiam*, 66 N.J. 448, 332 A.2d 596 (1975).

51. *See*, infra ch. 10.

52. For a compilation of the statutes, *see* Note, 24 Vand. L. Rev. 645, 649-50 (1971); Franklin, supra note 49, at 474-75.

products are, after all, free to do so, and to charge for the additional protection provided.

*Unknowable and Undiscoverable Hazards*

One exceptionally difficult challenge to the principles of implied-in-fact assumption of risk comes from cases in which drugs (and some other products) turn out upon prolonged use to present hazards that were unknowable and undiscoverable at the time they were first marketed. What is involved here, of course, is not some miscarriage of preparation or inspection, but harm from the very *generic* properties of the drug which were thought to be, and which may in fact have been, essential to the original usefulness of the product. Strict liability principles rightly govern the risks of formulation and preparation, but with respect to these generic risks, the general caution of the Restatement and the case law seems well founded.[53] Strict liability works well whenever the defendant can, with sensible inspection and testing, control and limit the incidence of product hazards. In this context, the rule channels resources to compensation, and away from the question of how much inspection was appropriate.

Strict liability assumes, however, a very different aspect with respect to unknowable and undiscoverable hazards, for now the implied distribution of risks cuts in precisely the opposite direction. The number of cases in which the undiscoverable defect is apt to cause damage may well be huge, and these cases will usually occur, as allegedly is the case with diethylstilbestrol (D.E.S.), years after the drug was placed on the market. The problems of proof raised on all collateral issues (for example, did plaintiff take defendant's drug; what warnings were given) are apt to be severe, if only because of the immensity of the distances in both space and time. The massive financial burden that these cases could impose can deter the development of other drugs which, in spite of the ever-present possibility of undetected hazards, may well prove beneficial in both the long and the short run. Consumers are as a group better off if they absorb certain losses in the hope of reaping greater gains; and there is no doubt that such risks would be assumed by them.

The point here is not that all the risks of undisclosed defects should be shifted to the consumers. Rather, some effort must be made to identify those instances in which the risk should be shifted from those in which it should not. It is possible, of course, to shift the risk to the manufacturer whenever the expected benefits of further testing and research exceed the costs that they entail. That cost benefit analysis is, however, unworkable even with simple construction defects; there is little reason to think that it

53. *See* Restatement (Second) of Torts § 402A, comment *k*, which represents a partial, although fully justified retreat from the strict liability principle announced in § 402A itself.

can be applied in a responsible fashion to the vast multidimensioned inquiries that are the norm in drug cases. The sensible approach in this area is to hold the defendant responsible whenever research was not in conformity with the high (if not excessive) standards for drug research imposed by the Food and Drug Administration or, when applicable, the higher standards of drug research generally accepted by the scientific community, of which the drug companies are only a single part. These tests are not perfect, and they depart from the strict liability rule applicable in most products contexts. They will, however, catch thalidomide and MER/29.[54] This departure from strict liability is not, as has already been noted, the sign of any logical or legal inconsistency, as an implied contract theory need not be uniform across different product contexts even if a tort theory, concerned with the protection of innocent bystanders, should be. The position taken here is in effect the one adopted today,[55] and nothing about the internal logic of products liability requires a different approach to what promises to become an ever more important problem in the future.

54. For an account of the MER litigatrion, *see* Rheingold, *The MER/29 Story—An Instance of Successful Mass Disaster Litigation*, 56 Calif. L. Rev. 116 (1968).

55. *See Terhune v. A. H. Robins Co.*, 90 Wash. 2d 9, 577 P.2d 975 (1978) in which the plaintiff unsuccessfully sought to hold strictly liable the manufacturer of an intrauterine contraceptive device. The Washington Supreme Court held that the device was an unavoidably unsafe product under the theory of §402A, comment *k*.

CHAPTER

# 10

# PROCEDURE AND PROOF

The core of any system of products liability law lies in its substantive rules of liability. The complete operation of the system, however, entails far more than substantive rules: rules of procedure and proof are needed as well. Decisions on the admissibility of evidence or on the assignment of burdens of proof can have important effects not only on individual cases but also upon the operation of the overall system. Not surprisingly, matters of procedure and proof have been extensively litigated in recent years. Indeed, the pattern of their development has in marked degree reinforced the strategic gains made by plaintiffs in the areas of substantive law of products liability: not only have defendants' legal duties been made more onerous, but proof of their breach has been made easier as well.

This chapter studies three of the most important rules of procedure and proof in order to determine the magnitude and desirability of these procedural changes. The first section deals with the rules that answer a hitherto neglected issue: whether the product in question was one that was supplied by this particular defendant; the second section deals with the proof of an original construction defect and its causal connection to the plaintiff's harm; and the third section deals with the rules that govern the admissibility of subsequent changes in a product's design or in the warnings and labels with which it is sold.

## PRODUCT IDENTIFICATION

The identification of the manufacturer, distributor or retailer of a given product arises in principle in all products liability actions. A plaintiff may well have been injured by an admittedly defective product, but supplier A can no more be held responsible for the defective products of B than for his debts. Identifying the proper product defendant will in most instances be a trivial affair, as most products leave behind them visible indicia of their origin: labels, bills of sale, distinctive features, and the like. Yet product identification can become the source of intense factual dispute needing a fair bit of detective work. An exploding soft drink bottle may have been supplied by one of several bottling firms; the inflammable fabrics of a burnt coat may have been provided by one of several independent suppliers; and the replacement wheel bearings for an automobile may have come from any one of several parts distributors.

The divergent patterns of litigation are well illustrated by two cases. In *Drayton v. Jiffee Chemical Corp.*,[1] the infant plaintiff was severely burned when some caustic drain cleaner, while in the possession of the plaintiff's father, was in some undetermined manner poured over her face. There was testimony from both the plaintiff's parents and the parents' landlord who had originally purchased the drain cleaner in question that the drain cleaner was "Liquid-plumr," manufactured by the defendant. The chemical evidence presented by the defendant suggested that the plaintiff's burns were more consistent with exposure to the sulphuric acid base of a rival product than the sodium hydroxide base of the defendant's. The evidence in question was in clear conflict on the matter of product identification, and matters were further confused by the defendant's procedural failure to raise that matter during discovery. The Court of Appeals held that there was sufficient evidence on the record to allow this question to go to the jury.

The opposite result was reached in *Schmidt v. Archer Iron Works, Inc.*[2] The plaintiff, an employee at a bridge construction site, was injured when struck by a falling concrete-pouring chute which broke loose from the high tower to which it was attached. The undisputed cause of the fall was a defective metal eye pin used to secure the chute to the tower. The only issue of fact was whether the defendant, which had furnished the tower and its accessories, had furnished the defective pin as well.

The evidence on the point revealed that the purchase order placed on the plaintiff's employer's account with the defendant did not make any reference to the type of eye pin in question. It showed further that the tower in question had on one previous occasion been assembled and disassembled, and that its dismantled pieces, unboxed and untended, had been left by a river bank. The defendant's officers also testified without contradiction that they did not make or sell the type of pin in question. The only evidence in favor of the plaintiff was that the pin in question had not been repaired or rewelded in the field, and that it was painted the same rust color as the equipment admittedly supplied by the defendant.

The Illinois Supreme Court followed a rule that directed verdicts or judgments n.o.v. should be entered "only in those cases in which all of the

1. 591 F.2d 352 (6th Cir. 1978).

2. 44 Ill.2d 401, 256 N.E.2d 6 (1970). The case is extensively annotated in 51 A.L.R. 3d 1344 (1973).

evidence, when viewed in its aspect most favorable to the opponent, so overwhelmingly favors [the] movant that no contrary verdict based on that evidence could ever stand."[3] As stated, the standard seems too stringent for formal review, given that there are few if any litigated cases in which all the evidence can meet such an exacting standard. The use of the standard in *Schmidt*, however, gave content to the bare verbal formula. The trial court directed a verdict for defendant; the intermediate appellate court reinstated the judgment for the plaintiff; and the Illinois Supreme Court in turn restored the directed verdict entered by the trial judge.

In its opinion the Illinois Supreme Court recognized that some evidence was consistent with the plaintiff's theory. The paint colors matched; the product in question was ordered "complete" from the defendant; and there was always the possibility that one of the defendant's agents had inserted the eye pin from an alien source to fill the order. Yet the possibilities the other way were far greater. Other firms used the same color paint; the order for a "complete" boom was accompanied by a request for several operational accessories, but not the pin; and, most importantly, some third party—be it distributor or user—could have incorporated the eye pin into the defendant's product during the thirteen months after it left the defendant's possession.

It is difficult to know whether the presence or absence of any of these factors would have tilted the decision of the court to allow the case to go to the jury. Indeed the plaintiff might have been able to establish that the defendant had indeed supplied the defective pin if it had ordered a spectrographic analysis which showed that all the paint had come from the same original batch. What is important for our purposes is that the court showed its willingness to keep the case from the jury on its own independent assessment of *all* the undisputed evidence, not only that favorable to the plaintiff. No single such decision of course can set the outer boundaries of the appropriate sphere of jury control, but a set of such decisions can, far more than any form of words, affirm the proposition that such boundaries do exist, and give some sense of their approximate location.[4]

The problem of supplier identification assumes much more controversial

3. Id. at 405, 256 N.E.2d at 8, citing *Pedrick v. Peoria & Eastern R.R. Co.*, 37 Ill.2d 494, 510, 229 N.E.2d 504, 513-14 (1967).

4. Throughout this section I am assuming that the same standard of jury control is being applied regardless of the procedural way in which the question arises, that is, the same standard applies whether the moving party (usually, but not necessarily the defendant) asks for a summary judgment, a directed verdict, a judgment notwithstanding the verdict, or a reversal on appeal. Arguments can be made to suggest that the burdens should differ at the different stages of a lawsuit. It might, for example, be urged that there be a very stringent standard applied on appellate review given the opportunity to make motions before the trial judge. *See generally* on these motions, F. James & G. Hazard, *Civil Procedure* §7.12-§7.22 (2d ed. 1977).

dimensions where the question is which of several possible defendants has supplied a given standardized product, such as a drug or a vaccine, that has allegedly injured the plaintiff. In one of these cases is it asserted that all the defendants have combined together to cause the harm in question; but in all it is insisted that the responsible party is one of the defendants joined in the suit.

This particular problem of identification need not, of course, arise only in connection with products liability law. Indeed, discussion of the subject begins properly with the 1948 California case of *Summers v. Tice*,[5] a negligence action in which exhaustive evidence failed to establish which of the two defendant hunters shot the plaintiff. The two defendants, moreover, did not act in concert, so that both could not be held responsible no matter who had fired the shot. On this record, the ordinary rules on burdens of proof required dismissing the actions against both defendants because neither case was supported by a preponderance of the evidence. Yet on the narrow facts of this case the court found this double nonsuit unacceptable, because the evidence conclusively established (1) that the plaintiff was the victim of some tort, and (2) that each defendant had a 50 percent chance of being the tortfeasor. In these circumstances the rigorous rule of "all or nothing" on matters of proof only *guaranteed* a *wrong* result, which the court then avoided by holding the defendants jointly and severally liable. If both defendants are solvent, there is an undeniable elegance to the judicial result. The plaintiff collects fully, as he ought, and each defendant pays precisely the probable costs of his own wrong: 50 percent of the total damages.

Notwithstanding its commendable elegance, *Summers* was incorrect in its insistence that each hunter could be liable for the full damages. Suppose that the first defendant had not been joined in the action or was unable to satisfy any judgment entered against him. It is most awkward to allow the plaintiff full payment from the second party, for if that defendant had been sued alone, the plaintiff presumably could have recovered nothing at all. It is hard, therefore, to see why the addition of a second insolvent defendant should suddenly saddle the first defendant with the plaintiff's total damage award. The explicit probabilistic justification for the outcome in *Summers* requires the corresponding reduction in liability: in principle each defendant should be held only for his own pro rata share of the loss, and no more.[6] The plaintiff's price for the extraordinary dispensation of *Summers*

5. 33 Cal.2d 80, 199 P.2d 1 (1948).

6. The court tried to escape this result by noting that both defendants had been negligent toward the plaintiff. Id. at 84, 199 P.2d at 5.

Yet even if both parties were careless, the conduct of only one party was tortious, given the need to make out the causal connection between carelessness and harm. Even if the court's argument were accepted in negligence cases, it could not apply to strict liability actions where negligence itself is immaterial.

*v. Tice* now becomes the risk of the insolvency of any given defendant. This pro rata limitation upon recovery does not, it must be stressed, in any way undermine the traditional rule that holds each of two defendants responsible for the total loss where both assume distinct places in the chain of causation.[7] *Summers v. Tice* does not reach the case where defendants A *and* B are responsible for the plaintiff's loss; it only governs the case where defendant A *or* B, but not both, is responsible. With joint causation the risk of defendant A's default properly falls on defendant B; with *Summers v. Tice* the risk of defendant A's default should fall on the plaintiff.

The difference between these modes of allocating risk becomes apparent when the number of possible defendants is increased. The rule in *Summers* would make each of one hundred defendants responsible for the full extent of a given loss on the 1 percent chance that he is responsible. The alternative rule holds each defendant for 1 percent of the loss, no matter how many other defendants are insolvent.

There is, however, a real question, both in the products liability context and throughout the tort law, whether it is appropriate to follow even this restrained reinterpretation of *Summers v. Tice.* The issue arose, for example, in the important case of *Hall v. E. I. Du Pont De Nemours & Co., Inc.*[8] In that case, each of thirteen plaintiffs brought suit against six corporations who had manufactured and distributed blasting caps which had exploded and injured the plaintiffs. The trade association, of which the individual corporate defendants were all members, was also joined as a party defendant, because it had been responsible for the collection of information about the level of accidents to children and had opposed legislation to place warnings on individual blasting caps, claiming that the other modes of warnings (placards, leaflets) then used were adequate. The caps themselves were unidentified as to source. Some caps, perhaps all, may have been supplied by the named corporate defendants; some, or all, may have been supplied by other foreign and domestic manufacturers, several of which had gone out of business before the suit.

Without an aggressive extension of *Summers v. Tice*, the plaintiffs clearly faced a directed verdict because of their inability to identify the proper defendant. The district court, however, held that the plaintiffs could shift the burden of proof to the defendants as a class simply by showing that it was more likely than not that one of the named defendants furnished the cap involved in each particular instance.[9] With the shift of the original burden each defendant could then seek to escape liability by showing that its cap was not involved. If, however, the further evidence introduced in the

7. *See, e.g.*, Restatement (Second) of Torts, § 441 (2), commend *d.* (1965).

8. 345 F. Supp. 353 (E.D. N.Y. 1972).

9. Id. at 380. Note that the cap which injured the plaintiff Hall was in fact identified. The caps which injured other defendants were, however, not so identified. Id. at 383.

case failed to displace the original burden, then all defendants who remained under suspicion remained jointly and severally liable for the loss. This solution has a strong formal elegance, even if each defendant's liability is limited to its pro rata share (a matter normally unimportant with large corporate defendants).

A simple example shows the basic point. Assume that twelve plaintiffs each suffer $100,000 in damages. Assume, further, that each of six defendants has injured exactly two plaintiffs, but it is uncertain which two. Applying rigid rules of proof means that none of the plaintiffs recovers anything, when all that is missing is the coupling of an individual plaintiff and defendant. By applying the rule in *Summers v. Tice*, each defendant pays $200,000 into the pool, and each plaintiff collects $100,000. No plaintiff collects more than his due; no defendant pays more than he owes. Although the precise causal linkages are not established, the benefits and burdens are distributed precisely as they would have been if they had been known all along.

Matters are, however, greatly complicated when only some of the relevant defendants are amenable to suit. Suppose for example that defendants with an assumed 60 percent share of the market are joined in the individual action. Is the proper course to hold the group responsible for only 60 percent of the total damages on the ground that the absent defendants are in all likelihood responsible for the remainder? If so, should these defendants be held responsible for 40 percent of the loss if they represent that share of the market even though no single defendant could ever be held responsible if its own market share was 40 percent?

In the alternative, it might be suggested that the defendants representing 60 percent of the market be held responsible for the full amount of the loss. Yet this is clearly inconsistent with the basic premise of *Summers v. Tice*, that the absence of particular product identification should not increase the burdens upon any defendant or the benefits to any plaintiff. And it creates an enormous instability at the 50 percent point, as enormous sums of money can turn upon the very imprecise science of determining market shares.

There is then no neat way to extend alternative liability beyond the simple case that gave rise to its birth. Yet even if these theoretical problems could be overcome, the rule's extension is still unacceptable because of the enormous administrative costs that it creates, especially when large numbers of plaintiffs are pitted against large numbers of defendants.

In *Summers v. Tice*, the rule of division was applied only after an extensive trial failed to establish which defendant shot the plaintiff. In the blasting cap case, the parallel initial factual inquiry must of necessity assume much greater dimensions. Each defendant tries to show that its caps were not supplied to particular contractors; that its market share in a given region at the relevant time was low; or that testimony from the injured party or those with him can show that someone else's cap was involved. A task of this complexity has no promise of success. Nor is it proper to forbid each defendant from denying the product was his, for wholly apart from the substantive unfairness in such a dramatic position, the rule is an open invitation to the plaintiff to win its suit against the parties of its choice simply by joining them into the suit. Even if the mathematics of *Summers v. Tice* can be generalized, its administrative workability cannot.

The basic problems are further complicated because the separate defendants may be in very different positions on other substantive questions of liability raised by the basic duty to warn or design defect action. There are of course unavoidable choice of law questions when the different injuries take place in different jurisdictions.[10] Yet even if some uniform "national" products liability law were adopted, important factual differences remain in the different cases. Thus the costs of placing warnings on the different caps may be a function of time, cap type and size, and company of manufacture. How then can evidence be taken on the question when the very identification of the cap is unknown? Then too some defendants may have issued appropriate warnings; others may not. Some caps may have been used by knowledgeable intermediates; others may not. Some caps may have been manufactured with inferior materials; others may not. Some caps may have been made for some purposes; others for very different purposes. The inability to identify the proper defendant for each injury insures the complete degeneration of courtroom procedure. *Hall v. Du Pont* was wrongly decided. Some cases are simply better left untried.

The issues raised by the blasting cap cases promise to loom large in the emergent diethylstilbestrol (DES) litigation. While some of these cases involve allegations of vaginal cancers, most of them involve the admitted causation of vaginal adenosis, a condition in which normal columnar epithelial tissue is found in the vagina instead of in its usual location in the cervix, which does not, on the state of the evidence to date, appear to be a precursor of any form of cancer.[11] The basic cause of action rests upon a variety of theories, of which failure to warn and to test are the most common. Implicit in each case remains, however, the requirement that the plaintiff prove that the DES in question was supplied by the defendant whom she seeks to hold responsible for the harm in question. Given this identification

10. Indeed it was precisely on these grounds that the district court in a subsequent decision "severed and transferred" each individual claim to the federal district court sitting where each individual accident occurred. *Chance v. E.I. Du Pont De Nemours & Co.*, 371 F. Supp. 439 (E.D. N.Y. 1974).

11. Department of Health, Education and Welfare, Questions and Answers About DES Exposure Before Birth, Publication # (NIH) 76-1118. There have been many recent studies upon DES daughters that confirm that general pattern of frequent adenosis and rare cancers (adenocarcinomas). *See, e.g.*, P.C. O'Brien et al., *Vaginal Epithelial Chantes in Young Women Enrolled in the National Cooperative Diethylstilbestrol Adenosis (DESAD) Project*, 53 Obstetrics & Gynecology 300 (1979).

issue, the DES cases raise exactly the same problems that are presented by *Hall v. Du Pont*. Here, too, it is possible to invent elaborate theories of joint responsibility based upon the parallel activities of each drug manufacturer in the preparation and distribution of its own goods, but these do not in general contain any supportable allegations that the defendants engaged in any concerted activities about the testing, labeling, or marketing of the defendants' products.

The California Supreme Court, in its recent decision in *Sindell v. Abbott Labs*,[12] recognized the force of the defendant's case with respect to the concerted action theory, but nonetheless accepted the plaintiff's argument, well presented in a student note in the *Fordham Law Review*,[13] that the principle of *Summers v. Tice* can be extended to the drug cases, even though it means that the presumptive apportionment between defendants must be determined by market share, with each defendant still free to absolve himself if he can. Yet here the administrative concerns do seem decisive. It has been variously estimated that over a period from 1947 to 1971 DES was taken by between 500,000 to 3,000,000 women, with most of the usage being concentrated in the years before 1960.[14] Since the drug in question was first developed by English researchers, it has always been in the public domain, and in fact has been produced by perhaps as many as several hundred firms, some of whom have been major suppliers in a national market, and others who have operated only in one or another regional market. The share of every firm may well have shifted both from year to year and from place to place because of the competition among the various defendants. DES, moreover, has been prescribed (as it is still prescribed today) for a variety of conditions other than the stabilization of pregnancy, so it is difficult if not impossible to make any inference about the number of pregnant women who took a given defendant's products even if accurate information about market share could be acquired in the first instance. To make matters worse it is doubtful that there is any very raw data on market share for products that were sold twenty or more years ago.

Even if some reliable estimate of market share can be made in each individual case in which it is raised, the defendant still has, under the rule of *Summers v. Tice*, the opportunity to absolve himself if he can. This question

12. 26 Cal. 3d 588, 607 P.2d 924, 163 Cal. Rptr. 132 (1980). There is now a parallel suit in Michigan, *Abel v. Eli Lilly Co.*, 94 Mich. App. 59, 289 N.W. 2d 20 (1980), in which the plaintiffs prevailed on the same theory. The defendants have now moved for a hearing by the Michigan Supreme Court. I have set out at greater length the arguments developed here in an amicus curiae brief on behalf of the American Insurance Association.

13. Comment, *DES and a Proposed Theory of Enterprise Liability*, 46 Ford. L. Rev. 963 (1978).

14. The estimate given by the California Supreme Court in *Sindell*, based on the Fordham note, is between 1,500,00 and 3,000,000. 26 Cal. 3d 588, ______, 607 P.2d 924, 927, 162 Cal. Rptr. 132, 135 (1980).

cannot be put off until the plaintiff has collected judgment from the defendant of his choice, as the very gist of the identification defense is the complete *denial* of the central element of the plaintiff's basic cause of action: the defendant says, "I did not supply this product." Moreover, when it is asked what type of evidence will suffice to rebut the presumption, new difficulties will emerge. Can the defendant produce evidence that shows it operates in a special submarket which has different percentages from that in which the plaintiff has made her calculations, as by offering evidence that a given plaintiff obtained a pill from a pharmacy that used only 15 percent of its pills, even though this defendant had 30 percent of the relevant metropolitan market? What should be done if the plaintiff can show that there is a 50 percent (30 percent or 20 percent?) chance that the pill was both red and round? Are all defendants who made non-red non-round pills dismissed from the case; or are efforts made to take into account all available information, both as it relates to market share and particular identification evidence? Questions of this sort are sure to arise in abundance if only because of the sheer number of defendants presumptively involved in any case, especially if those suppliers not sued by the original plaintiffs are brought into the case by the original defendants. And even if the questions are resolved, there still remains a very difficult lawsuit on matters of negligence, causation, and damages for all the parties involved. The administrative problems overwhelm every other aspect of the case. There is no question but that these difficulties would have been decisive in any era but our own. Yet even a court that is prepared to assay the enormous complexities of an individual design defect or duty to warn case should be well advised of the possible consequences of having large numbers of plaintiffs each pursuing parallel actions against multiple defendants. The system of private adjudication breaks down with litigation of this scope and magnitude. The courts should not struggle to keep it alive with the dubious extension of alternative liability theories beyond the narrow confines of *Summers v. Tice.*

## IS THERE A DEFECT CAUSING HARM?

If the identificaiton of the proper defendant is but of occasional, if dramatic, concern, the further question of linking up the plaintiff's injury with the defect in the defendant's product is raised frequently in much products liability litigation.[15]

The unavoidable evidentiary complications presented by the defect question are well illustrated by *Moore v. Jewel Tea Co.*[16] In that case the plaintiff was blinded when a can of Drano, manufactured by the Drackett Companies and distributed by Jewel Tea, exploded just as the plaintiff was about to use it. One of the central questions was, whether the moisture was inside the can

15. *See generally* Rheingold, *Proof of Defect in Product Liability Cases*, 38 Tenn. L. Rev. 325 (1971). There is also an exhaustive compilation of cases in 51 A.L.R.3d 8 (1973).

16. 116 Ill. App. 2d 109, 253 N.E. 2d 636 (1969).

when it left the factory, or had worked its way into the container only after it had sat for a year, first in Jewel's possession and then in the plaintiff's. The can in this case was a far cry from the Coca-Cola bottle presumed defective in *Escola v. Coca-Cola Bottling Co.*[17] No can has ever received such close scrutiny, as teams of experts testified for both sides, addressing themselves to the significance of the rust on the can and the opportunities for moisture to enter the can at each point in the chain of manufacture, distribution, and use. Given the closeness of the evidence, the question was left for the jury, and a large plaintiff's verdict was properly upheld on appeal.

The recent trend in these cases has, however, been to relax the proof requirements for the plaintiff far beyond these traditional limits. Aided by a great deference to the jury on all questions of fact, the plaintiff has been able to get to the jury on evidence which seems weak and unpersuasive, especially in those cases in which there is no clear evidence of product defect.

Consider in particular two recent fact patterns. In *Tweedy v. Wright Ford Sales, Inc.*,[18] the plaintiff recovered for bodily injuries when his Ford automobile went out of control at an intersection and struck a tree. The plaintiff testified that the brakes had failed unaccountably as he approached the intersection, even though they had worked several times previously on the same trip. He also introduced evidence that they had failed earlier that morning when the car was driven by his daughter; that in none of the mechanical work done on the car since its original purchase had the brakes been tampered with; and that the emergency brake had been pushed to the floor. No specific product defect was identified; indeed the plaintiff did not introduce the car into evidence. Standing alone, the case for some unidentified construction defect in the braking system was very weak, resting solely on the testimony of the plaintiff and his daughter. Some undisclosed event may have caused the accident, or the plaintiff, having daydreamed at the intersection, may have been unable to save himself, even with the use of the emergency brake.

The balance of probabilities shifted sharply against the plaintiff with the defendant's evidence. After the accident the plaintiff junked the car, which the defendant then retrieved with some efficient detective work. Even then, the braking system still worked. Notwithstanding the physical evidence, the Illinois Supreme Court affirmed the judgment entered below for the plaintiff on the jury's verdict, saying:

> Here the evidence shows that the brakes of an automobile driven approximately 7,500 miles, inspected by Wright [the dealer] prior to delivery, inspected again at 6,000 miles, and subjected to no abnormal use prior to the occurrence failed to function

17. 24 Cal.2d 453, 150 P.2d 436 (1944).

18. 64 Ill. 2d 570, 357 N.E.2d 449 (1976); for a similar result, *see Brownell v. White Motor Corp.*, 260 Or. 251, 490 P.2d 184 (1971), where the Oregon court allowed proof of an unidentified product defect by circumstantial evidence alone.

in the manner reasonably to be expected. Plaintiff was driving carefully at a reasonable rate of speed, the weather was good, the roads were dry, he knew the intersection well, and there was no evidence of any reasonable secondary cause.[19]

A second case involves a somewhat different fact pattern. In *Jagmin v. Simonds Abrasive Co.*[20] the plaintiff was struck in the face by a grinding wheel that disintegrated while he was using it. The plaintiff presented evidence that he had used the grinding wheel properly, that no other worker had used the wheel, that the wheel still had several hours of useful life in it, and that no stranger had tampered with the wheel. No direct evidence was introduced as to the specific defect, if any, in the wheel which was destroyed in the accident. The Wisconsin Supreme Court regarded the case as "exceedingly close" but allowed it to go to the jury on the theory that the evidence presented excluded the possibility that something other than an unidentified defect in the grinding wheel caused the damage.

The subject matter of these two cases is quite different; yet their patterns of argument are remarkably similar. In both, the question is whether it is possible to trace the plaintiff's mishap back to a defect of the product in its original condition. In both, no evidence is introduced by the plaintiff to identify any particular product defect. In both cases the line of proof rests upon the elimination of all other possible causes that might have been involved. In *Tweedy* the plaintiff testified as to his own proper conduct and as to the normal road conditions. In *Jagmin* the plaintiff testified to his own proper care, and the unlikelihood that his coworkers would have used the wheel (but *not* the possibility that it was damaged in shipping or storage while in the possession of a third party). From the *exclusion* of these alternatives, the claimed inference is that the harm could only be attributed to some original product defect for which the defendant is responsible.[21]

Such arguments are not wholly novel in the law. They are similar to those commonly advanced by plaintiffs under the banner of res ipsa loquitur in ordinary negligence actions, where the usual requirements of proof are: (1) that the accident would not ordinarily happen in the absence of negligence, (2) that the instrumentality in question was within the exclusive control of the defendant, and (3) that no voluntary action of the plaintiff contributed to his own harm.[22] The first of these conditions is designed to rule out the simple act of God; the second is designed to rule out the possibility of culpable conduct of some third party, and the third is designed, of course, to rule out conduct by the plaintiff himself.

19. 64 Ill.2d 570, 574-75, 357 N.E.2d, 449, 452 (1976).

20. 61 Wis.2d 60, 211 N.W.2d 810 (1973).

21. For an earlier case in which efforts to prove causation by an exclusion of alternatives were rebuffed, *see DeVere v. Parten*, 222 Minn. 211, 23 N.W.2d 584 (1946).

22. See W. Prosser, *Handbook of the Law of Torts*, 214 (4th ed. 1971).

The first of these three issues is of no relevance in the products liability context, as the strict liability principle precludes any defense based upon the reasonable care of the defendant. Yet the second and third of these points are of constant concern, as the product in question passes through the hands of many third parties—dealers, repairmen, shippers, the plaintiff himself as well as other users.

The relative weakness of the res ipsa loquitur arguments in the context of *Tweedy* is well illustrated if its plaintiff-driver is cast in the role of defendant who is sued by the owner of the tree that was damaged in the crash. In this hypothetical action, res ipsa loquitur is quite powerful; the tree was passive and nothing intervened between its being struck and being broken. In the absence of good explanation, moreover, even the defense of "no negligence" by the driver would probably not prevail, either as a matter of law or before the jury. By the same token, the tree owner would have a very difficult action against the original automobile manufacturer, notwithstanding the doctrine of strict liability toward bystanders; now the intervening causal conduct, including the acts of the driver, would render very shaky any inference from the tree's damage to the alleged automobile defect. The method of proof against the manufacturer is in principle the same as that against the driver, but the length added to the causal chain seriously, if not fatally, weakens the strength of the required inference. As between the driver and the manufacturer, the tree owner surely has the stronger case against the driver, even though that action requires the proof of negligence unnecessary in the product liability case.

The question therefore arises: how do matters change when the action in question is brought by the driver against the manufacturer? One obvious change is that now the burden of proof is placed upon the driver, which should make his case all the more difficult. The other problems still remain. The plaintiff's testimony may be fraudulent, however difficult to expose by independent evidence; some unidentified third-party causation remains a live possibility; and (on the facts of *Tweedy*) the braking system still operated after the collision.

The same basic line of argument applies to *Jagmin*. The plaintiff's testimony is only about his own conduct, and is, even if in good faith, hardly decisive about the way in which he dealt with the product. The evidence about third-party conduct is also skimpy: some unidentified operators of the wheel may have placed it under improper stress; the wheel itself may have been damaged during either shipment or installation.

In both *Tweedy* and *Jagmin* verdicts should have been directed for the defendant; while each plaintiff may have been correct on his factual allegations, the strong probabilities suggest that such was not the case. Yet as these two cases show, such directed verdicts are difficult indeed to obtain. The root of the problem lies in the appropriate standards for taking cases away from the jury. The oft-quoted language of the California Supreme Court is again illustrative.

> A nonsuit in a jury case or a directed verdict may be granted only when disregarding conflicting evidence, giving to the plaintiffs' evidence all the value to which it is legally entitled, and indulging every legitimate inference which may be drawn from the evidence in plaintiffs' favor, it can be said that there is no evidence to support a jury verdict in their favor.[23]

The standard as announced is a bulwark against one form of error: denying the plaintiff recovery when such recovery is due. Yet, by the same token it is the source of a second form of error by inviting the jury to find for the plaintiff when the vast bulk of the evidence is against him. An evenhanded system of procedure must be impartial between plaintiffs and defendants. As with all rules of evidence, the key question here is how to minimize the *sum* of two types of error: keeping the plaintiff from juries when he should get there; and allowing plaintiff to reach the jury when he should not. A rule of "indulgence" reduces the first type of error but at the cost of vastly increasing the second. What is needed is a rule of substantial evidence, applicable to both plaintiff's and defendant's motions, that places a better balance between the parties.

This substantial evidence rule will no doubt reduce the expected value of a plaintiff's claim in a contested situation, but it should not place an excessive barrier to all recovery. Thus scientific and physical evidence is usually available for the proof of a construction defect. But it may be objected that the rule frustrates the plaintiff by keeping a case from the jury whenever the allegedly defective product is destroyed in the accident. Yet here it is equally true that the same want of evidence also complicates the defendant's efforts when a jury trial is allowed. In some instances, where the defendant has exclusive control of the particular product, or exclusive access to evidence about its condition, it is proper on that ground to shift the burden of proof to him. Yet in the typical products liability case the defendant has no special advantage on either score, as the product in question has spent as much time out of the defendant's possession as it has in it. Indeed as the plaintiff is often in possession and control of the product before injury occurs, there is, if anything, an additional reason not to allow him to escape the burden of proof which he must routinely overcome. There is, for example, no doubt that the plaintiff's circumstantial case for a defect can be far more attractive than that presented in *Tweedy*: the automobile in question might have run out of control as it was driven out of the showroom. Likewise, the plaintiff's

23. *Elmore v. American Motors Corp.*, 70 Cal. 2d 578, 583, 451 P.2d 84, 87, 75 Cal. Rptr. 652, 655 (1969). Note that the statement in the text limits the application of the indulgence rule to the plaintiff's benefit only.

case would be further strengthened if a neutral party could testify as to the proper conduct by the plaintiff in the operation of the vehicle in question. By the same token his case for reaching the jury is further weakened if there is some independent cause for the harm, as when the plaintiff strikes a pothole on a back road while driving at high speeds.[24]

The possible variations on the original theme are, of course, infinite, and there is clearly no single verbal test which will eliminate the need for judicial judgment whether jury determinations are appropriate. Nonetheless a well-reasoned line of cases can offer real guidance on this vital question and thereby improve the quality of civil litigation even if the substantive rules of product liability are left unaltered. Any call for greater judicial supervision of jury verdicts may sound undramatic when set against the weightier issues of products liability law. Yet such control could go a long way toward righting the balance of the liability system.

## SUBSEQUENT IMPROVEMENTS[25]

The last of the three issues in this chapter is the question of whether the defendant's product, when challenged in a design defect or duty to warn case, meets appropriate standards for product safety. The basic judicial standards for defectiveness in design and warning are, to say the least, very fluid in the wake of the recent revolution of substantive doctrines. Yet while the state of the substantive law now permits the plaintiff to advance an impressive array of scientific and technical evidence on the defect question, it also permits the defendant to introduce a comparable wealth of evidence with, of course, precisely the opposite effect.

Amid this welter of conflicting evidence, the plaintiff has a strong incentive to clinch his case with dramatic evidence of improper warning or design. One type of evidence well calculated to have this effect rests upon the proposition that the defendant has virtually *admitted* some defect in his original

24. *See, e.g., Holloway v. General Motors Corp.*, 403 Mich. 614, 271 N.W.2d 777 (1978), where the court allowed the jury to draw the inference of original product defect after the front wheel assembly cracked under such circumstances.

25. *Moore v. Jewel Tea*, supra note 16, might well be paired with another decision of the Illinois Appellate Court, *St. Paul Fire & Marine Ins. Co. v. Michelin Tire Corp.*, 12 Ill. App. 3d 165, 298 N.E.2d 289 (1973). There the question was whether Michelin's tire had failed because of external puncture or "internal ply separation," the latter counting as a product defect. The plaintiff's expert introduced some weak evidence in support of ply separation, but his testimony was thoroughly rebutted by the defendant's expert witnesses. Under the *Elmore* test of extreme indulgence, the case should have gone to the jury. Yet the court "at the close of all the evidence" quite rightly ordered a judgment for the defendant.

On the general issue of subsequent repairs or improvements, *see generally*, Note, *Products Liability and Evidence of Subsequent Repairs* [1972] Duke L.J. 837 (1972); Annot. 74 A.L.R.3d 1001 (1970).

product by having subsequently altered its design or warnings in some essential feature. In essence the function of such evidence, if admitted, is to have the strengths of the newer product set the standards by which the asserted defects of the older product are judged. A new component shows the dangers of the older component it replaced. A strengthened warning in a drug case shows the inadequacy of the warnings originally given. The trier of fact need not adopt the chain of inference urged by the plaintiff, but it is, of course, free to do so. Given some likelihood that this will happen, the admissibility of this type of evidence can only increase the plaintiff's possibilities for success and thus enhance the settlement value of his case.

Before the recent enormous growth of products liability litigation, evidence of such post-accident product modifications and improvements could not be introduced. Such evidence was, broadly speaking, regarded as tainted on two counts. First, as a straight matter of proof, it was generally urged that such evidence might not be probative of original improper conduct by the defendant. In essence the rule rejected the proposition that "because the world gets wiser as it gets older, therefore it was foolish before."[26] Second, it was thought that the rule could have an adverse effect upon the conduct of the defendant who might be deterred from making beneficial post-accident improvements because of the fear of adverse tort judgments.[27]

More to the point here, the courts applied this same rule about subsequent repairs and improvements to products liability actions, which traditionally were based upon negligence theories. This traditional ban has, however, eroded with great speed in the context of strict liability actions since the important California case of *Ault v. International Harvester Co.*[28]

In *Ault* the plaintiff was injured when his "Scout" vehicle, manufactured by the defendant, went over the side of a steep mountain road. After the accident it was discovered that the Scout's aluminum gear box had been badly smashed. The plaintiff contended that the choice of improper materials for the gear box had led to the accident. In order to show the defectiveness of the box, plaintiff was allowed at trial, over defendant's objection, to introduce evidence that three years after this accident the defendant had changed the materials used in the construction of gear boxes from aluminum to malleable iron. The defendant's objection rested upon Section 1151 of the California Evidence Code, understood to be a codification of the basic common law rule. The section provides as follows:

26. *Hart v. Lancashire & Yorkshire Ry. Co.*, 21 L.T.R. (NS) 261, 263 (Ex. 1869). As stated, the observation is tailored to negligence cases only, but it can easily be modified to apply to design defect or duty to warn cases in which reasonableness at the time of manufacture or sale is built into the test of product defect. On the application of the subsequent improvement rule to strict liability actions, *see* below.

27. For a discussion of the exceptions. *see* below.

28. 13 Cal.3d 113, 528 P.2d 1148, 117 Cal. Rptr. 812 (1974).

> When after the occurrence of an event, remedial or precautionary measures are taken, which, if taken previously would have tended to make the event less likely to occur, evidence of such subsequent measures is inadmissible to prove negligence or culpable conduct in connection with the event.

The precise question of statutory construction was whether a design defect action based upon strict liability principles was covered by the expression "culpable conduct." The California Supreme Court admitted the evidence, holding that section 1151 did not govern strict liability actions, because the words "culpable conduct" referred only to conduct that was "morally blameworthy." It then fortified its conclusion by a discussion of the underlying issues of public policy raised in the decision.

> When the context is transformed from a typical negligence setting to the modern products liability field, however, the "public policy" assumptions justifying this evidentiary rule are no longer valid. The contemporary corporate mass producer of goods, the normal products liability defendant, manufactures tens of thousands of units of goods; it is manifestly unrealistic to suggest that such a producer will forego making improvements in its product, and risk innumerable additional lawsuits and the attendant adverse effect upon its public image, simply because evidence of adoption of such improvement may be admitted in an action founded on strict liability for recovery on an injury that preceded the improvement. In the products liability area, the exclusionary rule of section 1151 does not affect the primary conduct of the mass producer of goods, but serves merely as a shield against potential liability. In short, the purpose of section 1151 is not applicable to a strict liability case and hence its exclusionary rule should not be gratuitously extended to that field.[29]

The opinion of the California Supreme Court has been widely followed on this point, but is not for that reason immune from criticism. On the straight question of the interpretation of section 1151, the court may be faulted because of the way in which it has in effect read the words "culpable conduct" out of the statute. These words were used in opposition to the term negligence and seem to cover strict liability actions. It is hardly likely that evidence of subsequent improvements is needed in actions alleging deliberate harms, and the words "culpable conduct" seem to cover the case of a defendant charged with making or marketing the defective product, even under a strict liability theory.

More than a textual point is at stake, as the issue here goes to the very heart of modern products liability litigation. We have already noted the want of any significant difference between negligence and strict liability causes of action, both in design defect and duty to warn cases.[30] The com-

29. Id. at 120, 528 P.2d at 1151-52, 117 Cal. Rptr. at 815-16.
30. *See* chs. 4, 7, and 8.

mon generalization that strict liability places the product and not the manufacturer on trial only obscures some of the central features of modern products liability law. Thus the modern design defect and warning cases require courts and juries to consider the relevant alternatives (and their associated costs) available to the manufacturer at the time that the particular goods were made. The rationales for strict product liability, moreover, explicitly raise the question of incentives for proper behavior of manufacturers and suppliers. The question in the end is, therefore, whether the justifications advanced in support of the traditional ban in ordinary negligence actions carry over to products liability actions based upon strict liability theories. There is good reason to think that they do.[31]

First, evidence of subsequent repairs and improvements could be quite prejudicial, given that the ultimate standard of liability is whether the product is unreasonably dangerous when measured against the technical and cost constraints faced by the firm *at the time* such product was manufactured and marketed. Thus the evidence in question might well show that the new product was indeed safer than the old one, but that is not the same as a demonstration that the old product was unreasonably dangerous. Likewise, with the impressive rate of technical change, it is quite possible that the new product depends on technologies that were either unavailable or unaffordable when the product involved in the lawsuit was first made or sold. Then again the changes may have nothing to do with safety at all. A defendant might have chosen to consolidate his sources of supply in order to reduce his costs of production, or changes may have been made in response to public regulations, such as those concerned with the level of pollutant emissions in automobiles. Last, the changes in product standards may well reflect the substantive changes in the common law. The substantive standards of liability are far more exacting than they were even a generation ago. And the valuation of human life and limb has climbed more rapidly than the rate of inflation. All in all, the chain of inference from subsequent improvement to original defect is long, uncertain, and prey to abuse and misinterpretation.

In a similar vein, it is doubtful that the California court has analyzed completely the complex set of incentives created by the admissiblity of evidence of post-accident improvements. For one thing, the change in the rule affects all products, not only those "normal" products that are manufactured by mass-production techniques. For another, even with mass-production goods, the incentives upon manufacturers are very difficult to determine. Thus if the firm is faced with tens, or even hundreds, of suits involving a given product defect, it may well be in its interest to forestall the introduction of some improvement until those cases are either settled or

31. Arguments along these lines are forcefully developed by Clark, J. in his dissent in *Ault*. Id. at 195-96, 528 P.2d at 1156-57, 117 Cal. Rptr. at 819-20.

tried. If, moreover, some change in product design is warranted, the range of choices open to the firm is not limited to just making or not making a given change. Thus the firm could make product changes more extensive than otherwise necessary, solely to frustrate any direct comparison between the old and new product design: instead of redesigning a simple washer, a whole assembly might be changed. These changes will, of course, cost more money to implement and may in some instances introduce new errors that could have been avoided by keeping more closely to tested methods of design. In the end, one point remains clear. The introduction of post-accident improvements into evidence *must* increase the costs of making those improvements, and this in turn *must* decrease the willingness of firms to make those improvements. The shift from negligence to strict liability, or that from individual to mass-produced items, does not change the central point.

Notwithstanding these criticisms, there is some force to the position of the California Supreme Court. Whether we deal with negligence or strict liability theories, or with old premises liability cases or modern products liability cases, the evidence of subsequent improvements may be just what is needed for the plaintiff to clinch a sound case. The question therefore arises whether it is possible to identify some intermediate position that might do something to minimize the rigors of the two extremes. One approach, which is to carve certain limited exceptions to the absolute ban on subsequent improvements, has been taken in many common law jurisdictions, and is embodied in the recent Federal Rules of Evidence that provide:

**Rule 407. Subsequent Remedial Measures**

When, after an event, measures are taken which, if taken previously, would have made the event less likely to occur, evidence of the subsequent measures is not admissible to prove negligence or culpable conduct in connection with the event. This rule does not require the exclusion of evidence of subsequent measures when offered for another purpose, such as proving ownership, control, or feasibility of precautionary measures, if controverted, or impeachment.[32]

The first of these exceptions, relating to proof of ownership and control, may be of some use in premises liability cases (so long as the court does not admit evidence of the nature of the repairs and improvements made) but is of little relevance to products liability actions where the manufacturer or supplier has typically parted with possession and control before the accident

32. Federal Rules of Evidence, Rule 407. Note that the federal courts have followed the California Supreme Court's view of "culpable conduct" and thus have freely allowed in evidence of subsequent repairs in strict liability causes of action. *See Robbins v. Farmers Union Grain Terminal Ass'n*, 552 F.2d 788, 793 (8th Cir. 1977).

took place. The second exception, going to the question of feasibility, is, however, of great importance in that the question of alternative designs or warnings is of vital importance in most modern products liability litigation.[33] Here the exception is so drafted as to eliminate the very protection which originally justified the rule. There is simply no way that evidence cannot be admitted on the question of feasible alternatives without its being admitted on the question of product defect or (in the jurisdictions where it is relevant) negligence as well. Nor will the matter be eased by any limiting instruction, since it is impossible to draw the conceptual distinction between questions of feasibility and questions of design or warning defect, even if a jury were eager to respect it.

The third of the mentioned exceptions, that relating to impeachment, is also troublesome. In one sense such a limitation is clearly needed. If the defendant announces that it remains impossible even at the time of trial to improve his product, evidence of subsequent improvement should be admitted to rebut the extravagance of the false claim. Yet, the defendant who makes the more limited claim that improvement was not possible or feasible at the time the product was marketed is not impeached by evidence of subsequent improvement without some further proof that its earlier introduction was possible, an inquiry that raises the familiar doubts about using evidence of subsequent improvements in the first place. The impeachment exception loses its appeal as we move further and further away from the case of outright falsehood.

The use of substantive exceptions, then, does not offer a consistently successful escape from the rigors of the total ban upon the admissibility of post-accident improvements. Another approach to the matter might cut back on the unyielding structure of the rule, ridding it of some injustices without gutting its essential strength. In looking at the merits of the rule, it seems clear that the *temporal gap* between the time of sale (not the accident) and the time of subsequent improvement is a key determinant in passing upon the relevance of the evidence.[34] Where the improvement is made shortly after the original distribution of the product, there seems greater reason to treat the improvement as evidence of a product defect, simply because there are fewer other legitimate reasons that might account for the change. There is, for example, less likelihood of technological change, of changes in relative costs, of changes in general patterns of product use, of changes in regulatory controls. It might, therefore, be appropriate to use a rule that is in some cases more stringent than that adopted at common law. In essence the

33. *See, e.g., Incollingo v. Ewing*, 444 Pa.263, 282 A.2d 206 (1971), supra at 101.

34. Indeed here there is a real question of whether even this date pushes the matter too far forward, as with the case of a company which keeps old inventory on its shelf even after newer, improved products are created. It might well be, therefore, that the date of individual product manufacture is relevant.

proposed rule *allows evidence of improvements to be introduced if they are made within, say, three years after the date of the product sale, no matter when the accident in question takes place.*

The rule, as reformulated, treats as decisive the moment the defendant parted with possession and control of the product and not the moment the plaintiff sustained injury. While post-accident conduct may be of special importance for the typical case of premises liability, it certainly has little relevance when what is being litigated is a change in the design or warnings associated with an entire product line. The proposed rule keyed to date of sale should be easily administered, and its temporal division seems to respond to some of the insistent pressures that are otherwise placed upon an iron rule of inadmissibility. There is, of course, some risk that firms will put off making improvements in order to take advantage of the three-year rule, but this tendency toward delay will be surely less than those created by allowing improvements made at any time to be introduced into evidence. The possibilities of abuse that still remain, moreover, will be further mitigated as the firm must continue to deal with competitive pressures and the real risk that its current line of products will be found defective for other reasons when measured against industry or statutory standards. Where the evidence is admitted, the defendant is, of course, free to explain away the changes by pointing to independent circumstances that justify the change, and the jury is, of course, free to weigh the evidence as it chooses. The rule will create some new errors, even as it avoids older ones. The guess here is that it will improve the balance on an overall basis.

CHAPTER

# 11

# COMPENSATORY AND PUNITIVE DAMAGES

This chapter is devoted to a discussion of the principles that govern the award of actual and punitive damages in products liability cases. While these two types of damages are bracketed together for purposes of convenience, it is widely recognized that they raise very different types of issues. Actual damages are primarily a question of the plaintiff's loss, an inquiry that presupposes the resolution of all basic liability issues. The central tasks of this inquiry are to identify those heads of damages that are proper for recovery and to specify the proper principles for determining their amount. Punitive damages, on the other hand, address the conditions appropriate for imposing additional liability upon the defendant, not as redress for the plaintiff's injuries but for the outrageous manner in which the defendant has inflicted them. The discussion of actual damages is kept brief both because the issue has been often reviewed, and because I have little disagreement with the general ideals of the tort law, even if from time to time excessive dollar awards escape appropriate judicial review. The discussion of punitive damages will be somewhat more extensive, as the case law offers some evidence that the traditional limitations upon punitive damages are being eroded in products liability cases. We begin then with actual damages and conclude with punitive damages.

## ACTUAL DAMAGES

Of actual damages it has been well said that their major purpose is to afford full compensation to the injured plaintiff. "The rule of damages is a practical instrumentality for the administration of justice. The principle on which it is founded is compensation. Its object is to afford the equivalent in money for the actual loss caused by the wrong of another."[1] In essence a

1. *Sullivan v. Old Colony Street Railway Co.*, 197 Mass. 512, 516, 83 N.E. 1091, 10-92 (1908).

tort judgment on a plaintiff's behalf is tantamount to an assertion that the defendant has wrongfully taken the life, limb, or property of the injured party. What has been so taken must be restored; since redress in kind is beyond the power of the law in personal injury actions, money, the only available substitute, must be awarded instead. The payment of total damages places the innocent party, to the extent that money can do it, in the position that he was in before the tort. Life and limb are dear; likewise the damage awards that function as their equivalent should be high. It must be stressed that damages in the law of tort do not serve a welfare function. They are not designed to give the plaintiff some minimum guarantee of future well-being; they are meant to give him the full measure of well-being he had before the tort took place.

The obstacles that stand in the way of the implementation of this program are, to be sure, formidable. It is quite clear, for example, that there can never be compensation to a person who has been killed by the actions of another, even if payment can be made to his dependents. And with bodily injuries, it is difficult if not impossible to place an appropriate value upon pain and suffering, even if some greater measure of precision can be attached to the two other major components of value, lost earnings and medical expenses. Yet difficulties of evaluation do not require an abandonment of the basic ideal of full compensation. There is, for example, no reason to accept the common suggestion that all rewards for pain and suffering be disallowed.[2] There is no question but that injured persons would pay dearly to be rid of their injuries and that persons free of affliction would pay dearly to avoid possible suffering. The inherent difficulties of valuation may make arbitrary the precise dollar figures that are awarded. Yet the case for full compensation remains undiminished, as the one estimate of pain and suffering that is sure to be wrong is zero.

This much established, the case for lost earnings and medical expenses is easy. There are, to be sure, questions about the choice of the relevant discount rate for future expenditures, as well as endless disputes about whether certain medical expenditures are properly included in recovery, or whether accurate predictions can be made of the lifetime earnings of college students. These and other problems have been faced in other contexts, and there is no reason why they should prove insurmountable here.

In connection with products liability therefore, the full compensation ideal imposes only these two demands:

First, the same level of damage awards appropriate elsewhere should be used in products liability cases. Simply put, the point is that an arm is an

2. *See*, for an attack on the proposition that pain and suffering constitutes an appropriate head for tort damages, Jaffe, *Damages for Personal Injury: The Impact of Insurance*, 18 Law & Contemp. Prob. 219, 224-25 (1953).

arm. If that arm is worth $400,000, it is worth $400,000, no matter who the defendant. The product liability defendant should not find himself saddled with a $1,000,000 verdict when the homeowner escapes with $200,000. The "deep pocket" has nothing to do with damage awards.

Second, (and the point is a general one) there should be some internal consistency between awards based on the relative severity of the harm. At one level the injunction is obvious enough. The more serious the case, the greater the damages. What is more, appropriate dollar differentials should be adhered to as well. If the total loss of mind and body, coupled with racking pain, is worth, say, $5,000,000, then it is difficult to think that the loss of a leg should be worth $750,000. The point cannot be transformed into an ironclad rule, but it should be both brought to the attention of the jury and taken into account in any review of awards challenged as either excessive or inadequate.

The previous paragraphs have set out what is in essence a defense of the traditional rules for tort damages and argued that they can apply even in cases in which verdicts of several million dollars or more (though surely not commonplace) are proper and acceptable. There is, however, one challenge to this model that does require some consideration. Both workers' compensation systems and automobile no-fault plans rest upon a well-recognized legislative bargain.[3] The injured party receives compensation in a whole host of cases in which recovery would be barred under the tort law. In exchange for the increased coverage, that party in turn agrees to accept a lower level of benefits than otherwise would be available. Ex ante it is thought that all parties are made better off by the system. The administrative costs may be reduced, as are the uncertainties of recovery and the unevenness of compensation amongst injured individuals.

The question, therefore, is whether such a legislative bargain might be pressed into service to place some limitation upon tort damages in products liability cases. An argument of this sort has no particular appeal where the system of tort liability insures an adequate balance of rights and duties between the parties. High tort damages can be strongly defended both because they respond to a sense of corrective justice and because they sharpen the incentives for appropriate conduct. With respect to the law of products liability, however, the case is unfortunately not so clear, given the enormous changes in substantive doctrines that have occurred within the past ten or fifteen years. In fact it could be argued that in the first half, the workers' compensation bargain, broad coverage has been imposed by judicial revisions in products liability law. Note the evident parallels. In the workers' compensation bargain two elements dominate. First, the plaintiff need not

3. *See New York Central R.R. Co. v. White*, 243 U.S. 188 (1917). For the basic parallel structure of the automobile no-fault plans, *see Pinnick v. Cleary*, 360 Mass. 1, 271 N.E.2d 592 (1971).

show the negligence or other wrongful conduct of the employer. It is quite enough to show that the injury arose out of and within the scope of employment, broadly construed. Second, the defenses of assumption of risk and contributory negligence do not prevent any compensation award, so that only deliberate self-infliction of harm (like voluntary suicide) bars recovery. The parallels to product liability law should by now be obvious. The expansion of the defect concept makes it possible (though not necessary) to treat any product-related injury as though it were caused by a product defect. The defenses of assumption of risk and contributory negligence in many jurisdictions have been whittled away to the point where they are little larger than what remains of the analogous defenses of workers' compensation. The liability rules in the product area have thus by degrees approached the compensation rules. It could well be argued that the quid pro quo of limited damages should follow.

At one level the parallel stated fails because it is quite clear that the modern products liability law has not yet adopted the automatic no-fault coverage rules characteristic of both automobile no-fault plans and workers' compensation law. It could, of course, be urged that the transition should be completed by removing the last traces of the defect requirement and the remaining products liability defenses.[4] Yet even a little reflection shows the massive instability, not to say astronomical costs and wholesale inequities, associated with any such misguided venture. Is every drug-related condition to be compensable, even when known to be an inevitable by-product of treatment? Does every fall from a ladder generate a no-fault recovery? And *which* manufacturer should pay if a tipsy man wearing smooth shoes falls off a sturdy ladder when his glasses slip off his ears?[5]

The only sensible solution, then, is to undo the first side of the implicit bargain in products liability cases. The rules of liability should be cut back from their current reach. When that is done, the question of damages will be reduced in significance, as a great many expensive and dubious cases can be properly taken out of the products liability system, to be handled by workers' compensation or ordinary health and disability payments. Should that line of reform fail, then it might be necessary to consider some limitations of damages, although they will doubtless be more complicated than the simple caps on damages that have been proposed to deal with the analo-

4. *See*, for statements on this scheme, J. O'Connell, *Ending Insult to Injury*, 97-106 (1975). For a draft of a possible statute, see O'Connell, *An Elective No-Fault Liability Statute,* [1975] Ins. L. J. 261, 267-93. The elective feature, whereby manufacturers could choose whether or not to be governed by the scheme, is designed to ease the no-fault system into place without undue institutional dislocations. It does not, however, eliminate any of the insuperable difficulties in defining the compensable event.

5. *See*, for this and other criticisms of the O'Connell plan, Blum, *Review of Ending Insult to Injury*, 43 U. Chi. L. Rev. 217 (1975).

gous explosion of liability in medical malpractice cases.[6] However, these possible limitations on damages should be viewed as a last resort. While there may be some general consensus that the levels of tort damages are simply too high, there is no case for moving to impose fixed limitations upon such damage awards. The better path toward controlling the problems of products liability is to concentrate upon the reform of both its substantive liability rules and its rules of procedure and proof.

## PUNITIVE DAMAGES

Although the major office of the law of torts, and of products liability in particular, is to determine the circumstances under which compensatory damages should be awarded, the common law has long recognized that there are some extraordinary cases in which it is proper to allow a plaintiff to recover punitive, or exemplary, damages as well.[7] In the early years of tort liability these damages were most often awarded in those situations in which one individual vented his spleen or hatred against the person or property of another. Deliberate beatings without any color of justification or excuse and spitting in public in order to show contempt and disrespect were two such circumstances.[8] While punitive damages do seem most natural in cases of such personal confrontation, it does not follow, by negative implication, that they ought never to be awarded when personal spite, hatred, or malice is absent from the case. To the contrary, as against certain institutional defendants it seems quite proper, at the very least, to award

6. The basic problem with the simple cap on damages is that its impact is confined only to the most serious cases. Where the cap is for $500,000, the plaintiff with a $1,000,000 recovery will lose 50 percent of his tort damages, while a plaintiff with a $500,000 recovery will be unaffected by the scheme. For reasons such as this, the Illinois statute [Ill. Rev. Stat. Ann. ch. 70, §101 (Smith-Hurd Supp. 1980)], calling for a $500,000 cap in medical malpractice cases, was held unconstitutional in *Wright v. Central DuPage Hospital Ass'n*, 63 Ill. 2d 313, 347 N.E.2d 736 (1976). The dissent in effect argued that the cap on damages was needed in order to insure the continuation of the delivery of medical services at reasonable costs, which could be reduced as well by a reformation of the substantive rules of medical malpractice. I have dealt with such possible reforms in Epstein, *Medical Malpractice: The Case for Contract*, [1976] Am. Bar Found. Res. J. 87.

7. On punitive damages generally, *see* Morris, *Punitive Damages in Tort Cases*, 44 Harv. L. Rev. 1173 (1931). The most recent and exhaustive review of punitive damages in products liability cases is Owen, *Punitive Damages in Products Liability Litigation*, 74 Mich. L. Rev. 1258 (1976), which generally takes a more favorable view to the award of punitive damages than is adopted here. For further literature on the subject *see*, Owen, id., n. 9 and n. 16. For a collection of the relevant cases, *see* 29 A.L. R.3d 1021 (1970).

8. *See*, W. Prosser, *Handbook of the Law of Torts*, 10-11 (4th ed. 1971) where it is noted that punitive damages may be awarded for "assault and battery, libel and slander, deceit, seduction, alienation of affections, malicious prosecution, and intentional interferences with property such as trespass, private nuisance, and conversion."

punitive damages where the evidence reveals that such defendants acted in conscious, flagrant disregard of the safety or welfare of the public at large or some segment of it. It seems, for example, wholly appropriate to assess punitive damages against a railroad whose high officials authorize the reckless speeding of locomotives through densely populated areas, and there is no reason in principle why products liability should form an enclave safe from such punitive damage awards for injuries that stem from the same improper motives.

It is not, however, enough just to observe that punitive damage actions should in principle lie against products liability defendants. It is also necessary to say something of the three possible theories upon which these punitive damage awards should be based. One theory is that the damages in essence are not really punitive at all but in effect are disguised compensatory damages designed to make good the shortfall in the actual damages typically awarded in ordinary tort actions. A second theory is that the damages are justified because they perform the important social function of deterring business enterprises from engaging in socially harmful activities. The third theory is that they are appropriate as a kind of substitute punishment for conduct which is, or should be, punishable under the criminal law but which may well escape detection and punishment by the public authorities. As the actual shape of the law of punitive damages will depend in large measure upon the uses to which it is put, it is important to consider the arguments for and against these different approaches in some detail. As will become clear, the third of these theories offers the most appropriate foundation for punitive damage awards.

The argument that punitive damages are in essence a form of disguised compensation rests on the assumption that the actual damages awarded in the ordinary tort action will not provide full compensation.[9] Thus it is said that accurate calculation of the major elements of damages—loss of earnings, medical expenses, and pain and suffering—leaves unaccounted one and possibly two elements. First, the law makes no explicit provision for the plaintiff's legal fees and other costs incurred in obtaining relief; and second, except for the loss of consortium between spouses, damages are not allowed to other persons—mainly children and parents—who suffer from the loss of full familial relationships. Punitive damages, it can be argued, would help fill this gap.

This position is subject, however, to several objections. With respect to legal fees, for example, it should be noted first, that legal fees can to some degree be embedded in the generous awards for pain and suffering, and second, that the unsuccessful plaintiff is likewise under no obligation to reimburse the successful defendant for the costs incurred in the defense of the

9. *See*, in support of the position, Owen, *Punitive Damages*, supra note 7, 1295-99.

suit. It may be said, of course, that this balm to the undeserving plaintiff is of no concern to the deserving one, but the argument misses the mark in two respects. Thus before the final resolution of the suit, the knowledge that costs need not be paid in the event that the defendant prevails will no doubt strengthen the resolve of all plaintiffs to continue. More importantly, the absence of appropriate compensation for costs does not argue for the routine award of punitive damages, but argues instead for a complete modification of the costs rules which, ideally, should be, on the English and European model, routinely awarded to the winner, wholly apart from any showing of the frivolous or captious nature of any claim or defense. Where the rules are so revised, the question of explicit accounting for one set of costs can be taken care of without any modification of the punitive damages rules, and in ways that promise to reduce the overall costs of litigation.[10] The well-tailored remedy is preferable to the overbroad one.

The treatment of familial losses raises similar issues. These losses—like those for legal fees—could be built into the general award for pain and suffering, especially in light of the unavoidably loose standards by which pain and suffering are determined. Even if they are not, it seems that the proper approach is to face the question of their recognition head on, wholly apart from the question of special liabilities for defendants who act in manifestly improper ways. If it is thought that current damage awards are too high or that there is too much speculation in determining these awards once we pass beyond the case of harm to spouses, then no such damages should be awarded. Such, somewhat surprisingly, was the recent view of the California Supreme Court.[11] If, however, it is thought that these damages are both measurable and appropriate, then they should be awarded generally to all eligible plaintiffs against all eligible defendants. There seems to be no case to use the asserted weaknesses of the law of costs and of general damages to justify punitive damage awards.

The arguments from deterrence also need close scrutiny. Here the basic form of the argument is that the award of punitive damages in appropriate cases counts as an extra spur that insures that all manufacturers will take appropriate steps to insure the general safety of their products. In particular it is claimed that there is a general underenforcement of the ordinary tort action, as many injured parties, owing to the perils of litigation and to the availability of other sources of compensation, may simply choose not to bear

10. For my views on the question, *see* R. Epstein, *Medical Malpractice; The Case for Contract*, [1976] Am. Bar Found. Res. J. 87, 135-36.

11. *Borer v. American Airlines, Inc.*, 19 Cal. 3d 441, 563 P.2d 858, 138 Cal. Rptr. 302 (1977), which refused to allow children to maintain actions for the loss of the consortium of their parents.

the heartache and effort of pursuing a meritorious cause of action.[12] This point is bolstered by noting that in a certain predictable fraction of cases, the jury will excuse those defendants who ought to be held liable, thereby further weakening the deterrent effect of the products liability law. Remedying both of these perceived defects is thought to be one useful function of punitive damages.

One great weakness of these deterrence arguments is that they take an incomplete view of the set of incentives under which products liability defendants in particular labor, selecting for consideration only those which point to the possible underenforcement of the tort law. Matters, however, take on quite a different aspect if due note is made of the extensive regulatory apparatus already in place, for example, with drugs, airplanes, and automobiles, where additional sanctions and penalties are imposed upon potential tort defendants wholly apart from the occurrence of actual damages in individual cases.[13] Also omitted from consideration are those features of current products liability system which point to the overenforcement of tort remedies. There is, for example, a certain number of cases in which the plaintiff will, if only because of jury error, recover when the defendant should have been exonerated. More importantly perhaps, there is a good reason to believe that the substantive organization of the products liability law—whether in setting standards for design defects, warnings, and plaintiff's conduct, or in treating evidentiary issues—is unduly biased in the plaintiff's favor. When all the pros and cons of the current system are netted out, there is no a priori reason to think that the level of enforcement

12. The argument, for example, is made as well in connection with medical malpractice cases; *see* Schwartz & Komisar, *Doctors, Damages, and Deterrence: An Economic View of Medical Malpractice*, 298 New Eng. J. of Med. (1978).

13. A manufacturer distributing a drug to many thousands of users under government regulation scarcely requires this additional measure [punitive damages] for manifesting social disapproval and assuring deterrence. Criminal penalties and heavy compensatory damages, recoverable under some circumstances even without proof of negligence, should sufficiently meet these objectives.

Friendly, J. in *Roginsky v. Richardson-Merrell, Inc.*, 378 F.2d 832, 840-41 (2d Cir. 1967). Judge Friendly also expressed a strong concern that multiple punitive damage awards against manufacturers could well bankrupt a firm for a single misdeed. This argument, while surely relevant to the caution appropriate for punitive damage awards, need not however mean that they should *never* be awarded against a manufacturer of mass-produced articles. *See* Owen, *Punitive Damages*, 1322-25, who suggests that greater awards could be made to the earlier plaintiffs who first establish the defendant's basic liability, a suggestion that is taken up in the draft Uniform Model Product Liability Act, § 120(B) (7). Owen also notes that in the MER/29 cases, the only mass disaster litigation to have run its course, only eleven cases out of fifteen went to jury trial, and only three of these resulted in punitive damages awards, one of which was reversed on appeal in *Roginsky*. How the possibility of such awards influenced the settled cases is not known.

is below the social optimum: indeed in light of the enormous increase in products liability litigation in the past decade and the great divergence between American products liability law and that found elsewhere in the industrial world, it is more likely that the reverse is true. Therefore, if it is thought that the incentives created by the current law are to some degree underdeveloped, then the proper response is, again, not punitive damages in the odd case but some increase in the level of actual damages in all cases—beyond the current high levels that they have reached.

In the end the strongest, indeed the only, justification for punitive damages is, as the name itself suggests, as a substitute for the direct criminal sanctions that might be brought against defendants. As the criminal law functions best when it operates on retributivist principles,[14] so, too, should these principles govern the operation of punitive damage awards. It is not so much that the plaintiff is entitled to this extra measure of compensation as it is that the defendant, in light of his wholly improper conduct, should be required to pay it. This windfall could be avoided if the state took the initiative through its criminal law enforcement, but this is in fact improbable, as its resources are in large measure tied up in the fight against street and organized crime, where the need for public intervention is more urgent. It remains possible, of course, to provide that the punitive damages in any given case be awarded to the state, or perhaps to some worthy charity; but stripping the plaintiff of his only financial gain guarantees by indirection that no punitive damage actions will ever be brought. Moving to the opposite extreme, any person, wholly apart from the suffering of actual injury, might be allowed to maintain punitive damage actions. Yet this approach becomes manifestly unworkable, as there is no way to decide which of the literally hundreds of eager plaintiffs should be allowed to impose the serious costs of defending such suits upon the targeted defendants. Therefore, if we are to have punitive damage actions, they must be through the traditional method of private enforcement by injured parties.

The choice of the basic—retributive—theory for these actions has important consequences for the doctrinal structure of punitive damages law, especially in products liability cases. Now the basic theme of the area must be to make the substantive law of punitive damages approach, if not conform to, the basic features of criminal law doctrine. The consequences on

14. *See* Hart, *The Aims of the Criminal Law*, 23 Law & Contemporary Problems 401 (1958) which makes the case in the strongest possible terms. *See also* for my defense of the important differences between tort and criminal liability, Epstein, *Crime & Tort: Old Wine in Old Bottles*, in *Assessing the Criminal*, 231-57 (R. Barnett & J. Hagel III, eds., 1977). In this connection it should be noted that it is proper to speak of deterrence of criminal actions, i.e., those performed with the appropriate mental state, but not to speak of the deterrence of certain types of particular harms, which should be the subject of either tort sanctions or *civil* statutory fines.

doctrine are important. One obvious point concerns the basic burden of proof. While the standard in most civil actions is the preponderance of evidence on the facts of the case, punitive damages should be subjected to a higher standard of proof—if not proof beyond a reasonable doubt, then surely, as is the dominant standard today, proof by clear and convincing evidence.[15]

A second consequence concerns the basic standard by which punitive damages should be judged. Where the deterrence goal is recognized there is a strong tendency to argue that the standard for punitive damages should be something less than a conscious and flagrant disregard for the public health and safety and something more akin to objective, gross negligence.[16] Yet, once it is clear that deterrence is the proper province of the basic tort action or certain explicit forms of administrative and regulatory controls, there is no case for weakening the standards of subjective wrongdoing that are normally applied in criminal cases. The defendant's conduct should not only be wrongful in its consequence, but it should be clear also that the defendant knew that the conduct was wrongful (that is, knew that he regarded the risk as wholly inappropriate) at the time it was undertaken and nonetheless decided for reasons of self-interest to continue that conduct until caught red-handed.

In this connection it is useful to inquire into the relationship between punitive damages, common practice, and statutory obligations. Thus one possible implication of the basic position is that a product that complies with both the standards of common practice and government regulation should rarely, if ever, be the subject of a punitive damage attack. So much follows a fortiori in a legal system that treats these standards as decisive of the question of product defect: for if there can be no liability (whether on a design defect or duty to warn theory), then there can hardly be a case for punitive damages. The point, however, goes further. Even if a product that complies with both common practice and statute may be found defective, it is wholly inappropriate to assert that a party who has complied with the only fixed standards for conduct should be treated as reckless, or worse, for doing so. To expose such defendants to punitive damages (not to men-

15. On the effects of the standard of proof, *see e.g., Sabich v. Outboard Marine Corp.*, 131 Cal. Rptr. 703 (1976), where the punitive damage award for the plaintiff was reversed on appeal on burden of proof grounds. The case, it might be noted, is another of the strong design defect cases, in which the vehicle made by the defendant had its center of gravity so far forward that it toppled over when going down the very inclines that it was designed to operate on. This case was withheld from official publication, 60 Cal. App. 3d 591 (1976). *See*, on this subject, ch. 7.

16. *See* Owen, *Punitive Damages*, at 1365-69, where in place of the conscious and reckless disregard language, it is urged that courts adopt the phrase "reflecting a flagrant indifference to public safety." Id. at 1368. *See also* infra at 187-88.

tion the criminal liability unsuccessfully sought in the Pinto prosecutions in Indiana)[17] is not only to attack the defendant for his conduct, but by the same token to impugn everyone associated with the formulation of products standards, including the federal government, with the same degree of reckless indifference. If, to be sure, it could be shown that the defendant in question influenced the formation of the applicable standards by submitting fraudulent information to governmental bodies, then of course the question of damages becomes relevant, but only if the firm's position influenced the setting of the standard in a way which in fact enhanced the risk of injury to the particular plaintiff in question. Apart from this narrow exception, conformity with applicable standards must be an absolute defense to all punitive damage claims.

The argument, moreover, might be pushed one degree further, for conscious noncompliance with an applicable safety standard is by no means tantamount to the reckless disregard of the safety of others required for a punitive damages case against a product liability defendant. It is well known that the safety standards in question are often formulated in ways that do not promote the ends for which they are advanced or do so only at a wholly unreasonable cost. The weakness of the punitive damage claim should surely become manifest where the alternative precautions taken by the defendant are more effective than (not to mention inconsistent with) those that are required by the statute. And, while the matter is more problematical, a powerful case against punitive damages can be made even where the defendant thinks regulatory standards are too high, as with a firm that continues to follow its older and cheaper practices, secure in the knowledge that they have resulted but rarely in bodily injury or property damage. Whatever the undesirable exposure of the defendant to statutory fines, the case for punitive damages continues to require the clear demonstration of the defendant's belief that the risks that it imposed upon members of the public were by any acceptable standard, unwarranted, and known to be such.

As a third point, the basic criminal analogy makes it advisable—by adoption of the so-called "complicity rule"—to limit the liability of corporate defendants to those cases in which the senior officials have authorized, participated in, or thereafter ratified the basic policy choices that form the basis of the criminal conduct charged to the corporation.[18] Here it is, of course, somewhat odd to hold the shareholders of a corporation, normally

17. I have given my criticisms of the misguided prosecution in the Ford Pinto case in Epstein, *Is The Pinto A Criminal?* Regulation, March-April 15 (1980).

18. The "complicity" rule was adopted by the American Law Institute, Restatement (Second) Torts, §909 (Draft No. 19, 1973). That rule was supported by Morris, *Punitive Damages in Personal Injury Cases*, 21 Ohio St. L.J. (1960), but is rejected in favor of a broader vicarious liability rule in Note, *The Assessment of Punitive Damages Against an Entrepreneur for the Malicious Torts of His Employees*, 70 Yale L. J. 1296 (1961), and in Owen, *Punitive Damages*, 1301, 1303.

innocent in all respects, to the financial consequences for wrongs committed by some of the corporate employees. Yet such an anomaly must be tolerated if there is ever to be any use of punitive damage awards against corporate defendants. Since the superior officers take us as close as we can get to the alter ego of the corporation, it does not seem too improper to levy punitive damages (or criminal fines) against the corporation for especially flagrant conduct.

The uneasy case for corporate criminal liability makes it important to take special care with the application of the principles of vicarious liability. Where tortious liability alone is involved, products liability actions should of course be governed by the usual principle that holds the corporation responsible for the torts of the servant committed in the course of employment, even, as has been repeatedly held, where the servant has acted in direct contravention to the command of the employer in carrying out his assigned task. Yet punitive damages against the corporation (and of course against the superior officer) should not rest simply upon proof that the servant's improper conduct fell within the scope of employment. Instead every link in the chain of responsibility should bear the imprint of the conscious wrongdoing with which the corporate defendant is charged. It should therefore be a requirement that the challenged conduct was deliberately authorized or ratified by a superior officer who had full knowledge of its criminal and improper nature. The standard of responsibility is an exacting one and should not be satisfied by simply showing that certain practices by certain low-level employees had taken place for long periods of time. While some acts of corporate irresponsibility may escape scrutiny under the restrictive standard urged here, it should be possible with both direct testimony of inferior officials and documentary evidence to show complicity of the higher-level corporate officials in the wrongful conduct in most cases. Such proof has in fact been presented in the two major cases that have raised this issue,[19] and there is no reason to believe that this rule will fatally hinder efforts to unearth such evidence in future cases. And where it does, it should be remembered that the quasi-criminal nature of a punitive damage case requires that the defendant receive the benefit of the doubt.

Where the deterrence rationales are used, of course, this limitation of punitive damages to high-level officials is much less severe. Once the concern is with the simple prevention of certain forms of harm, it may seem easy and convenient to use the strict principles of vicarious liability to hold the corporation responsible for the conscious misdeeds of any of its inferior

19. *See*, *Gillham v. Admiral Corp.*, 523 F.2d 102 (6th Cir. 1975); *Toole v. Richardson-Merrell, Inc.*, 251 Cal. App. 2d 689, 60 Cal. Rptr. 398 (1967) reaches a similar result, one that Friendly, J. strongly resisted in *Roginsky v. Richardson-Merrell, Inc.*, 378 F.2d 832, 844-45.

employees. In principle this additional criminal liability can be said to work to inject senior officials of a corporation into the safety decisions of the firm instead of relegating these matters to lower echelon employees. Yet, that objective may already have been achieved by the constant—indeed excessive—regulatory concern with product safety and by the vast increase in ordinary litigation for compensatory damages. Nor is it obvious that such further involvement, when brought about, would be sensible. There is no apparent relationship between the participation of top management in safety decisions and the safety of the product that is produced. Constant intervention on a day-to-day basis might simply result in interference with the orderly progress of safety development. Indeed it might not even lead to protection against punitive damage suits, as it would then become that much easier for the plaintiff to allege with great rhetorical flourish that any conscious wrongdoing *had* to involve high officials, since they were so intimately involved with the detailed decisions of product development and marketing. Today demands are being made upon top corporate management from every quarter—foreign bribes, affirmative action, environmental protection—to the point where it is impossible to satisfy them all simultaneously while running a business. Where by studied silence and the blind eye, high-level officials do authorize or condone patently antisocial practices, the traditional doctrines, both of substantive law and civil procedure, seem adequate for the task. Punitive damages should be reserved for the exceptional case only.

The general principles appropriate to punitive damage awards must be applied to particular cases. Indeed, in addition to cases settled before trial, a substantial number of punitive damages actions have reached the appellate courts in recent years. By and large, the courts have shown the proper sensitivity in their treatment of these cases and have been able to distinguish, especially at the extremes, those cases in which punitive damages are and are not appropriate. There have, however, been a number of troublesome cases in which the principles of liability appear to have been extended beyond their proper sphere. Though there is need for some additional caution and restraint, the case law is by no means as disquieting as that raised by, say, modern design defect litigation. An analysis of particular litigation is especially difficult, given the constant inquiry into complicated mental states over long periods of time. Nonetheless, it is possible to say something tentative about the general pattern of cases.

Perhaps the most convincing case in which the plaintiff has been awarded punitive damages is *Gillham v. Admiral Corporation.*[20] The plaintiff was a seventy-five-year-old woman who was seriously burned and otherwise injured while trying to put out a fire that started when her Admiral television set caught fire while she was in another room. The immediate cause

20. 523 F.2d 102 (6th Cir. 1975).

of the fire was a defective "horizontal output transformer" that incorporated certain wax and paper components unsuitable (under industry standards) for use at the high temperatures at which the transformer operated. Apart from some minor causal complications raised by the plaintiff's efforts to put out the fire, the case falls within the paradigm of the strong design defect case in that the product in question contained a latent defect that made it unfit for its ordinary use.

The evidence in the case takes on a more sinister aspect when directed not to the product itself but to the circumstances under which it was first developed and then marketed. The defendant's project manager admitted that he knew that the set as designed might catch fire in customers' homes, but only futile and inadequate steps were taken to protect against this contingency. From the time that the television was first marketed until the plaintiff was injured some four years later, the defendant, moreover, had received a total of some ninety-one reports of similar spontaneous fires in the television model in question. The response of the defendant to the adverse information was to continue to market the set without any design change, even though the company's highest officials knew of the substantial fire hazard that it presented. To make matters worse, the company, apparently with the knowledge of its president, continued to instruct its dealers to assure consumers that the product was safe even though it believed to the contrary. The only possible defense for the defendant's conduct was that the company did not have any personal ill will to its customers. The Court of Appeals rightly reversed the judgment entered for the defendant in lower court and ordered reinstatement of the jury's award of $100,000 in her favor. On the strength of the reported facts, the decision seems unquestionably correct.

If *Gillham* represents the type of case in which punitive damages are properly awarded, then *Thomas v. American Cystoscope Makers, Inc.*[21] represents the type of case in which the court properly intervenes to overturn the jury's extensive punitive damage award. In that case the plaintiff was a physician who used a medical instrument (a "resectoscope") manufactured by the defendant. The instrument was allegedly defective because it produced an electrical current "arc" that ran from the end of the instrument into the plaintiff's eye, thereby injuring the plaintiff's cornea. The liability for actual damages was itself contested, given that the plaintiff performed the operation using an eyepiece that allowed direct viewing through the resectoscope—instead of the photographic eyepiece with which the machine was properly outfitted—and did so with knowledge that the machine had malfunctioned on previous occasions. He did not have any particular knowledge of the source of the electrical defect nor of the arcing effect which in fact caused injury.

21. 414 F. Supp. 255 (E.D. Pa. 1976).

The plaintiff's evidence for punitive damages was essentially that some two years before his accident, the defendant had begun to receive notice that physicians were using uninsulated resectoscopes without the appropriate viewing attachments. In response to the possible dangers the company introduced a new eyepiece of nonconductive materials which reduced but did not eliminate the shock problem. It did not, however, send out any warnings to users of its instruments to alert them of any special problem. Yet, in sharp opposition to the situation in *Gillham*, there was no previous report of any injury similar in severity to the plaintiff's, and the minor mishaps that did occur were attributable at least in part to some other malfunction or break in the electrical circuit. The plaintiff also introduced some obscure reference in the early medical literature about the possibility of electrical shocks but none which related specifically to the type of incident involved in the particular case. The evidence introduced shows at most some negligence in the failure of the company in preparing the product's warnings and design, but nothing whatsoever suggests that the defendant itself perceived any extreme risk that required immediate attention and drastic action. Whatever negligence the case may reveal is a far cry from the callous disregard of the interests and welfare of others so evident in *Gillham.*

It is possible, however, to find cases, whatever the actual facts, that show a tendency to lapse toward a negligence or even strict liability standard in the award of punitive damages. Illustrative in this connection is *Hoffman v. Sterling Drug, Inc.*[22] There the defendant marketed the drug "Aralen"

22. 485 F.2d 132 (3d Cir. 1973).

Deliberately omitted in this discussion is the question of whether punitive damages were appropriate against the defendant Richardson-Merrell in the MER/29 litigation. Contrast here the summary of the evidence that is presented in *Toole v. Richardson-Merrell*, 251 Cal. App. 689, 60 Cal. Rptr. 398 (1967), with that offered in *Roginsky v. Richardson-Merrell, Inc.*, 378 F.2d 832 (2d Cir. 1967). In *Toole* the California Court of Appeals found substantial evidence of a deliberate campaign to deceive the public, the medical profession, and the F.D.A. concerning the potentially harmful effects of MER/29. Reviewing a substantially identical trial record, Friendly, J. after a merciless dissection of the evidence concluded that what the record showed, "apart from negligence in policing subordinates and a somewhat stiff-necked attitude toward the F.D.A., is rather that [the defendant's chief officers] were so convinced of the value of the drug both to the public welfare and to the company's finances that they maintained a sanguine view longer than prudence warranted." 378 F.2d at 850. (Indeed several of defendant's officers used the drug regularly. 378 F.2d at 844, n. 22.) The radical difference in the conclusions in the two opinions reflects the abundant possibilities for interpretation that can be placed on the words and decisions of highly placed corporate officials. It also points to the degree of passion that can be aroused when the issue of bad faith conduct is litigated in punitive damage cases. One sign of the passions generated by the case concerned the proper interpretation to be placed on a surprise F.D.A. examination of the defendant's plant just days before the drug was removed from the market, a point made much of in *Toole*. In *Roginsky*, however, the plaintiff on its petition for rehearing described the court's efforts to minimize the impact of the surprise visit as "laughable," only to provide a strong and pointed response which to this reader, at least, was persuasive. 378 F.2d. at 853, n.4.

(chloroquine phosphate) which was taken by the plaintiff over a period of years. The plaintiff used the drug, designed to control certain skin conditions, in sufficient dosages to cause serious eye damage. The complaint alleged that the drug had not been sufficiently tested before it has been released into the general market, and that the appropriate F.D.A. clearances for this new use—the drug had long been used to treat malaria—had not been obtained.

Of interest here, however, were the allegations on the question of punitive damages. The plaintiff contended that the defendant, once it began to accumulate information about the adverse consequences of the drug, did what it could to keep the drug on the market as long as possible. He then supported this claim in two particular respects. First, he argued that the warning letters and notices that were in fact sent out did not convey the full seriousness of the possible dangers. Second, he argued that the method used to convey the information was inappropriate to the risk at hand. In fact the defendant had included warnings in its promotional literature and upon certain product cards, but it delayed for several years to make the parallel changes in its entry in the Physicians Desk Reference, which doctors regularly consult to determine appropriate uses and contraindications for given treatments. There is good reason to doubt any campaign of systematic suppression in light of the efforts to warn the public that the defendant had initiated, even if the means chosen were inadequate. Yet, even if the plaintiff's action for punitive damages was in principle maintainable, there seems to be serious error in the grounds on which the court let the case go to the jury. Here, on the strength of expert testimony that physicians tend to disregard the warnings that they receive from detail men, the court concluded, first, that "defendants must be charged with knowledge of the workings of the distribution system by which they chose to state the dangerous effects of Aralen and the shortcomings therein," and, second, that "defendants, knowing of the danger of chloroquine retinopathy, knew or should have known that their mode of communicating warnings would not effectively reach the medical profession."[23]

Both these statements show how easy it is to slide over the gulf that lies between the willful and flagrant conduct suitable for a punitive damage award to the type of mistaken decision that supports at most a negligence cause of action. In essence *Hoffman* raises the spectre of the following type of abuse in punitive damage actions. First, the court announces general rules for design and warning cases that require the defendant, as a responsible manufacturer, to weigh consciously the risks associated with all forms of corporate conduct. Dealing with the question of actual damages, such reasonableness rules allow the defendant to show that the risks that ma-

23. Id. at 146, 147.

terialized in any given case were worth running because of the other benefits that were obtained. They allow, in a word, a trade of lives for dollars. Yet let the liability for actual damages be established, and it becomes all too easy to argue that the very fact that the defendant made, as demanded, a conscious decision about product design with the full knowledge of some possible resulting harm might in itself be sufficient to warrant an award of punitive damages. This view of the mental element in punitive damage cases wholly misconceives the theory on which these damages should be awarded. What must be shown is not that the defendant knew of certain risks, much less that he had means to learn of them. Instead it must be shown, as was shown in *Gillham*, that the defendant himself regarded the risks as *unwarranted* and took them even though he believed that his own conduct was in reckless and flagrant disregard for the safety of the public at large.

The failure to observe the essential distinctions in the area can lead to important judicial errors. Thus in *Moore v. Jewel Tea Co.*, the Illinois Appellate Court first announced that the "question of willful and wanton conduct is essentially whether the failure to exercize care is so gross that it shows a lack of regard for the safety of others."[24] Using what is in essence a gross negligence standard, the court then affirmed the $10,000 punitive damage award for the plaintiff on the following analysis of the evidence:

> The caustic soda contained in Drano was known by Drackett to be greatly destructive to human tissue, particularly the eyes. Drackett employees handling caustic soda were directed to wear cotton clothing and goggles properly adjusted to the contour of the face. No such warnings were given to the public. Drano was known by Drackett to generate gas and thus pressure when moisture was added. Drackett knew the importance of whether the cap or the seam of the can would withstand less pressure, yet it employed this can without knowing its ability to withstand pressure although manufacturers of products in cans as a custom knew the properties of their containers. This knowledge by the defendants of the potential dangerousness of their product, coupled with the notice to them of prior claims of spontaneous explosions and their failure to warn the public as they did their own employees presented a question for the jury to determine whether the defendants were guilty of wanton and wilful conduct.[25]

The record does not support this award. In the first place, the level of risk to which employees are routinely exposed in their daily work, measured by both the extent and nature of the contact, is far greater than that faced by ordinary consumers. The difference in the risk levels—explicitly taken into account in the general defect formulations of both design and warning

24. 116 Ill. App. 2d 109, 136, 253 N.E. 2d 636, 649 (1969).
25. Id. at 136-37, 253 N.E.2d at 649.

cases—easily justifies the differential warnings given in the two situations. Then, too, the allegation of insufficient testing is at most a classic allegation of negligence that in no way goes to the issue of whether the company believed that it should have marketed its product in some other kind of container. Finally, the firm's knowledge of claims of previous spontaneous explosions of unused Drano cans does not even begin to show conscious and flagrant disregard of consumer safety. Three such reported instances of explosions out of the hundreds of thousands of cans that had been sold is hardly evidence of systematic failure. These explosions, moreover, differed in important respects from the explosion here. All had taken place before the cans had been shipped to the ultimate consumer, and none had caused any serious injury. In essence the evidence is consistent at most with the assertion that the occasional miscarriages of manufacture and delivery resulted in "inevitable accidents" for which only actual damages should be allowed on a strict liability theory. Indeed the evidence suggests a close case on a negligence theory. In light of the small amount of punitive damages awarded—$10,000 against $900,000 in actual damages—it seems likely that the jury itself had substantial doubts about the wisdom of its award.

Similar errors assumed a greater role in the recent decision of the Missouri Appellate Court in *Rinker v. Ford Motor Co.*,[26] where a $460,000 award of punitive damages (as against $100,000 in actual damages) was sustained in an opinion that, if anything, was sketchier than that in *Moore.* In *Rinker* the only evidence used to support the claim was that the defendant had received notice of some twenty-nine claims of an allegedly identical product defect: a broken cam that forced the carburetor into an open position when the accelerator was depressed, about which the defendant did not provide warnings. Even viewed "in the light most favorable to plaintiff"—surely the wrong standard for a punitive damage case—the evidence presented shows at most that the defendant knew of the basic problem. Yet such evidence does not tend to show that the defendant's response to the question revealed its willingness to take unpardonable license with the safety of the public at large. In order to make out the claim of punitive damages, it becomes necessary at the very least to show how the defendant investigated the complaints, the degree of risk the defendant thought attached to the given hazard, and the treatment of the entire matter before the National Transportation and Highway Safety Board to which all such claims have to be referred. Yet on these issues the opinion of the appellate court remained silent.

The unwillingness to consider the full record on the punitive damages

26. 567 S.W.2d 655 (1978).

issue in *Rinker* points up the need for safeguards against the improper award of such damages. It seems appropriate to instruct the jury on the difference between gross negligence and willful and flagrant disregard of public safety, and on the high burden of proof required in these cases. Similarly, it is proper to demand of the reviewing court that it consider all undisputed evidence introduced by the defendant in passing on the merits of the award of the trial court. It might also be wise at trial to have the judge make the determination of the amount of punitive damages, or to have close judicial scrutiny of all the evidence in the record, both at trial and appeal, to see that excessive awards are not given. Lastly, it might be desirable to require punitive damages to be separately stated and to limit them to, say, twice the actual damages in any given case, in order to control the possible dangers of multiple punitive damages awards.[27] The principles governing punitive damages are difficult enough to apply even in the best of circumstances. The requirements for punitive damages should not be watered down to the extent that it becomes possible to make a punitive damage count a routine part of the typical products liability case.

27. The proposed standards in the Model Uniform Product Liability Act (Section 120) agree with these recommendations in some respects, but depart from them in others. In particular the Model Act adopts a general "reckless disregard" standard, which should be viewed as but a verbal variation of the willful and flagrant disregard standard supported in the text. *See* Section 120(A). The act also provides that the actual determination of the amount of punitive damages should be made by the judge and not the jury. Section 120(B).

The act differs from the proposals herein contained in that it does not propose any flat limitation upon the amount of punitive damages that might be awarded in any individual case, but instead instructs the judge to take into account the "total effect" of all punishments, fines, and sanctions that have been or are likely to be imposed upon the defendant. The point of this provision is commendable in that it provides some protection against the possibility that a massive punitive damage award might well absorb all the assets of a tort defendant, even to the exclusion of compensatory damage awards to other plaintiffs. But the task of coordination among the many payments that might be imposed upon a given defendant is so difficult it seems advisable to impose the strict upper limit even if, within that limit, expected severity of additional sanctions is still to be taken into account. The Model Act also introduces into the calculation of damages elements that ring of ordinary negligence or at most gross negligence, such as the "likelihood at the relevant time that serious harm would arise from the seller's misconduct." Model Act 120 (B) (1). The great danger here is that these objective factors will filter into the original determination of punitive damages. The subjective belief, not the objective fact should be controlling.

# AFTERWORD

The eleven chapters of this book have traced the major themes in the growth and development of the modern products liability law. The early chapters explained why the common law of products liability was right in extending the liability of manufacturers and other sellers beyond the narrow limits to which it was confined in the last part of the nineteenth century. The later chapters, dealing with the law since the watershed of the Restatement (Second) of Torts, took a very different position, arguing that many, but by no means all, modern doctrinal innovations represent unwarranted extensions of liability. The principles upon which I have based that conclusion bear some brief restatement.

First, there is a sense in which products liability law should be regarded as a species of "contracts at a distance," dealing with the allocation of losses associated with the manufacture, distribution, and use of a wide range of individual products. Viewed in this way the central task of the courts—at least where no statute or public regulation is involved—is to find the set of shared expectations that have governed the behavior of the relevant parties in the chain of distribution and to use them as the basis for allocating loss in any given case. These expectations may be found in the common practices of certain business communities, in the web of regulations that govern the use of particular products, in the representations that defendants make about their own products—whether in the form of product specifications, product warranties, product warnings and instructions or even in the appearance of the product itself. In the context of the different theories of product defect, and of affirmative defenses, this concern with shared expectations often reduces itself to one recurrent theme: *A defendant should normally be held liable for injuries caused by latent defects in the manufacturer's product which result in injury in ordinary use, and not otherwise.*

There is no question that plaintiffs can and do recover in products liability actions that conform to this general model. Indeed it is the approach to products liability cases that was taken as recently as 1963 in *Greenman v. Yuba Power Co.* The real question is the extent to which courts are prepared to allow recovery in cases that go beyond this traditional mode. That question, in turn, requires the formulation of new judicial standards of product fitness and user conduct, and these the courts have quite simply not been able to provide in terms that can be consistently and sensibly applied. The point receives special force in those frequent cases in which statutes (or even common practice) set a standard for product safety. Today, inordinate attention is paid to the possible imperfections of such standards while little attention is paid to the greater weaknesses of the more stringent judicial alternative. It simply will not do to say that the various rules of custom and common practice may well "lag" behind some hypothetical ideal, when there are in fact far graver risks in trying to use the individual lawsuit as the forum to judge the suitability of entire product lines. Broad formulations of reasonableness may aid an administrative body in deciding what particular safety standards are required with new drugs, automobiles, or airplanes, but they are pitifully inadequate when applied on a case-by-case basis to any given drug, automobile, or airplane sold after it already has been subjected to administrative scrutiny. There may well be reason to doubt the binding force of administrative standards that are known by all to be outdated or which were prepared on the strength of inaccurate information submitted by the very parties to be regulated. But it is a mistake to assume that such occasional imperfections make it appropriate to subject every product and every standard to de novo review in an individual product liability lawsuit. The importance of certainty and predictability may not be absolute; but they are surely undervalued in much of modern products liability litigation.

The treatment of plaintiff's conduct in products liability actions raises a different but equally insistent set of concerns. While there are many ordinary tort actions in which the plaintiff's only involvement in the case is as victim, product liability actions—especially the vast bulk brought by users and consumers—typically arise from situations in which the conduct of the injured party is one of the main sources of his own injury. Where such is indeed the case, it becomes imperative that the plaintiff be held accountable for his own conduct, just as the defendant is held accountable for the defective products that he places on the market. Fortunately, an increasing number of courts recognize that the task of insuring product safety is one that falls on all parties in the chain of distribution and use, with the consequence that the defenses of contributory negligence (or responsibility), even its comparative form, and of assumption of risk still have some role to play in the adjudication of product liability cases. Notwithstanding this recognition, however, it is true that too many courts tend to disregard these defenses—especially contributory negligence—or to hem them in with limitations that reduce their effectiveness precisely where, as with "foreseeable" product misuse, their application is most needed. The substantive fairness of the system and its ability to control accident and administrative costs make it imperative that these defenses be treated as an integral and proper part of any general set of products liability rules and not as regrettable obstacles over which astute courts and juries are eager to hurdle. The products liability system is not a pure compensation system that treats the deep pocket of the defendant as a sufficient reason to impose liability. It is a system of tort law, one in which it is improper to regard a defendant's ability to pay as any kind of justification for imposing or expanding liability.

The last two general points have to do with judicial administration. The first of these is that the courts do not seem to have properly appreciated the enormous administrative costs associated with the application of modern products liability doctrines to litigated cases. Even though accurate cost figures are notoriously difficult to find, properly calculated, greater sums may well be spent in the litigation of a complicated design defect or drug case than is paid out in compensation to injured parties. Clearly, no court would be prepared to offer a remedy where the costs of administration are $1,000,000 and the amount of compensation $100. And if the extreme case is clear, then surely some of the modern cases should give rise to great pause. Somewhere along the continuum these costs should be taken into account.

The second point has to do with the treatment of error. Each case raises the prospect of two types of error: that a deserving plaintiff might go without relief; that a deserving defendant might have to pay an unwarranted judgment. There is, moreover, no way to guard against the first type of error unless courts are prepared to decide for plaintiffs in every case. Again the extreme case lays bare the weakness of the principle. Yet the only way to escape the consequence is to recognize that errors against the defendant are entitled to clear weight, indeed to a weight equal to that of errors for the plaintiff: such is the reason that the normal burden of proof rests upon the plaintiff and not the defendant. Yet here too the recent tendency of the judicial decisions is to weight the evidentiary scales even more heavily in favor of plaintiff's recovery. Again the modest solution—some degree of balance, or evenhandedness between parties—is the most effective cure.

In spite of its many weaknesses, the modern law of products liability contains a core of good sense that seems well worth preserving. Indeed, it seems fair to say that we are in the midst of a legal revolution that has both obvious strengths as well as obvious weaknesses. It can only be hoped that through further judicial and legislative action, steps will be taken, as some first steps have been taken, to bring greater structure and cohesion to modern products liability law. Whatever the final reckoning on the state of American products liability law, one point seems clear: its greatest errors lie in its boldest innovations.

# TABLE OF CASES

*Coughtry v. Globe Woolen Co.*, 56 N.Y. 124 (1874), *page 18.*

*Cronin v. J. B. E. Olson Corp.*, 8 Cal.3d 121, 501 P.2d 1153, 104 Cal. Rptr. 433 (1972), *page 65n.18.*

*Dalke v. Upjohn Co.*, 555 F.2d 245 (9th Cir. 1977), *page 105n.2.*

*Daly v. General Motors Corp.*, 20 Cal.3d 725, 575 P.2d 1162, 144 Cal. Rptr. 380 (1978), *pages 123-126, 129, 132-33, 135n.29.*

*Davis v. Wyeth Laboratories, Inc.*, 399 F.2d 121 (9th Cir. 1968), *pages 100, 107-110.*

*Derry v. Peek*, 14 App. Cas. 337 (H.L. 1889), *page 20n.3.*

*DeSantis v. Parker Feeders, Inc..*, 547 F.2d 357 (7th Cir. 1976), *page 71n.6.*

*DeVere v. Parten*, 222 Minn. 211, 23 N.W. 2d 584 (1946), *page 162n.21.*

*Devlin v. Smith*, 89 N.Y. 470 (1882), *pages 18-21.*

*Dillon v. Legg*, 68 Cal.2d 728, 441 P.2d 912, 69 Cal. Rptr. 72 (1968), *page 14n.12.*

*Dimond v. Caterpillar Tractor Co.*, 65 Cal. App. 3d 173, 134 Cal. Rptr. 895 (1976), *page 106n.22.*

*doCanto v. Ametek, Inc.*, 367 Mass. 776, 328 N.E.2d 873 (1975), *page 72n.8.*

*Drayton v. Jiffee Chemical Corp.*, 591 F.2d 352 (1978), *page 153.*

*Dudley Sports Co. v. Schmitt*, 151 Ind. App. 217, 279 N.E. 2d 266 (1972), *pages 71-73.*

*E. Hulton & Co. v. Jones*, [1909] 2K.B. 444, [1910] A.C. 20, *page 27n.9.*

*Elmore v. American Motors Corp.*, 70 Cal.2d 578, 451 P.2d 84, 75 Cal. Rptr. 652 (1969), *pages 54n.5, 164.*

*Escola v. Coca-Cola Bottling Co.*, 24 Cal.2d 453, 150 P.2d 436 (1944), *pages 7, 26, 35, 36-48, 57, 98, 161.*

*Evans v. General Motors Corp.*, 359 F.2d 822 (7th Cir. 1966), *page 88n.38.*

*Farwell v. The Boston and Worcester R.R. Corp.*, 45 Mass. (4 Metc.) 49 (1842), *page 13n.8.*

*Fields v. Volkswagen of America, Inc.*, 555 P.2d 48 (Okla. 1976), *pages 77, 141.*

*Finnegan v. Havir Manufacturing Corp.*, 60 N.J. 413, 290 A.2d 286 (1972), *page 99n.9.*

*Fletcher v. Rylands*, L.R. 1 Ex. 265 (1866), *pages 27n.8, 124.*

*Foster v. Ford Motor Co.*, 139 Wash. 341, 246 P. 945 (1926), *page 71.*

*Fulbright v. Klamath Gas Company*, 271 Or. 449, 553 P.2d 316 (1975), *pages 113-114.*

*Garst v. General Motors Corp.*, 207 Kan. 2, 484 P.2d 47 (1971), *pages 85n.34.*

*Gillham v. Admiral Corp.*, 523 F.2d 102 (6th Cir. 1975), *pages 183n.19, 184-186.*

*Givens v. Lederle*, 556 F.2d 1341 (5th Cir. 1977), *pages 108-111.*

*Goldberg v. Kollsman Instrument Corp.*, 12 N.Y.2d 432, 191 N.E.2d 81, 240 N.Y.S. 2d 592 (1963), *pages 41, 47.*

*Gray v. Zurich Insurance Co.*, 65 Cal.2d 263, 419 P.2d 168, 54 Cal. Rptr. 104 (1966), *page 52n.11.*

*Greenberg v. Lorenz*, 9 N.Y.2d 195, 173 N.E.2d 773, 213 N.Y.S. 2d 39 (1961), *page 34.*

*Greenman v. Yuba Power Products, Inc.*, 59 Cal.2d 57, 377 P.2d 897, 27 Cal. Rptr. 697 (1963), *pages 7, 26, 35, 36-48, 70-71, 73, 81-82, 90, 98, 120n.2, 122, 192.*

*Greiner v. Volkswagenwer Aktiengeselleschaft*, 540 F.2d 85 (3rd Cir. 1976), *remanded*, 429 F. Supp. 495 (E.D. Pa. 1977), *pages 117-118.*

*Gyerman v. United States Lines Co.*, 7 Cal.3d 488, 498 P.2d 1043, 102 Cal. Rptr. 795 (1972), *page 145n.44.*

*Haft v. Lone Palm Hotel*, 3 Cal.3d 756, 478 P.2d 465, 91 Cal. Rptr. 745 (1970), *page 106n.22.*

*New York Central R.R. Co. v. White*, 243 U.S. 188 (1917), *page 173n.3.*

*Noel v. United Aircraft Corp.*, 342 F.2d 232 (3rd Cir. 1964), *page 60n.8.*

*Outboard Marine Corp. v. Schupbach*, 93 Nev. 158, 561 P.2d 450 (1977), *page 114.*

*Peck v. Tribune Co.*, 214 U.S. 185 (1909), *page 27n.9.*

*Pedrick v. Peoria & Eastern R.R. Co.*, 37 Ill. 2d 494, 229 N.E.2d 504 (1967), *page 154n.3.*

*Pike v. Frank G. Hough Co.*, 2 Cal.3d 465, 467 P.2d 229, 85 Cal. Rptr. 629 (1970), *page 90.*

*Pinnick v. Cleary*, 360 Mass. 1, 271 N.E. 2d 592 (1971).

*Poggi v. Scott*, 167 Cal. 372, 139 P.815 (1914), *page 27n.10.*

*Price v. Niagara Machine & Tool Works*, 136 Cal. Rptr. 535 (1977), *deleted from official reporter, page 48n.27.*

*Priestly v. Fowler* 3 M. & W. 1, 150 Eng. Rep. 1030 (Ex. 1837), *page 13n.8.*

*Reyes v. Wyeth Laboratories, Inc.*, 498 F.2d 1264 (5th Cir. 1974), *pages 100, 107-110.*

*Reynolds v. Clarke*, 1 Str. 634, 92 Eng. Rep. 410 (1/26), *page 12n.7.*

*Richenbacher v. California Packing Corporation*, 250 Mass. 198, 145 N.E. 281 (1924), *pages 31-32, 37.*

*Rinker v. Ford Motor Co.*, 567 S.W.2d 655 (1978), *pages 189-190.*

*Robbins v. Farmers Union Grain Terminal Ass'n*, 522 F.2d 788 (8th Cir. 1977), *page 168n.32.*

*Rodiguez v. Besser Co.*, 115 Ariz. 454, 565 P.2d 1315 (1977), *page 114.*

*Rogers v. Unimac Co., Inc.*, 115 Ariz. 304, 565 P.2d 181 (1977), *pages 78-80, 114n.33.*

*Roginsky v. Richardson-Merrell, Inc.*, 378 F.2d 832 (2d Cir. 1967), *pages 179n.13, 183n.19, 186n.22.*

*Rudisaile v. Hawk Aviation, Inc.*, 92 N.M. 575, 592 P. 2d 175 (1979), *pages 122-123.*

*Rylands v. Fletcher*, L.R. 3 E. & I. App. 330 (1868), *pages 27n.8, 124.*

*Sabich v. Outboard Marine Corp.*, 131 Cal. Rptr. 703 (1976), *deleted from official reporter, page 181n.15.*

*Scheller v. Wilson Certified Foods, Inc.*, 114 Ariz. 159, 559 P.2d 1074 (1977), *pages 147-148.*

*Schmidt v. Archer Iron Works, Inc.*, 44 Ill.2d 401, 256, N.E.2d 6 (1970), *pages 153-154.*

*The Schooner Catharine v. Dickinson*, 58 U.S. (17 How.) 170 (1854), *page 136n.30.*

*Self v. General Motors Corp.*, 42 Cal. App. 3d 1, 116 Cal. Rptr. 575 (1974), *pages 88n.39, 91-92.*

*Siegler v. Kuhlman*, 81 Wash.2d 448, 502 P.2d 1181 (1972), *page 132n.25.*

*Sindell v. Abbott Laboratories*, 26 Cal. 3d. 588, 607 P. 2d 924, 163 Cal. Rptr. 132 (1980), *page 159.*

*Smith v. Peerless Glass Co.*, 259 N.Y. 292, 181 N.E. 576 (1932), *page 23.*

*Spruill v. Boyle-Midway, Inc.*, 308 F.2d 79 (4th Cir. 1962), *page 16n.36.*

*St. Paul Fire & Marine Insurance Co. v. Michelin Tire Corp.*, 12 Ill. App.3d 165, 298 N.E.2d 289 (1973), *page 165n.25.*

*Stevens v. Parke, Davis & Co.*, 9 Cal.3d 51, 507 P.2d 653, 107 Cal. Rptr. 45 (1973), *page 111n.26.*

# BIBLIOGRAPHY

## BOOKS

American Law Institute, *Restatement (Second) of Torts* (1965).
Frumer, Louis R. and Friedman, Melvin II, *Products Liability* (New York: Matthew Bender, 1979).
Holmes, Oliver Wendell, Jr., *The Common Law* (Boston: Little, Brown, 1881).
Hursh, Robert D., and Bailey, Henry J., *American Law of Products Liability* (Rochester: The Lawyer's Cooperative Publishing Co.—Bancroft Whitney, 2nd ed. 1975).
Insurance Services Office. *Product Liability. Closed Claim Survey: A Technical Analysis of Survey Results* (1977).
O'Connell, Jeffrey, *Ending Insult to Injury* (Urbana: University of Illinois, 1975).
Prosser, William L., *Handbook of the Law of Torts* (St. Paul: West Publishing Co., 4th ed. 1971).
United States Department of Commerce, *Interagency Task Force on Product Liability*, Final Report (1977).

## ARTICLES

Ames, James Bar. *Law and Morals*, 22 Harv. L. Rev. 97 (1908).
Birnbaum, Sheila. *Legislative Reform or Retreat? A Response to the Product Liability Crisis*, 14 Forum 251 (1978).
Blum, Walter J. *Review of Ending Insult to Injury*, 43 U. Chi. L. Rev. 217 (1975).
Bohlen, Francis H. *Liability of Manufacturers to Persons Other Than Their Immediate Vendees*, 45 Law. Q. Rev. 343 (1929).
Demsetz, Harold. *When Does the Rule of Liability Matter?*, 1 J. Legal Stud. 13 (1972).
Epstein, Richard A. *Coordination of Worker's Compensation Benefits with Tort Damage Awards*, 13 The Forum 464 (1978).
______. *Defenses and Subsequent Pleas in a System of Strict Liability*, 3 J. Legal Stud. 165 (1974).

______. *Medical Malpractice: The Case for Contract*, 1976 Am. Bar. Foundation Res. J. 87 (1976).

______. *Nuisance Law: Corrective Justice and Its Utilitarian Constraints*, 8 J. Legal Stud. 49 (1979).

______. *Products Liability: The Search for the Middle Ground*, 56 N. Car. L. Rev. 643 (1978).

______. *A Theory of Strict Liability*, 2 J. Legal Stud. 151 (1973).

______. *Unconscionability: A Critical Reappraisal*, 18 J. L. & Econ. 293 (1975).

Franklin, Marc. *Tort Liability for Hepatitis: An Analysis and a Proposal*, 24 Stan. L. Rev. 439 (1972).

______, and Mais, Joseph E. *Tort Law and Mass Immunization Programs: Lessons from the Polio and Flu Episodes*, 65 Calif. Law Rev. 754 (1977).

Green, Leon. *Strict Liability Under Section 402A and 402B: A Decade of Litigation*, 54 Tex. L. Rev. 1185 (1976).

Griffith, L. E. and Griffith, B. E. *Doctrine of Res Ipsa Loquitur in Negligence Actions —Old Solutions for New Problems*, 48 Miss. L. J. 259 (1977).

Henderson, James. *Judicial Review of Manufacturers' Conscious Design Choices: The Limits of Adjudication*, 73 Colum. L. Rev. 1531 (1973).

______. *Manufacturers' Liability for Defective Product Design: A Proposed Statutory Reform*, 56 N. Car. L. Rev. 625 (1978).

Hoenig, Michael. *Product Designs and Strict Tort Liability: Is There a Better Approach?*, 1976 Ins. L. J. 282 (1976); 8 Sw. U. L. Rev. 109 (1976).

Jaffe, Louis. *Damages for Personal Injury: The Impact of Insurance*, 18 Law & Contemporary Problems 219 (1953).

James, Fleming. *Products Liability*, 34 Tex. L. Rev. 44 (1955).

Kessel, Reuben. *Transfused Blood, Serum Hepatitis, and the Coase Theorem*, 17 J. Law & Econ. 265 (1974).

Kessler, Friedrich. *Contracts of Adhesion—Some Thoughts About Freedom of Contract*, 43 Colum. L. Rev. 629 (1943).

Klemme, H. C. *Enterprise Liability Theory of Torts*, 47 U. Colo. L. Rev. 153 (1976).

McCoid, Allen H. *The Care Required of Medical Practitioners*, 12 Vand. L. Rev. 549 (1959).

Montgomery, John E., and Owen, David G. *Reflections on the Theory and Administration of Strict Tort Liability for Defective Products*, 27 S. Car. L. Rev. 803 (1976).

Morris, Clarence. *Punitive Damages in Personal Injury Cases*, 21 Ohio St. L. J. 216 (1960).

______. *Punitive Damages in Tort Cases*, 44 Harv. L. Rev. 1173 (1931).

Noel, Dix. *Defective Products: Extension of Strict Liability to Bystanders*, 38 Tenn. L. Rev. 1 (1970).

O'Connell, Jeffrey. *An Elective No-Fault Liability Statute*, 1975 Ins. L. Journal 261 (1975).

______. *Expanding No-Fault Beyond Auto Insurance: Some Proposals*, 59 Va. L. Rev. 749 (1973).

Oi, Walter. *The Enconomics of Product Safety*, 4 Bell Journal of Economics 3 (1973).

Owen, David G. *Punitive Damages in Products Liability Litigation*, 74 Mich. L. Rev. 1258 (1976).

Pelzman, Sam. *The Effects of Automobile Safety REgulations*, 83 J. Political Economy 677 (1975).

Phillips, Jerry J. *An Analysis of Proposed Reform of Products Liability Statutes of Limitations*, 56 N. Car. L. Rev. 663 (1978).

______. *Standard for Determining Defectiveness in Products Liability*, 46 U. Cin. L. Rev. 101 (1977).

______. *A Synopsis of the Developing Law of Products Liability*, 28 Drake L. Rev. 317 (1979).

Posner, Richard A. *A Theory of Negligence*, 1 J. Legal Stud. 29 (1972).

Prosser, William L. *The Assault Upon the Citadel (Strict Liability to the Consumer)*, 69 Yale L. J. 1099 (1960).

______. *Comparative Negligence*, 41 Calif. L. Rev. 1 (1953).

______. *The Fall of the Citadel (Strict Liability to the Consumer)*, 50 Minn. L. Rev. 791 (1966).

Rheingold, Paul D. *The MER/29 Story—An Instance of Successful Mass Disaster Litigation*, 56 Calif. L. Rev. 116 (1968).

______. *Proof of Defect in Products Liability Cases*, 38 Tenn. L. Rev. 325 (1971).

Sachs, Reynold M. *Product Liability: An Economic View*, 14 Trial 48 (March 1978).

Schwartz, Alan. *Products Liability and Judicial Wealth Redistribution*, 51 Ind. L. J. 558 (1976).

Schwartz, Gary T. *Contributory and Comparative Negligence: A Reappraisal*, 87 Yale L. J. 697 (1978).

______. *Understanding Products Liability*, 67 Calif. L. Rev. 435 (1979).

Schwartz, William, and Komisar, Neal. *Doctors, Damages and Deterrence, An Economic View of Medical Malpractice*, 298 New Eng. J. of Med. (1978).

Shapo, Marshall. *A Representational Theory of Consumer Protection: Doctrine, Function and Legal Liability for Product Disappointment*, 60 Va. L. Rev. 1109 (1974).

______. *Swine Flu and Legal Policy*, 63 A.B.A. J. 51 (1977).

Smith, *Relation of Emotions to Injury and Disease: Legal Liability for Psychic Stimuli*, 30 Va. L. Rev. 193 (1944).

Terry, Henry. *Negligence*, 29 Harv. L. Rev. 40 (1915).

Twerski, Aaron D. *From Defect to Cause to Comparative Fault—Rethinking Some Product Liability Concepts*, 60 Marq. L. Rev. 297 (1977).

______. *The Use and Abuse of Comparative Negligence in Products Liability*, 10 Ind. L. Rev. 797 (1977).

______, and Weinstein, A. S. *A Critique of the Uniform Product Liability Law—A Rush to Judgment*, 28 Drake L. Rev. 221 (1979).

______, Weinstein, A. S., Donaher, W. A., and Piehler, H. R. *The Use and Abuse of Warnings in Products Liability—Design Defect Litigation Comes of Age*, 61 Cornell L. Rev. 495 (1976).

Wade, John W. *On the Nature of Strict Tort Liability for Products*, 44 Miss. L. J. 825 (1973).

## NOTES AND COMMENTS

*The Assessment of Punitive Damages Against an Entrepreneur for the Malicious Torts of His Employees*, 70 Yale L. J. 1296 (1961).

*DES and a Proposed Theory of Enterprise Liability*, 46 Ford. L. Rev. 963 (1978).

*Package Inserts for Prescription Drugs as Evidence in Medical Malpractice Suits*, 44 U. Chi. L. Rev. 398 (1977).

*Product Liability and the Choice of Law*, 78 Harv. L. Rev. 1452 (1965).

*Products Liability—The Patent-Latent Defect Rule: Strict Liability for Misrepresentation*, 1977 Ann. Survey of Am. L. 85 (1977).

*Products Liability and Evidence of Subsequent Repairs* (1972) Duke L. J. 837 (1972).

*Strict Products Liability to the Bystander: A Study in Common Law Determinism*, 38 U. Chi. L. Rev. 625 (1971).

24 Vand. L. Rev. 645 (1971).

## MISCELLANEOUS

*Setting Safety Rules for Products Proves Costly and Complicated*, Wall Street Journal, Aug. 11, '77. p. 1.

# INDEX

**About the Author**

RICHARD A. EPSTEIN is Professor of Law at the University of Chicago. He is the author of many books including *Cases and Materials on Torts*, 3d ed., with Charles O. Gregory and Harry Kalven, Jr., and his articles include "A Theory of Strict Liability" (1973) and "Medical Malpractice: The Case for Contract" (1976). Richard Epstein is also a member of the California Bar and a Special Consultant on Products Liability to the American Insurance Association.